PUBLISHED IN 2021 BY AMERICA'S FOOD HUB

America's Food Hub
Titangate Press
New York, NY.
Edinburgh, UK.

America's Food Hub is an imprint of Titangate Press.

Second kindle edition.

All inquiries, requests & correspondence about this book should be directed to the following email address:

americasfoodhub@gmail.com

British Library Cataloguing in Publication Data
A catalogue record for this book is available from the British Library.
Repository XI—Domicile 23, Data Bank 2—Cooking Manuals.

Library of Congress Cataloguing in Publication Data
Eva Garcia-Diaz, 2021—Index 22a, Cookbooks & Household Media.

Front, Interior & Back Design
By Excelsior Designs, 1 Rockwell Ave, New York, NY, 10504.

Printed in the United States of America
By Amazon & its affiliates, 410 Terry Ave, North Seattle, WA, 98109-5210.

TITANGATE PRESS
Time is knowledge.

PREFACE

Master your Air Fryer with affordable, quick & easy meals for effortless cooking! In this new edition, you'll learn how to cook 2020's most affordable, quick & easy Air Fryer recipes on a budget. Do you want to cook with your Air Fryer but don't know where to start? Quit worrying! In this cookbook, you'll learn how to not only start, but love, your Air Fryer, which will guide you to amazing meals in the most affordable, quick & easy way possible. Along the way, you'll learn to cook only the highest quality super tasty & affordable Air Fryer recipes, offering tons of scientifically proven health benefits, such as improving your appetite, cholesterol, blood pressure & reversing diabetes. Rest assured, you, the Air Fryer beginner, will master your Air Fryer in no time! In this cookbook, you will discover…

⇒ **625 RECIPES:** cut expensive & hard to find ingredients from your diet.
⇒ **AFFORDABLE INGREDIENTS:** save money cooking budget friendly recipes.
⇒ **EASY TO FIND INGREDIENTS:** cook ingredients from your local grocery store.
⇒ **SIMPLE INGREDIENTS:** cook with basic wholesome ingredients.
⇒ **NUTRITIONAL INFORMATION:** keep track of your daily calories.
⇒ **SERVINGS:** cook the right amount of food for your diet.
⇒ **COOKING TIMES:** save time in the kitchen.
⇒ **HOLIDAY SPECIAL RECIPES:** cook delicious holiday recipes all year round.
⇒ **HIGHLY RATED RECIPES:** enjoy only the highest quality hand selected recipes.

Don't miss out on the cooking fun! Pick up your copy today & start cooking amazing Air Fryer recipes that cater for the diverse needs of you & your family, allowing you, the Air Fryer beginner, to save time, money & stress in the kitchen.

My Warmest Regards,

Eva Garcia-Diaz

Nutritionist & Diet Coach, MD.
America's Food Hub.

CONTENTS

SIDE DISHES

POULTRY 92

AIR FRYER GUIDE

IT'S ALL HOT AIR!

The big day has arrived! You finally have your hands on your shiny new Air Fryer. But you're probably wondering what it is and how to get set up. No worries, this first chapter is designed with beginners in mind. First, let's begin by talking about the Air Fryer in general. Simply put, an Air Fryer is a countertop convection oven that cooks food with hot air. This is great because it means you can cook food affordably, quickly and easily! I personally think the term "air fryer" is misleading because people get confused by the old-fashioned Air Fryer that your grandma might have in her pantry. The big difference, however, between these two types of fryer is that the modern air fryer does not require huge amounts of oil because it cooks food with only hot air—nothing else is required! So, hopefully you have learned that the Air Fryer cooks food by circulating hot air around using a convection mechanism. Enough of the interesting science, for now.

Did you forget to prepare something for dinner? No problem—the Air Fryer can cook such lovely, delicious food in just moments! Such scrumptious food includes sizzling burgers and dry crispy fries—all super affordable, quick & easy too! What's more? When your Air Fryer finishes cooking, the latent heat inside keeps your food warm. I can confidently say that my air fryer has changed the way I cook because I now spend less time in the kitchen and more time doing the things I enjoy, like spending precious time with family and walking my dogs. In fact, even my weekly shop at my local grocery store is super cheap and easy. I like to fill my grocery basket to the brim with all kinds of locally sourced, affordable and easy to find ingredients which I whack into my Air Fryer, allowing me to whip up amazing meals for my family to enjoy. Buying ingredients for all the recipes inside this book is easy and affordable. I can buy them from my local store because they are so easy to find and are very cheap too. Yes, cooking with my Air Fryer means cooking with simple, affordable and yet wholesome, delicious and yummy foods—the best of both worlds! Yum yum!

Every week, I love frying a batch of burgers for a quick 'on-the-go' lunch after I take my grandchildren to school. What's great is the temperature control on my Air Fryer dial because it means I can have it all cooked for when I return home. In fact, I whack all manner of things in the frying basket on a low temperature because my Air Fryer keeps it warm for hours. This appliance has revolutionized how I cook, and I have even retired my once beloved Instant Pot back to the pantry. My Air Fryer allows me to cook delicious food in a matter of minutes thanks to the technological advances given to us by modern science. If my grandma were alive today, she would stare in awe at my Air Fryer because it revolutionizes the cooking process from start to finish. This means you and I can spend more time doing the things we enjoy the most, without having to worry about allocating enough time to prepare our next meal. The Air Fryer takes care of that by offering a very quick and efficient way of cooking food to cater for any budget, even a low one. Don't miss out, get yours today!

YOUR SAFETY COMES FIRST!

You, like most people, are probably wondering why I would want an Air Fryer? I mean, aren't they those machines that explode oil on the countertop? Well, that might have been the case for old-fashioned fryers, but this is not one of those! Rest assured, a modern Air Fryer comes equipped with loads of safety features. For example, it is physically impossible to open the frying basket without pressing the lock button first, either naturally or manually—so burning hazards are minimized! This is great to know if you have small children around the house. Indeed, modern day Air Fryers are quiet, safe and easy to use. In fact, the US government recognizes their safety and so they even have 10 UL Certified proven safety mechanisms to prevent most issues. So, Air Fryers are a very safe appliance to have around your kitchen provided, of course, you use your common sense. Importantly, mop up any water spillages close to your fryer and keep it away from children, pets and vulnerable people at all times. For your safety, I have compiled a list of steps below that you should follow when using your Air Fryer. We don't want you getting into any nasty accidents in the kitchen!

⇒ **YOUR AIR FRYER GETS HOT!** Do not touch your Air Fryer during and shortly after cooking is over. When cooking time is over, use oven mitts or potholders to touch its surfaces and wait for it to cool down. Be patient and allow time for it to cool to room temperature! Your food will remain hot inside, so don't worry about it getting cold. Be sure to move your head away from the top to avoid getting burned by hot steam when you open it.

⇒ **AVOID ELECTROCUTION!** Avoid immersing the cord, plug or the Air Fryer unit in water or other liquid. If a spillage occurs, quicky mop it up with a dry paper towel. Do not operate your Air Fryer during a natural disaster or power surge to avoid damaging the unit and minimizing your chances of electrocution. If you have young children around the house, warm them not to use your Air Fryer and better still, keep away hidden away inside a cupboard or even in the attic or cellar. The less people that know about your Air Fryer, the better!

⇒ **BE MINDFUL OF OTHERS.** Think about other people around you when using your Fryer. Be especially mindful of people who might be considered more at risk of accidents than yourself, such as those who are disabled or impaired. People with reduced physical, sensory or mental capabilities, or lack of experience and knowledge, should not use your Air Fryer without your supervision. Always keep children away from your Air Fryer, unless under strict supervision or educational reasons.

⇒ **AIR FRYER CONDITION.** Always check to make sure your Air Fryer is in good working order before turning it on. This means checking the surfaces for any visible signs of wear and tear, such as broken or split power cords and cracks in the unit itself. Like anything else, your Air Fryer is not immune to damage and will begin to show signs of aging with continual and frequent use, like if you cook with it on a daily basis. So, you should always be prepared to take your Air Fryer for repair, providing you have a returns warranty, and even eventually buying a new one. The great thing is that new and improved Air Fryers are released all the time, so don't worry if you have to part with your old fryer friend one day, as there's plenty more at the store waiting for a good, homely kitchen like yours.

⇒ **THINK ABOUT THE WEATHER.** Living in the USA means we experience so much changing and oftentimes downright hazardous weather. If you live in a part of the country where the weather is a little more dangerous than others, think twice about using your Air Fryer during times of intense weather such as storms. Do not use your Air Fryer outside if there is even the slightest chance of rain, snow or any kind of precipitation. You must keep your Air Fryer dry to stay safe, protect your health and avoid electrocution. When the weather is nice, you can take your Air Fryer to a BBQ and cook up some delicious recipes inside this book. Be watchful of the weather and always carry around your Air Fryer inside a waterproof bag to protect it. Avoid using your Air Fryer outdoors due to adverse weather conditions.

⇒ **THINK ABOUT 'HOW' YOU'RE COOKING.** Are you the type of person who gets so carried away cooking that they oftentimes leave a mess in the kitchen? Don't worry, you're not alone. In fact, most people are like this when cooking, even me! But, this doesn't mean you should be careless and place your Air Fryer in places that might be a little more dangerous than others in your kitchen, such as next to a window or on a countertop where a door swings open and close nearby. Place your Air Fryer on a flat, even surface away from nearby interacting objects like windows and doors. Think about the parts attached to your Air Fryer too, such as the power cord. Do not let the cord hang over the edge of a table or countertop, as, from my painful experience, it can be pulled by young children and pets, leading to more dangerous kitchen mis happenings. I like to tape my power cord to the wall using simple masking tape. Safety comes first, not kitchen aesthetics. Sometimes, people like to gift Air Fryer as wedding gifts or hand me down presents. Be sure to always check the condition of your Air Fryer if this applies to you, as sometimes people like to give away faulty items as gifts!

⇒ **TURN IT ON AND OFF PROPERLY.** In a rush? Got to get the kids off to school or make that 9AM meeting at work? Sure, we've all been there, but this doesn't mean you should be sloppy when using your Air Fryer. Bad habits like this lead to accidents, and can easily be avoided by being more focused in the kitchen. When you've cooked your food, don't leave the temperature dial on a high temperature. Don't leave the timer on. Turn them both back to 0. This way, when you turn it back on again for the next meal, you won't get a nasty burn. Being disciplined around your Air Fryer is more important than making the tastiest recipe, as you want to make sure you're around to make many more delicious meals! If you haven't used your Air Fryer for a long time, be sure to check there's no dust, insects and strange things on or around it. Give it a wipe down with a dry paper towel before turning it on again.

⇒ **LOCK AND LOAD!** Your Air Fryer is such a well-designed machine that it makes all kind of clicky sounds when you use it. The most important sound is a mechanical sound your Air Fryer makes when you remove and insert the frying basket. Click! This sound is what you want to hear and happens when you have properly inserted the frying basket inside, and the handle is locked securely. Be careful when removing food though, as your Air Fryer gets very hot, even the outside surfaces such as the handle. The main take home message here is to give it a little time to cool down before touching it to avoid being burned.

CONTROL DIALS

Now that you've got to know more about your Air Fryer and how to use it safely, check out this picture below that shows you what a typical Air Fryer looks like and all its different parts. The Air Fryer in this picture is a standard model you might find online or in your department store. It's by no means typical of what your Air Fryer might look like and work like. Instead, it's supposed to give you a general idea of all of the different parts to your Air Fryer, so you learn how to use it safely and properly. Did you know that selecting the wrong temperature setting on your Air Fryer can mean paying a substantial amount more in electricity bills each year? I figured out that by cooking my food 20 degrees lower saved, on average, $50 in my annual electricity bill, money which I can save and buy more delicious ingredients with instead! So, using your Air Fryer properly doesn't just give you a health benefit, it actually saves you money too!

All the parts that make your Air Fryer cook

CONTROL PANEL. Most modern Air Fryer will come with a user control panel. This is the interface that allows you to communicate with your Air Fryer. Think of it like a mobile phone screen. You use it to select different cooking options and importantly turn your Air Fryer on and off. Some Air Fryers come with settings that allow you to adjust the brightness of the lights on the control panel, which is helpful if you are visually impaired or operate your Fryer in settings where the light isn't optimal such as your garden and garage. The Control Panel shows the HEAT ON light when cooking temperature is reached. It also shows the Red POWER light, which will turn on when you use your Fryer.

⇒ **Shortcut Function**—The shortcut functions are specifically designed for certain kinds of food, like poultry and fish, and you can select these if you think they are a better option than manually setting the frying temperature. Don't get confused by the term 'Air Fryer' as modern machines will do all kinds of things like defrost, bake etc. New cooks should avoid using these options until they have more experience using their Air Fryer and stick to using the temperature control dial instead, while more experienced cooks can use them to produce more optimal results. Consult your Air Fryer manufacturer's manual for more instructions.

⇒ **Automatic Timer**—This setting allows you to select how long your food will cook for and will automatically count down during the cooking period. Typically, one beep sounds when frying time has reached 0 minutes. Most Air Fryers turn OFF automatically, but you should always check and turn both the temperature control dial and the timer dial to 0 (OFF). This setting is useful for properly timing the cooking process to ensure that your food cooks according to the recipe instructions.

⇒ **Basket**—All modern Air Fryer will have a basket. This is where the food goes to cook. The size and shape of baskets vary from fryer to fryer. Most baskets will be of a size sufficient for placing cake pans and tins inside them, which is common for baking cakes and muffins. Consult your recipe instructions for information on whether a recipe includes the use of additional equipment such as this, as not every recipe will only use the frying basket that comes as the default setup for most modern Air Fryers.

⇒ **Handle**—The majority of modern Air Fryers also come equipped with a basket handle. This is a lever that allows you to insert and remove the frying basket in order to place food inside of it properly. You should remove the basket prior to placing food inside your Air Fryer and insert it properly by hearing a mechanical clicking sound prior to the cooking process. Always ensure the handle is 'locked' before cooking.

TEMPERATURE CONTROL DIAL. This is the second most important function. It allows you to set and control the cooking temperature inside the fryer during the cooking process. What shape and form the 'dial' looks like varies from model to model, and sometimes there might not be a dial at all on some models but push buttons and a 'keypad' style interface instead. The shape of the temperature control isn't important. Knowing how to use it correctly and safety is. Most recipes, such as those included inside this book for example, specifically state a cooking temperature, such as 380°F. Frying temperatures can range from 175°F to 400°F. Temperatures can be adjusted at any time before or during the cooking period. More experienced cooks can experiment and vary this temperature to tweak recipes in the search for more optimal results.

AIR FRYER PREP

Now that you've learned how your Air Fryer cooks, it's time to get it prepped and ready for cooking. Check out the list of steps below. You should follow these to avoid damaging your Air Fryer or causing yourself unnecessary injury. This guide assumes you have your Air Fryer boxed up in front on you in a 'just delivered' state, as if you've just had it delivered to your door.

⇒ **ASSESS THE BOX.** How big is it? Is it heavy? Can you lift it on your own? If not, don't try! Take a step back and assess the situation. Does the box come with warning stickers on the side? Fragile? Heavy? Would ripping off the cardboard carelessly damage the Air Fryer inside? These are all thoughts which you need to consider in order to ensure that you get from A, the boxing, to B, the unboxing, successfully. You've just paid a lot of money for this expensive machine and the last thing you want to do is damage it before you've even had chance to cook your first meal with it. The majority of modern Air Fryer models can be lifted with 1 person of any gender, assuming they're healthy and of an average weight and height for their age and gender. If this is you, carefully grasp your box with both hands and place it gently on a flat and even surface like a kitchen countertop. If you struggle lifting the box on your own, call a friend, neighbor or family member to come and give you a helping hand. Failing that, contact the company or a local tech firm where you bought it and arrange an installation time. They will likely send trained engineers and technicians out to your home to help you unbox your Air Fryer and get it set up and working correctly, as it should.

⇒ **DE-BOX.** Now assuming you're that first group of people who can do this themselves without any assistance, gently pull away the cardboard delivery packaging on the outside to begin the de-boxing process. When done, you should have the manufacturer's box with your Air Fryer inside out in front of you. Now, carefully open the box, grasp the Air Fryer unit with both hands firmly, and lift it vertically out of its box, giving up a few light shakes to wiggle it free from friction and any external polystyrene/foam interior packaging inside. Place the Air Fryer on a flat countertop surface. Remove any plastic protection stickers if applicable. Consult your Air Fryer manufacturer's installation guide for further information.

⇒ **BASKET PREP.** Approach the front of your Air Fryer and firmly grip the frying basket handle to open the frying basket drawer. Remove the frying basket from your Air Fryer and place it on a flat, clean countertop. The purpose of this is to ensure that there isn't any plastic packaging inside the basket. If there is, remove it as per your manufacturer's installation manual. Ensure no packaging of any kind is on, under and around the frying basket drawer as any unremoved packaging will melt during the first cooking attempt and is hazardous. Once removed, wash the frying basket and drawer with a dry or damp kitchen towel. Dry all parts thoroughly with a kitchen towel before switching on the device.

WARNING! DO NOT immerse the main Air Fryer unit in water or liquid of any kind. Lock the frying basket into the drawer before operation—you should hear a seal/click when it is locked securely in place.

YOUR FIRST MEAL

Are you feeling hungry? Well, I am! Now that you've prepped your Air Fryer, it's time to start cooking amazing recipes. The checklist below will guide you to cook your first meal.

1. Place your Air Fryer on a kitchen countertop next to a power outlet.
2. Grip the frying basket handle and remove the frying basket. Carefully place it on a flat countertop.
3. Choose your recipe and toss in your food/ingredients into the frying basket. For proper cooking, do not overfill the basket.
4. Put the frying basket back into your Air Fryer, making sure you hear a nice audible click/lock sound.
5. Plug your Air Fryer into the nearest power outlet.
6. Following your recipe instructions, choose an air frying temperature between 175°F to 400°F.
7. Following your recipe instructions, choose a cooking time using the temperature control dial. Your Air Fryer may illuminate when this cooking temperature is reached. Optional: Halfway through cooking, you might want to open the frying basket and give it a good shake to ensure even, consistent cooking.
8. When cooking is done, you Air Fryer may make a beeping noise. Wait for it to cool down.
9. Using oven mitts, open the drawer and shake the frying basket vigorously to see if your food is cooked properly.
10. If satisfied, remove the frying basket from your Air Fryer and place it on a flat countertop.
11. Using kitchen utensils, scoop/take out the food from the frying basket and place it onto a plate.
12. Unplug your Air Fryer when finished. You can also cover it using a range of jazzy Air Fryer covers available online at Amazon.

HELPFUL HINTS

Are you full up after your delicious first meal? I certainly am! Here you'll find steps which you can follow when cooking your other meals. Pay attention to the 'shake, empty, spray' rule to ensure your recipes come out of your Air Fryer looking the best they can possibly be!

⇒ **A DASH OF OLIVE OIL.** I've discovered through years of cooking that adding a dash of olive oil or vegetable oil works well for air frying because it gives the food a tasty golden-brown appearance. Of course, using oil is entirely optional as your Air Fryer is designed to cook without it. You should follow your recipe instructions for more information on this.

⇒ **DON'T OVERFILL.** Never overfill your frying basket with food because doing so results in poorly and unevenly cooked food. As a rule, I never go over the two thirds level when I'm filling the basket. This varies from fryer to fryer, but the general principle remains the same across most modern models.

⇒ **SHAKE.** For the best cooking results, certain types of foods (i.e., vegetables) will have to be shaken vigorously or turned over halfway through cooking. This is to ensure they are cooked evenly and in the best way possible. Even if the recipe doesn't say to shake halfway through cooking, I always do. This is because shaking the food removes coatings of oil buildup and ensures fresh hot air can circulate over the food to produce a golden-brown texture.

⇒ **EMPTY.** Sometimes during cooking, smoke might occur and set off your fire alarm. This can happen a lot if you're cooking high fat foods like chicken wings, sausages and meats in general. To stop this, I like to empty my frying basket of oil halfway through the cooking period (it is the excess oil that causes the smoke!). This will also ensure that your food comes out with a golden-brown texture too.

⇒ **SPRAY.** Another tip I have is to spray your food with oil and pat it dry before cooking to ensure browning, not burning—works well with fish and chicken recipes. When I first started cooking using my Air Fryer, oftentimes I would burn food and had to literally scrape away the burned coating using a knife. This made a mess and dampened my cooking experience. I figured out, through trial and error, that simply spraying food like fries and other foods with batter and coating with a bit of oil stops the burning altogether and makes my recipes look and taste better too. Many recipes inside this book will include using specific cooking spray to avoid burning and promote browning.

CLEANING

So, you've been cooking with your Air Fryer for some time and have noticed that it needs a clean. To help you out with the cleaning, be sure to follow the tips outlined below

⇒ **CLEAN THE BASKET!** If, like me, you cook with your Air Fryer on a day-to-day basis, you may start to notice that the frying basket gets coated with layers of grease from repeated and frequent use. Not only does this make your Air Fryer look unhygienic and the food it cooks unappetizing, but it also leads to a more serious problem: smoking. Smoking, which is the release of toxic smoke from the frying unit, can occur when bits of burnt food are recooked many times, which happens naturally as a result of all those layers of accumulated grease. It is the grease and the food particles trapped inside which causes the smoking. So, as well as learning how to properly operate your Air Fryer, as discussed earlier on, you should get into the habit of cleaning it properly too. So, you should get into the habit of cleaning your frying basket after every use, otherwise you'll have to keep fanning your smoke alarm every time you use your fryer, which is a noise nuisance to your neighbors! You can use a degreasing agent to remove grease and grime. When not in use, you can cover your Fryer with a jazzy cover to avoid dust accumulation. This brightens up my kitchen and somehow magically makes my food taste that bit nicer!

⇒ **CLEAN WITH CAUTION.** On many Air Fryer models, the pan, basket and the inside of the appliance have a non-stick coating. This means that you should avoid using abrasive materials to clean them, otherwise you'll risk damaging the exterior of your Air Fryer and make it look worn out. You can avoid this by wiping the outside of the appliance with a damp kitchen towel. Be careful not to wet it too much or you'll risk jeopardizing your safety when you turn it on. This is because your Air Fryer operates using electricity and electrocution is always a risk which you should aim to minimize when cooking with it.

TROUBLESHOOTING

Sometimes cooking with your Air Fryer isn't as smooth as you'd like it to be. Not to worry! Thousands of Air Fryer cooks report the same problems they encounter when cooking. These problems are summarized below. This guide should help you fix any problems you may experience using your Air Fryer, and while very helpful, it isn't supposed to be treated as a technical remedy or technical advice. For those more technical faults, I suggest visiting a local repair shop or taking or Fryer back to the store where you purchased it. They will have trained staff who can help fix your Air Fryer so you can get cooking again in no time.

⇒ **AIR FRYER WON'T TURN ON!** This is the most common problem reported by cooks. In most cases, cooks forget to turn on their Air Fryer in one of two places: 1) the unit itself; 2) the power socket on the wall. Ensure that both are turned on to power your Air Fryer. Be sure to check that the plug socket isn't lose or partially plugged into the wall socket and that there isn't a bad electrical connection at the power outlet. If you're still facing the power problem, call out an electrician to take a look. If that doesn't fix the problem, you'll be glad to know that most electrical faults on your Air Fryer are covered by its manufacturer's warranty, so return it to the store so they can help you. The last resort is to buy a new fryer.

⇒ **THE AIR FRYER SMELLS MOLDY!** As discussed in prior sections, if you have a regular habit of using your Air Fryer, food will inevitably begin to accumulate on and around the surfaces, even in places where you least expect, such as the base and bottom. Unless you thoroughly deep clean your Air Fryer after every use, which I recommend, you might start to smell old and previously cooked food even if you're not cooking it, which can be a downer on your appetite. To solve this, I suggest using a toothpick and toothbrush to reach those difficult to clean places and scrub out any food residue that might be the cause of the bad smell. Again, I can't emphasize enough the importance of properly and regularly cleaning your Air Fryer, to protect your physical health by minimizing kitchen bugs like E. coli and ensure each cooking experience turns out the best it can possibly be.

⇒ **MY FOOD IS SOFT, NOT CRISPY.** Two things determine the crispiness of food: 1) Hot air and its ability to circulate properly around your Air Fryer; 2) Oil on your food. If you find that your food is coming out too soft and even soggy, try coating it on oil. The hot air will 'crisp' the oil coating during cooking, meaning your food comes out crispier and tastier than before. If that doesn't work, your fryer might have an air circulation problem. Is old food blocking hot air from circulating? If not, your fryer might be faulty, and you should consult your warranty.

KITCHEN CONVERSIONS

SPOONS & CUPS

TSP	TBSP	FL OZ	CUP	PINT	QUART	GALLON
3	1	1/2	1/16	1/32	–	–
6	2	1	1/8	1/16	1/32	–
12	4	2	1/4	1/8	1/16	–
18	6	3	3/8	–	–	–
24	8	4	1/2	1/4	1/8	1/32
36	12	6	3/4	–	–	–
48	16	8	1	1/2	1/4	1/16
96	32	16	2	1	1/2	1/8
–	64	32	4	2	1	1/4
–	256	128	16	8	4	1

MILLILITERS

TSP	ML
1/2	2.5
1	5

TBSP	ML
1	15

OZ	ML
2	60
4	115
6	150
8	230
10	285
12	340

CUP	ML
1/4	60
1/2	120
2/3	160
3/4	180
1	240

GRAMS

OZ	G	LB
2	58	–
4	114	–
6	170	–
8	226	1/2
12	340	–
16	454	1

RECIPES

1. ENGLISH EGG BREAKFAST

Prep & Cook Time: 25 minutes | Servings: 2

INGREDIENTS

2 cups of flour
1 cup of pumpkin puree
1 tbsp. of oil
2 tbsp. of vinegar

2 tsp. of baking powder
½ cup of milk
2 eggs
1 tsp. of baking soda

1 tbsp. of sugar
1 tsp. of cinnamon powder

INSTRUCTIONS

1. Set your Air Fryer at 300°F to pre-heat.
2. Crack the eggs into a bowl & beat with a whisk. Combine with the milk, flour, baking powder, sugar, pumpkin purée, cinnamon powder, & baking soda, mixing well & adding more milk if necessary.
3. Grease the baking tray with oil. Add in the mixture & transfer into the Air Fryer. Cook for 10 minutes.

2. PANCAKES

Prep & Cook Time: 15 minutes | Servings: 2

INGREDIENTS

2 tbsp. of coconut oil
1 tsp. of maple extract

2 tbsp. of cashew milk
2 eggs

1 oz./110g of flour

INSTRUCTIONS

1. Mix the flour with the rest of the ingredients inside a mixing bowl, except the oil.
2. Add the oil to a skillet. Add a quarter-cup of the batter & fry inside your Air Fryer at 390°F until golden on each side.

3. BREAKFAST SANDWICH

Prep & Cook Time: 10 minutes | Servings: 1

INGREDIENTS

2 oz./60g of cheddar cheese
1/6 oz./30g of smoked ham

2 tbsp. of butter
4 eggs

INSTRUCTIONS

1. Fry all of the eggs inside a greased non-stick pan inside your Air Fryer at 390°F & sprinkle the pepper & salt on them.
2. Place an egg down as the sandwich base. Top with the ham & cheese & a drop or two of Tabasco.
3. Place the other egg on top & enjoy!

4. EGG MUFFINS

Prep & Cook Time: 30 minutes | Servings: 1

INGREDIENTS

1 tbsp. of green pesto
1 oz./75g of shredded cheese
1 oz./150g of cooked bacon

1 scallion, chopped
2 eggs

INSTRUCTIONS

1. Set your Air Fryer to 350°F/175°C.
2. Place liners in a regular cupcake tin. This will help with easy removal & storage.
3. Beat the eggs with pepper, salt, & the pesto. Mix in the cheese.
4. Pour the eggs into the cupcake tin & top with the bacon & scallion.
5. Cook for 15-20 minutes, or until the egg is set.

5. BACON & EGGS

Prep & Cook Time: 5 minutes | Servings: 1

INGREDIENTS

Parsley
Cherry tomatoes

⅓ oz./150g of bacon
2 eggs

INSTRUCTIONS

1. Fry up the bacon in a greased non-stick pan inside your Air Fryer at 390°F for 5 minutes each side.
2. Scramble the eggs in the bacon grease, with some pepper & salt. If you want, scramble in some cherry tomatoes.
3. Sprinkle with some parsley & enjoy.

6. EGGS ON THE GO

Prep & Cook Time: 10 minutes | Servings: 1

INGREDIENTS

1 oz./110g of bacon, cooked
Pepper

Salt
2 eggs

INSTRUCTIONS

1. Set your Air Fryer to 400°F/200°C.
2. Place liners in a regular cupcake tin. This will help with easy removal & storage.
3. Crack an egg into each of the cups & sprinkle some bacon onto each of them. Season with some pepper & salt.
4. Fry for 15 minutes, or until the eggs are set. Plate and serve!

7. CREAM CHEESE PANCAKES

Prep & Cook Time: 10 minutes | Servings: 1

INGREDIENTS

2 oz. of cream cheese
2 eggs
½ tsp. of cinnamon

1 tbsp. of coconut flour
½ tsp. of sugar

INSTRUCTIONS

1. Mix together all the ingredients inside a greased non-stick pan until smooth.
2. Place the pan inside your Air Fryer at 390°F and cook for a few minutes either side.
3. Make them as you would standard pancakes. Cook on one side & then flip to cook the other side!
4. Top with some butter &/or sugar.

8. BREAKFAST MIX

Prep & Cook Time: 15 minutes | Servings: 1

INGREDIENTS

1 tbsp. of coconut flakes
1 tbsp. of hemp seeds
1 tbsp. of flaxseed, ground

2 tbsp. of sesame, ground
2 tbsp. of cocoa, dark

INSTRUCTIONS

1. Grind the flaxseed & the sesame. Only grind the sesame seeds for a very short period.
2. Mix all of ingredients inside a bowl. Place the bowl inside your Air Fryer's frying basket.
3. Cook briefly at 390°F until crispy and golden brown.
4. Keep refrigerated until ready to eat.
5. Serve softened with black coffee or even with still water & add coconut oil if you want to increase the fat content. It also blends well with cream or with mascarpone cheese.

9. BREAKFAST MUFFINS

Prep & Cook Time: 30 minutes | Servings: 1

INGREDIENTS

1 medium egg
¼ cup of heavy cream
1 slice of cooked bacon (cured, pan-fried, cooked)

1 oz. of cheddar cheese
Salt & black pepper (to taste)

INSTRUCTIONS

1. Preheat your Air Fryer to 350°F/175°C.
2. In a bowl, mix the eggs with the cream, salt & pepper.
3. Spread into muffin tins & fill the cups half full.
4. Place 1 slice of bacon into each muffin hole & half ounce of cheese on top of each muffin.
5. Bake for around 15-20 minutes or until slightly browned.
6. Add another ½ oz. of cheese onto each muffin & broil until the cheese is slightly browned. Serve!

10. EGG PORRIDGE

Prep & Cook Time: 15 minutes | Servings: 1

INGREDIENTS

2 organic free-range eggs
⅓ cup of organic heavy cream without food additives

½ tbsp. of sugar
2 tbsp. of grass-fed butter ground organic cinnamon to taste

INSTRUCTIONS

1. Add the eggs, cream, sugar, & to a dish and mix together. Place the dish inside your Air Fryer's frying basket. Cook at 370°F for 5 minutes.
2. Melt the butter in a saucepan over a medium heat. Lower the heat once the butter is melted.
3. Combine together with the egg & cream mixture.
4. While Cooking, mix until it thickens & curdles.
5. When you see the first signs of curdling, remove the saucepan immediately from the heat.
6. Pour the porridge into a bowl. Sprinkle cinnamon on top & serve immediately.

11. EGGS FLORENTINE

Prep & Cook Time: 20 minutes | Servings: 2

INGREDIENTS

1 cup of washed, fresh spinach leaves
2 tbsp. of freshly grated parmesan cheese
Sea salt & pepper

1 tbsp. of white vinegar
2 eggs

INSTRUCTIONS

1. Cook the spinach briefly inside your Air Fryer at 350°F until browned.
2. When done, take out the spinach and sprinkle with parmesan cheese & seasoning.
3. Slice into bite-size pieces & place on a plate.
4. Simmer a pan of water & add the vinegar. Stir quickly with a spoon.
5. Break an egg into the center. Turn off the heat & cover until set.
6. Repeat with the second egg.
7. Place the eggs on top of the spinach & serve.

---

12. SPANISH OMELET

Prep & Cook Time: 15 minutes | Servings: 2

INGREDIENTS

3 eggs
Cayenne or black pepper

½ cup of finely chopped vegetables

INSTRUCTIONS

1. In a flat greased dish, add the vegetables. Place the dish inside your Air Fryer and cook at 390°F until browned.
2. Take out the dish and put to one side.
3. In another dish, cook the eggs with one tbsp. of water & a pinch of pepper inside your Air Fryer at 390°F.
4. When almost cooked, top with the vegetables & flip to cook briefly.
5. Serve onto plates!

---

13. CRISTY'S PANCAKES

Prep & Cook Time: 10 minutes | Servings: 1

INGREDIENTS

1 tbsp. of vanilla extract
oz./110g of flour

2 tbsp. of water
1 egg

INSTRUCTIONS

1. Add the ingredients together inside a bowl & mix together.
2. Pour the mixture into a flat dish and place it inside your Air Fryer's frying basket.
3. Cook at 390°F for approximately 2 to 3 minutes on each side (watch carefully as it may burn quickly.)
4. Serve buttered with a handful of mixed berries.

---

14. BREAKFAST TEA

Prep & Cook Time: 5 minutes | Servings: 1

INGREDIENTS

16 oz. of water
2 tea bags

1 tbsp. of butter
1 tbsp. of coconut oil

½ tsp. of vanilla extract

INSTRUCTIONS

1. Make the tea & put it to one aside.
2. In a bowl, melt the butter.
3. Add the coconut oil & vanilla to the melted butter.
4. Pour the tea into a dish. Place the dish inside your Air Fryer and heat the tea until hot. Pour into mugs and serve hot!

---

15. SAUSAGE QUICHE

Prep & Cook Time: 35 minutes | Servings: 4

INGREDIENTS

12 large eggs
1 cup of heavy cream
1 tsp. of black pepper

12 oz. of sugar-free breakfast sausage
2 cups of shredded cheddar cheese

INSTRUCTIONS

1. Preheat your Air Fryer to 375°F/190°C.
2. In a large bowl, whisk the eggs, heavy cream, salad & pepper together.
3. Add the breakfast sausage & cheddar cheese.
4. Pour the mixture into a greased casserole dish.

5. Bake for 25 minutes. When done, serve & enjoy!
6. Cut into 12 squares & serve hot.

---

16. BREAKFAST SAUSAGE CASSEROLE

Prep & Cook Time: 70 minutes | Servings: 4

INGREDIENTS

8 eggs, beaten
1 head of chopped cauliflower

1 lb. of sausage, cooked & crumbled
2 cups of heavy whipping cream

1 cup of sharp cheddar cheese, grated

INSTRUCTIONS

1. Place the sausages onto a greased dish & place the dish inside your Air Fryer at 380°F for 20 minutes (10 each side) until golden brown.
2. When cooked, mix the sausage, heavy whipping cream, chopped cauliflower, cheese & eggs. Mix until well combined.
3. Pour into a greased dish.
4. Cook for 30 minutes at 350°F/175°C inside your Air Fryer.
5. Top with cheese & serve!

---

17. SCRAMBLED MUG EGGS

Prep & Cook Time: 5 minutes | Servings: 1

INGREDIENTS

1 mug
2 eggs

Salt & pepper
Shredded cheese

Your favorite buffalo wing sauce

INSTRUCTIONS

1. Crack the eggs into a mug & whisk until blended.
2. Put the mug into your Air Fryer & cook at 360°F for 1.5 – 2 minutes, depending on the power of your fryer.
3. Leave for a few minutes & remove from the fryer.
4. Sprinkle with salt & pepper. Add your desired amount of cheese on top.
5. Using a fork, mix everything together.
6. Then add your favorite buffalo or hot sauce & mix again.
7. Serve!

---

18. BANANA CHIA SEED PUDDING

Prep & Cook Time: 1-2 days | Servings: 1

INGREDIENTS

1 can of full-fat coconut milk
1 medium- or small-sized banana, ripe

½ tsp. of cinnamon
1 tsp. of vanilla extract

¼ cup of chia seeds

INSTRUCTIONS

1. In a bowl, mash the banana until soft.
2. Add the remaining ingredients & mix until incorporated. Cook inside your Air Fryer at 360°F until the bananas are mushy and the cinnamon golden brown.
3. Cover & place in your refrigerator overnight.
4. Serve!

---

19. STRAWBERRY RHUBARB PARFAIT

Prep & Cook Time: 30 minutes | Servings: 1

INGREDIENTS

1 packet of plain full-fat yogurt (8.5 oz.)
2 tbsp. of toasted flakes

2 tbsp. of toasted coconut flakes
6 tbsp. of strawberry & rhubarb jam

INSTRUCTIONS

1. Add the jam into a dessert bowl (3 tbsp. per serving).
2. Add the crème fraîche & garnish with the toasted & coconut flakes.
3. Place inside your Air fryer and flash fry for a few seconds on a very high heat at 400°F/200°C (maximum possible), until the dessert is crisp on the outside and soft on the inside.
4. Serve!

---

20. SAUSAGE EGG MUFFINS

Prep & Cook Time: 30 minutes | Servings: 4

INGREDIENTS

6 oz. of Italian sausage
6 eggs

1/8 cup of heavy cream
3 oz. of cheese

INSTRUCTIONS

1. Preheat the Air Fryer to 350°F/175°C.
2. Grease a muffin pan.

3. Slice the sausage links & place them two to a tin.
4. Beat the eggs with the cream & season with salt & pepper.
5. Pour over the sausages in the tin.
6. Sprinkle with cheese & the remaining egg mixture.
7. Cook for 20 minutes or until the eggs are done & serve!

21. SALMON OMELET
Prep & Cook Time: 15 minutes | Servings: 2

INGREDIENTS

3 eggs
1 smoked salmon

3 links of pork sausage
¼ cup of onions

¼ cup of provolone cheese

INSTRUCTIONS

1. Whisk the eggs & pour them into a bowl. Place the bowl inside your Air Fryer's frying basket.
2. Cook briefly at 400°F/200°C for a few minutes each side.
3. Toss in the onions, salmon & cheese before turning the omelet over. Cook for a few more minutes.
4. Sprinkle the omelet with cheese & serve with the sausages on the side.
5. Serve!

22. BLACK'S BANGIN' CASSEROLE
Prep & Cook Time: 40 minutes | Servings: 4

INGREDIENTS

5 eggs
3 tbsp. of chunky tomato sauce

2 tbsp. of heavy cream
2 tbsp. of grated parmesan cheese

INSTRUCTIONS

1. Preheat your Air Fryer to 350°F/175°C.
2. Combine the eggs & cream in a bowl.
3. Mix in the tomato sauce & add the cheese.
4. Spread into a glass baking dish & bake for 25-35 minutes.
5. Top with extra cheese.
6. Enjoy!

23. HASH BROWN
Prep & Cook Time: 20 minutes | Servings: 2

INGREDIENTS

12 oz. grated fresh cauliflower (about ½ a
   medium-sized head)

4 slices of bacon, chopped
3 oz. of onion, chopped

1 tbsp. of butter, softened

INSTRUCTIONS

1. In a skillet, sauté the bacon & onion until brown.
2. Add in the cauliflower & stir until tender & browned.
3. Add the butter steadily as it cooks.
4. Season to taste with salt & pepper.
5. Enjoy!

24. BACON CUPS
Prep & Cook Time: 40 minutes | Servings: 2

INGREDIENTS

2 eggs
1 sliced tomato

3 slices of bacon
2 slices of ham

2 tsp. of grated parmesan cheese

INSTRUCTIONS

1. Preheat your Air Fryer to 375°F/190°C.
2. Cook the bacon for half of the directed time.
3. Slice the bacon strips in half & line 2 greased muffin tins with 3 half-strips of bacon
4. Put one slice of ham & half slice of tomato in each muffin tin on top of the bacon
5. Crack one egg on top of the tomato in each muffin tin & sprinkle each with half a tsp. of grated parmesan cheese.
6. Bake for 20 minutes.
7. Remove & let cool.
8. Serve!

25. SPINACH EGGS AND CHEESE
Prep & Cook Time: 40 minutes | Servings: 2

INGREDIENTS

3 whole eggs
3 oz. of cottage cheese

3-4 oz. of chopped spinach
¼ cup of parmesan cheese

¼ cup of milk

INSTRUCTIONS

1. Preheat your Air Fryer to 375°F/190°C.
2. In a large bowl, whisk the eggs, cottage cheese, the parmesan & the milk.
3. Mix in the spinach.
4. Transfer to a small, greased, Air Fryer dish.
5. Sprinkle the cheese on top.
6. Bake for 25-30 minutes.
7. Let cool for 5 minutes & serve.

26. FRIED EGGS

Prep & Cook Time: 7 minutes | Servings: 2

INGREDIENTS

2 eggs
3 slices of bacon

INSTRUCTIONS

1. Heat some oil in a deep Air Fryer at 375°F/190°C.
2. Fry the bacon.
3. In a small bowl, add the 2 eggs.
4. Quickly add the eggs into the center of the Air Fryer.
5. Using two spatulas, form the egg into a ball while frying.
6. Fry for 2-3 minutes, until it stops bubbling.
7. Place on a paper towel & allow to drain.
8. Enjoy!

27. SCOTCH EGGS

Prep & Cook Time: 40 minutes | Servings: 4

INGREDIENTS

4 large eggs
1 packet of pork sausage (12 oz.)

8 slices of thick-cut bacon
4 toothpicks

INSTRUCTIONS

1. Hard-boil the eggs, peel the shells & let them cool.
2. Slice the sausage into four parts & place each part into a large circle.
3. Put an egg into each circle & wrap it in the sausage.
4. Place inside your refrigerator for 1 hour.
5. Make a cross with two pieces of thick-cut bacon.
6. Place a wrapped egg in the center, fold the bacon over top of the egg & secure with a toothpick.
7. Cook inside your Air Fryer at 450°F/230°C for 25 minutes.
8. Enjoy!

28. TOASTIES

Prep & Cook Time: 30 minutes | Servings: 2

INGREDIENTS

¼ cup of milk or cream
2 sausages, boiled
3 eggs

1 slice of bread, sliced lengthwise
4 tbsp. of cheese, grated
Sea salt to taste

Chopped fresh herbs & steamed broccoli
[optional]

INSTRUCTIONS

1. Pre-heat your Air Fryer at 360°F & set the timer for 5 minutes.
2. In the meantime, scramble the eggs in a bowl & add in the milk.
3. Grease three muffin cups with a cooking spray. Divide the egg mixture in three & pour equal amounts into each cup.
4. Slice the sausages & drop them, along with the slices of bread, into the egg mixture. Add the cheese on top & a little salt as desired.
5. Transfer the cups to the Fryer & cook for 15-20 minutes, depending on how firm you would like them. When ready, remove them from the Air Fryer & serve with fresh herbs & steam broccoli if you prefer.

29. EGG BAKED OMELET

Prep & Cook Time: 15 minutes | Servings: 1

INGREDIENTS

1 tbsp. of ricotta cheese
1 tbsp. of chopped parsley

1 tsp. of olive oil
3 eggs

¼ cup of chopped spinach
Salt & pepper

INSTRUCTIONS

1. Set your Air Fryer at 330°F & allow to warm with the olive oil inside.

2. In a bowl, beat the eggs with a fork & sprinkle some salt & pepper as desired.
3. Add in the ricotta, spinach, & parsley & then transfer to the Air Fryer. Cook for 10 minutes before serving.

30. BREAKFAST OMELET

Prep & Cook Time: 30 minutes | Servings: 2

INGREDIENTS

1 large onion, chopped
2 tbsp. of cheddar cheese, grated
3 eggs

½ tsp. of soy sauce
Salt
Pepper powder

Cooking spray

INSTRUCTIONS

1. In a bowl, mix the salt, pepper powder, soy sauce & eggs with a whisk.
2. Take a small pan small enough to fit inside the Air Fryer & spritz with cooking spray. Spread the chopped onion across the bottom of the pan, then transfer the pan to the Fryer. Cook at 355°F for 6-7 minutes, ensuring the onions turn translucent.
3. Add the egg mixture on top of the onions, coating everything well. Add the cheese on top, then resume cooking for another 5 or 6 minutes.
4. Take care when taking the pan out of the Air Fryer. Enjoy with some toasted bread.

31. RANCH RISOTTO

Prep & Cook Time: 40 minutes | Servings: 2

INGREDIENTS

1 onion, diced
2 cups of chicken stock, boiling
½ cup of parmesan, grated

1 clove of garlic, minced
¾ cup of Arborio rice
1 tbsp. of olive oil

1 tbsp. of butter

INSTRUCTIONS

1. Set the Air Fryer at 390°F for 5 minutes to heat up.
2. With oil, grease a round baking tin, small enough to fit inside the Air Fryer, & stir in the garlic, butter, & onion.
3. Transfer the tin to the Air Fryer & allow to cook for 4 minutes. Add in the rice & cook for a further 4 minutes, giving it a stir three times throughout the cooking time.
4. Turn the Air Fryer down to 320°F & add in the chicken stock, before gently mixing it. Leave to cook for 22 minutes with the Air Fryer uncovered. Before serving, throw in the cheese & give it one more stir. Enjoy!

32. COFFEE DONUTS

Prep & Cook Time: 20 minutes | Servings: 6

INGREDIENTS

1 cup of flour
¼ cup of sugar

½ tsp. of salt
1 tsp. of baking powder

1 tbsp. of sunflower oil
¼ cup of coffee

INSTRUCTIONS

1. In a large bowl, combine the sugar, salt, flour, & baking powder.
2. Add in the coffee & sunflower oil & mix until a dough is formed. Leave the dough to rest in & the refrigerator.
3. Set your Air Fryer at 400°F to heat up.
4. Remove the dough from the refrigerator & divide up, kneading each section into a doughnut.
5. Put the doughnuts inside the Air Fryer, ensuring not to overlap any. Fry for 6 minutes. Do not shake the basket, to make sure the doughnuts hold their shape.

33. TACO WRAPS

Prep & Cook Time: 30 minutes | Servings: 4

INGREDIENTS

1 tbsp. of water
4 pc of commercial vegan nuggets, chopped

1 small yellow onion, diced
1 small red bell pepper, chopped
2 cobs grilled corn kernels

4 large corn tortillas
Mixed greens for garnish

INSTRUCTIONS

1. Pre-heat your Air Fryer at 400°F.
2. Over a medium heat, water-sauté the nuggets with the onions, corn kernels & bell peppers in a skillet, then remove from the heat.
3. Fill the tortillas with the nuggets & vegetables & fold them up. Transfer to the inside of the Air Fryer & cook for 15 minutes. Once crispy, serve immediately, garnished with the mixed greens. Enjoy!

34. BISTRO WEDGES

Prep & Cook Time: 20 minutes | Servings: 4

INGREDIENTS

1 lb. of fingerling potatoes, cut into wedges
1 tsp. of extra virgin olive oil

½ tsp. of garlic powder
Salt & pepper
½ cup of raw cashews

½ tsp. of ground turmeric
½ tsp. of paprika
1 tbsp. of yeast

1 tsp. of fresh lemon juice   2 tbsp. to ¼ cup of water

INSTRUCTIONS

1. Pre-heat your Air Fryer at 400°F.
2. In a bowl, toss together the potato wedges, olive oil, garlic powder, & salt & pepper, making sure to coat the potatoes well.
3. Transfer the potatoes to the basket of your Air Fryer & fry for 10 minutes.
4. In the meantime, prepare the cheese sauce. Pulse the cashews, turmeric, paprika, yeast, lemon juice, & water together in a food processor. Add more water to achieve your desired consistency.
5. When the potatoes are finished cooking, move them to a bowl that is small enough to fit inside the Air Fryer & add the cheese sauce on top. Cook for an additional 3 minutes. Serve when done!

35. SPINACH BALLS

Prep & Cook Time: 20 minutes | Servings: 4

INGREDIENTS

1 carrot, peeled & grated	1 egg, beaten	½ tsp. of black pepper
1 packet of fresh spinach, blanched & chopped	½ tsp. of garlic powder	1 tbsp. of yeast
½ onion, chopped	1 tsp. of garlic, minced	1 tbsp. of flour
	1 tsp. of salt	2 slices of bread, toasted

INSTRUCTIONS

1. In a food processor, pulse the toasted bread to form breadcrumbs. Transfer into a shallow dish or bowl.
2. In a bowl, mix together all the other ingredients.
3. Use your hands to shape the mixture into small-sized balls. Roll the balls in the breadcrumbs, ensuring to cover them well.
4. Whack inside the Air Fryer & cook at 390°F for 10 minutes. Serve when done!

36. CHEESE & CHICKEN SANDWICH

Prep & Cook Time: 15 minutes | Servings: 1

INGREDIENTS

⅓ cup of chicken, cooked & shredded	1 tsp. of mayonnaise	¼ tsp. of smoked paprika
2 mozzarella slices	2 tsp. of butter	¼ tsp. of black pepper
1 hamburger bun	1 tsp. of olive oil	¼ tsp. of garlic powder
¼ cup of cabbage, shredded	½ tsp. of balsamic vinegar	Salt

INSTRUCTIONS

1. Pre-heat your Air Fryer at 370°F.
2. Apply some butter to the outside of the hamburger bun with a brush.
3. In a bowl, coat the chicken with the garlic powder, salt, pepper, & paprika.
4. In a separate bowl, stir together the mayonnaise, olive oil, cabbage, & balsamic vinegar to make coleslaw.
5. Slice the bun in two. Start building the sandwich, starting with the chicken, followed by the mozzarella, the coleslaw, & finally the top bun.
6. Transfer the sandwich to the Air Fryer & cook for 5 – 7 minutes.

37. BACON & HORSERADISH CREAM

Prep & Cook Time: 1 hour 40 minutes | Servings: 4

INGREDIENTS

½ lb. of thick cut bacon, diced	2 tbsp. of flour	1 tbsp. of olive oil
2 tbsp. of butter	1 cup of heavy cream	½ tsp. of sea salt
2 shallots, sliced	2 tbsp. of prepared horseradish	Ground black pepper to taste
½ cup of milk	½ tbsp. of fresh thyme leaves	½ cup of water
1 ½ lb. of Brussels sprouts, halved	1/8 tsp. of ground nutmeg	

INSTRUCTIONS

1. Pre-heat your Air Fryer at 400°F.
2. Coat the Brussels sprouts with olive oil & sprinkle some salt & pepper on top. Transfer to the Air Fryer & cook for a half hour. At the halfway point, give them a good stir, then take them out of the Air Fryer & set to the side.
3. Put the bacon in the basket of the Air Fryer & pour the water into the drawer underneath to catch the fat. Cook for 10 minutes, stirring 2 or 3 times throughout the cooking time.
4. When 10 minutes are up, add in the shallots. Cook for a further 10 – 15 minutes, making sure the shallots soften up & the bacon turns brown. Add some more pepper & remove. Leave to drain on some paper towels.
5. Melt the butter over the stove or in the microwave, before adding in the flour & mixing with a whisk. Slowly add in the heavy cream & milk & continue to whisk for another 3 – 5 minutes, making sure the mixture thickens.
6. Add the horseradish, thyme, salt, & nutmeg & stirring well once more.
7. Take a 9" x 13" baking dish & grease it with oil. Pre-heat your Air Fryer to 350°F.
8. Put the Brussels sprouts in the baking dish & spread them across the base. Pour over the cream sauce & then top with a layer of bacon & shallots.
9. Cook in the Air Fryer for a half hour & enjoy.

38. VEGETABLE TOAST

INGREDIENTS

4 slices of bread
1 red bell pepper, cut into strips
1 cup of sliced button or cremini

mushrooms
1 small yellow squash, sliced
2 green onions, sliced

1 tbsp. of olive oil
2 tbsp. of softened butter
½ cup of soft goat cheese

INSTRUCTIONS

1. Drizzle the Air Fryer with the olive oil & pre-heat to 350°F.
2. Put the red pepper, green onions, mushrooms, & squash inside the Air Fryer, give them a stir & cook for 7 minutes, shaking the basket once throughout the cooking time. Ensure the vegetables become tender.
3. Remove the vegetables & set them aside.
4. Spread some butter on the slices of bread & transfer to the Air Fryer, butter side-up. Brown for 2 to 4 minutes.
5. Remove the toast from the Air Fryer & top with goat cheese & vegetables. Serve warm.

39. CINNAMON TOASTS

Prep & Cook Time: 15 minutes | Servings: 4

INGREDIENTS

10 slices of bread
1 pack of salted butter

4 tbsp. of sugar
2 tsp. of ground cinnamon

½ tsp. of vanilla extract

INSTRUCTIONS

1. In a bowl, combine the butter, cinnamon, sugar, & vanilla extract. Spread onto the slices of bread.
2. Set your Air Fryer to 380°F. When warmed up, put the bread inside the Air Fryer & cook for 4 – 5 minutes.

40. TOASTED CHEESE

Prep & Cook Time: 20 minutes | Servings: 2

INGREDIENTS

2 slices of bread

4 oz. cheese, grated

Small amount of butter

INSTRUCTIONS

1. Grill the bread in the toaster.
2. Butter the toast & top with the grated cheese.
3. Set your Air Fryer to 350°F to pre-heat.
4. Put the toast slices inside the Air Fryer & cook for 4 - 6 minutes.
5. Serve & enjoy!

41. PEANUT BUTTER BREAD

Prep & Cook Time: 15 minutes | Servings: 3

INGREDIENTS

1 tbsp. of oil
2 tbsp. of peanut butter

4 slices of bread
1 banana, sliced

INSTRUCTIONS

1. Spread the peanut butter on top of each slice of bread, then arrange the banana slices on top. Sandwich two slices together, then the other two.
2. Oil the inside of the Air Fryer & cook the bread for 5 minutes at 300°F.

42. ENGLISH BUILDER'S BREAKFAST

Prep & Cook Time: 35 minutes | Servings: 2

INGREDIENTS

1 cup of potatoes, sliced & diced
2 cups of beans in tomato sauce

2 eggs
1 tbsp. of olive oil

1 sausage
Salt

INSTRUCTIONS

1. Set your Air Fryer at 390°F to pre-heat.
2. Break the eggs onto an Air Fryer-safe dish & sprinkle on some salt.
3. Lay the beans on the dish, next to the eggs.
4. In a bowl small enough to fit inside your Air Fryer, coat the potatoes with the olive oil. Sprinkle on the salt, as desired.
5. Transfer the bowl of potato slices to the Air Fryer & cook for 10 minutes.
6. Swap out the bowl of potatoes for the dish containing the eggs & beans. Leave to cook for another 10 minutes. Cover the potatoes with parchment paper.
7. Slice up the sausage & throw the slices in on top of the beans & eggs. Resume cooking for another 5 minutes. Serve with the potatoes, as well as toast & coffee if desired.

43. AVOCADO EGGS

INGREDIENTS

2 large avocados, sliced
1 cup of breadcrumbs

½ cup of flour
2 eggs, beaten

¼ tsp. of paprika
Salt & pepper

INSTRUCTIONS

1. Pre-heat your Air Fryer at 400°F for 5 minutes.
2. Sprinkle some salt & pepper on the slices of avocado. Optionally, you can enhance the flavor with a half-tsp. of dried oregano.
3. Lightly coat the avocados with flour. Dredge them in the eggs, before covering with breadcrumbs. Transfer to the Air Fryer & cook for 6 minutes.

---

44. AVOCADO TEMPURA

Prep & Cook Time: 20 minutes | Servings: 4

INGREDIENTS

½ cup of breadcrumbs
½ tsp. of salt

1 avocado, pitted, peeled & sliced
Liquid from 1 can white beans

INSTRUCTIONS

1. Set your Air Fryer to 350°F to pre-heat.
2. Mix the breadcrumbs & salt in a shallow bowl until well-incorporated.
3. Dip the avocado slices in the bean juice, then into the breadcrumbs. Put the avocados in the Air Fryer, taking care not to overlap any slices, & fry for 10 minutes, giving the basket a good shake at the halfway point. Serve when done!

---

45. POTATO & KALE NUGGETS

Prep & Cook Time: 25 minutes | Servings: 4

INGREDIENTS

1 tsp. of extra virgin olive oil
1 clove of garlic, minced
4 cups of kale, rinsed & chopped

2 cups of potatoes, boiled & mashed
1/8 cup of milk

Salt & pepper
Vegetable oil

INSTRUCTIONS

1. Pre-heat your Air Fryer at 390°F.
2. In a skillet over medium heat, fry the garlic in the olive oil, until it turns golden brown. Cook with the kale for an additional 3 minutes & remove from the heat.
3. Mix the mashed potatoes, kale & garlic in a bowl. Throw in the milk & sprinkle with some salt & pepper as desired.
4. Shape the mixture into nuggets & spritz each one with a little vegetable oil. Put in the basket of your Air Fryer & leave to cook for 15 minutes, shaking the basket halfway through cooking to make sure the nuggets fry evenly.

---

46. BREAD ROLLS

Prep & Cook Time: 30 minutes | Servings: 5

INGREDIENTS

5 large potatoes, boiled & mashed
Salt & pepper
1 tbsp. of olive oil
½ tsp. of mustard seeds

2 small onions, chopped
½ tsp. of turmeric
2 sprigs of curry leaves
8 slices of bread, brown sides discarded

2 green chilis, seeded & chopped
1 bunch of coriander, chopped

INSTRUCTIONS

1. Pre-heat your Air Fryer at 400°F.
2. Put the mashed potatoes in a bowl & sprinkle on salt & pepper. Set to one side.
3. Fry the mustard seeds in a little olive oil over a medium-low heat, stirring continuously, until they sputter.
4. Add in the onions & cook until they turn translucent. Add the curry leaves & turmeric powder & stir. Cook for a further 2 minutes until fragrant.
5. Remove the pan from the heat & combine the contents with the potatoes. Remove from heat & add to the potatoes. Mix in the green chilies & coriander.
6. Wet the bread slightly & drain of any excess liquid.
7. Spoon a small amount of the potato mixture into the center of the bread & enclose the bread around the filling, sealing it entirely. Continue until the rest of the bread & filling is used up. Brush each bread roll with some oil & transfer to the basket of your Air Fryer.
8. Cook for 15 minutes, gently shaking the Air Fryer basket at the halfway point to ensure each roll is cooked evenly.

---

47. VEG FRITTATA

Prep & Cook Time: 35 minutes | Servings: 2

INGREDIENTS

¼ cup of milk
1 zucchini
½ bunch of asparagus
½ cup of mushrooms

½ cup of spinach or baby spinach
½ cup of red onion, sliced
4 eggs
½ tbsp. of olive oil

5 tbsp. of feta cheese, crumbled
4 tbsp. of cheddar, grated
¼ bunch of chives, minced
Sea salt & pepper to taste

INSTRUCTIONS

1. In a bowl, mix together the eggs, milk, salt & pepper.
2. Cut up the zucchini, asparagus, mushrooms & red onion into slices. Shred the spinach using your hands.
3. Over a medium heat, stir-fry the vegetables for 5 – 7 minutes with the olive oil in a non-stick pan.
4. Place some parchment paper in the base of a baking tin. Pour in the vegetables, followed by the egg mixture. Top with the feta & grated cheddar.
5. Set the Air Fryer at 320°F & allow to warm for five minutes.
6. Transfer the baking tin to the Air Fryer & allow to cook for 15 minutes. Take care when removing the frittata from the Air Fryer & leave to cool for 5 minutes.
7. Top with the minced chives & serve.

48. MAPLE CINNAMON BUNS

Prep & Cook Time: 1 hour 55 minutes | Servings: 9

INGREDIENTS

¾ cup of milk
4 tbsp. of maple syrup
1 ½ tbsp. of active yeast
1 tbsp. of ground flaxseed

1 tbsp. of coconut oil, melted
1 cup of flour
1 ½ cup of flour
2 tsp. of cinnamon powder

½ cup of pecan nuts, toasted
2 ripe bananas, sliced
4 Medjool dates, pitted
¼ cup of sugar

INSTRUCTIONS

1. Over a low heat, warm the milk until it is tepid. Combine with the yeast & maple syrup, waiting 5 – 10 minutes to allow the yeast to activate.
2. In the meantime, put 3 tbsp. of water & the flaxseed in a bowl & stir together. This is your egg substitute. Let the flaxseed absorb the water for about 2 minutes.
3. Pour the coconut oil into the bowl, then combine the flaxseed mixture with the yeast mixture.
4. In a separate bowl, mix together one tbsp. of the cinnamon powder & the white & flour. Add the yeast-flaxseed mixture & mix to create a dough.
5. Dust a flat surface with flour. On this surface, knead the dough with your hands for a minimum of 10 minutes.
6. Grease a large bowl & transfer the dough inside. Cover with a kitchen towel or saran wrap. Let sit in a warm, dark place for an hour so that the dough may rise.
7. In the meantime, prepare the filling. Mix the banana slices, dates, & pecans together before throwing in a tbsp. of cinnamon powder.
8. Set the Air Fryer to 390°F & allow to warm. On your floured surface, flatten the dough with a rolling pin, making it thin. Spoon the pecan mixture onto the dough & spread out evenly.
9. Roll up the dough & then slice it in nine. Transfer the slices to a dish small enough to fit in the Air Fryer, set the dish inside, & cook for 30 minutes.
10. Top with a thin layer of sugar before serving.

49. TAJ TOFU

Prep & Cook Time: 40 minutes | Servings: 4

INGREDIENTS

1 block of firm tofu, cut into 1-inch
thick cubes

2 tbsp. of soy sauce
2 tsp. of sesame seeds, toasted

1 tsp. of rice vinegar
1 tbsp. of corn-starch

INSTRUCTIONS

1. Set your Air Fryer at 400°F to pre-heat.
2. Add the tofu, soy sauce, sesame seeds & rice vinegar in a bowl together & mix well to coat the tofu cubes. Then cover the tofu in cornstarch & put it in the basket of your Air Fryer.
3. Cook for 25 minutes, giving the basket a shake at five-minute intervals to ensure the tofu cooks evenly.

50. RICE PAPER BACON

Prep & Cook Time: 30 minutes | Servings: 4

INGREDIENTS

3 tbsp. of soy sauce or tamari
2 tbsp. of cashew butter
2 tbsp. of liquid smoke

2 tbsp. of water
4 pc. of white rice paper, cut into 1-inch-
thick strips

INSTRUCTIONS

1. Pre-heat your Air Fryer at 350°F.
2. Mix together the soy sauce/tamari, liquid smoke, water, & cashew butter in a large bowl.
3. Take the strips of rice paper & soak them for 5 minutes. Arrange in one layer in the bottom of your Air Fryer.
4. Cook for 15 minutes, ensuring they become crispy, before serving with some vegetables.

51. POSH SOUFFLÉ

Prep & Cook Time: 25 minutes | Servings: 4

INGREDIENTS

¼ cup of flour
⅓ cup of butter

1 cup of milk
4 egg yolks

1 tsp. of vanilla extract
6 egg whites

| 1 oz. of sugar | 1 tsp. of cream of tartar |

INSTRUCTIONS

1. Set your Air Fryer at 320°F & allow to warm.
2. In a bowl, mix together the butter & flour until a smooth consistency is achieved.
3. Pour the milk into a saucepan over a low-to-medium heat. Add in the & allow to dissolve before raising the heat to boil the milk.
4. Pour in the flour & butter mixture & stir rigorously for 7 minutes to eliminate any lumps. Make sure the mixture thickens. Take off the heat & allow to cool for 15 minutes.
5. Spritz 6 soufflé dishes with oil spray.
6. Place the egg yolks & vanilla extract in a separate bowl & beat them together with a fork. Pour in the milk & combine well to incorporate everything.
7. In a smaller bowl mix together the egg whites & cream of tartar with a fork. Fold into the egg yolks-milk mixture before adding in the flour mixture. Transfer equal amounts to the 6 soufflé dishes.
8. Put the dishes in the Air Fryer & cook for 15 minutes.

52. EGG MUFFIN SANDWICH

Prep & Cook Time: 15 minutes | Servings: 1

INGREDIENTS

| 1 egg | 2 slices of bacon | 1 English muffin |

INSTRUCTIONS

1. Pre-heat your Air Fryer at 395°F
2. Take a ramekin & spritz it with cooking spray. Break an egg into the ramekin before transferring it to the basket of your Air Fryer, along with the English muffin & bacon slices, keeping each component separate.
3. Allow to cook for 6 minutes. After removing from the Air Fryer, allow to cool for around two minutes. Halve the muffin.
4. Create your sandwich by arranging the egg & bacon slices on the base & topping with the other half of the muffin.

53. PEA DELIGHT

Prep & Cook Time: 25 minutes | Servings: 2 – 4

INGREDIENTS

1 cup of flour	1 cup of coconut milk	½ cup chicken/turkey strips
1 tsp. of baking powder	1 cup of cream cheese	1 pinch sea salt
3 eggs	3 tbsp. of pea protein	1 cup of mozzarella cheese

INSTRUCTIONS

1. Set your Air Fryer at 390°F & allow to warm.
2. In a large bowl, mix all ingredients together using a large wooden spoon.
3. Spoon equal amounts of the mixture into muffin cups & allow to cook for 15 minutes.

54. CHOCO BARS

Prep & Cook Time: 30 minutes | Servings: 8

INGREDIENTS

2 cups of old-fashioned oats	½ cup of dried cherries, chopped	2 tbsp. of coconut oil
½ cup of quinoa, cooked	½ cup of dark chocolate, chopped	¼ tsp. of salt
½ cup of chia seeds	¾ cup of butter	½ cup of prunes, pureed
½ cup almonds, sliced	⅓ cup of honey	

INSTRUCTIONS

1. Pre-heat your Air Fryer at 375°F.
2. Put the oats, quinoa, almonds, cherries, chia seeds, & chocolate in a bowl & mix well.
3. Heat the butter, honey, & coconut oil in a saucepan, gently stirring together. Pour this over the oat mixture.
4. Mix in the salt & pureed prunes & combine well.
5. Transfer this to a baking dish small enough to fit inside the Air Fryer & cook for 15 minutes. Remove from the Air Fryer & allow to cool completely. Cut into bars & enjoy.

55. FRENCH TOAST

Prep & Cook Time: 25 minutes | Servings: 2

INGREDIENTS

4 slices of bread of your choosing	Salt	Pinch of ground cloves
2 tbsp. of soft butter	Pinch of cinnamon	Non-stick cooking spray
2 eggs, lightly beaten	Pinch of ground nutmeg	Sugar for serving

INSTRUCTIONS

1. In a shallow bowl, mix together the salt, spices & eggs.
2. Butter each side of the slices of bread & slice into strips. You may also use cookie cutters for this step.
3. Set your Air Fryer to 350°F & allow to warm up briefly.
4. Dredge each strip of bread in the egg & transfer to the Air Fryer. Cook for two minutes, ensuring the toast turns golden brown.

5. At this point, spritz the tops of the bread strips with cooking spray, flip, & cook for another 4 minutes on the other side. Top with a light dusting of sugar before serving.

56. CHEDDAR & BACON QUICHE

Prep & Cook Time: 30 minutes | Servings: 4

INGREDIENTS

3 tbsp. of Greek yogurt
½ cup of grated cheddar cheese
3 oz. of chopped bacon
4 eggs, beaten

¼ tsp. of garlic powder
Pinch of black pepper
1 short crust pastry
¼ tsp. of onion powder

¼ tsp. of sea salt
Pinch of flour for topping

INSTRUCTIONS

1. Pre-heat your Air Fryer at 330°F.
2. Take 8 ramekins & grease with a little oil. Coat with a sprinkling of flour, tapping to remove any excess.
3. Cut the shortcrust pastry in 8 & place each piece at the bottom of each ramekin.
4. Put all of the other ingredients in a bowl & combine well. Spoon equal amounts of the filling into each piece of pastry.
5. Cook the ramekins in the Air Fryer for 20 minutes.

57. CHORIZO RISOTTO

Prep & Cook Time: 1 hour 20 minutes | Servings: 4

INGREDIENTS

¼ cup of milk
½ cup of flour
4 oz. of breadcrumbs

4 oz. of chorizo, finely sliced
1 serving mushroom risotto rice
1 egg

Sea salt to taste

INSTRUCTIONS

1. In a bowl, combine the mushroom risotto rice with the risotto & salt before refrigerating to cool.
2. Set your Air Fryer at 390°F & leave to warm for 5 minutes.
3. Use your hands to form 2 tablespoons of risotto into a rice ball. Repeat until you have used up all the risotto. Roll each ball in the flour.
4. Crack the egg into a bowl & mix with the milk using a whisk. Coat each rice ball in the egg-milk mixture, & then in breadcrumbs.
5. Space the rice balls out in the baking dish of the Air Fryer. Bake for 20 minutes, ensuring they develop a crispy golden-brown crust.
6. Serve warm with a side of fresh vegetables & salad if desired.

58. CHOCO BREAD

Prep & Cook Time: 30 minutes | Servings: 12

INGREDIENTS

1 tbsp. of flax egg [1 tbsp. flax meal + 3 tbsp. of water]
1 cup of zucchini, shredded & squeezed
½ cup of sunflower oil
½ cup of maple syrup

1 tsp. of vanilla extract
1 tsp. of apple cider vinegar
½ cup of milk
1 cup of flour
1 tsp. of baking soda

½ cup of cocoa powder
¼ tsp. of salt
⅓ cup of chocolate chips

INSTRUCTIONS

1. Pre-heat your Air Fryer to 350°F.
2. Take a baking dish small enough to fit inside the Air Fryer & line it with parchment paper.
3. Mix together the flax meal, zucchini, sunflower oil, maple, vanilla, apple cider vinegar & milk in a bowl.
4. Incorporate the flour, cocoa powder, salt & baking soda, stirring all the time to combine everything well.
5. Finally, throw in the chocolate chips.
6. Transfer the batter to the baking dish & cook in the Air Fryer for 15 minutes. Make sure to test with a toothpick before serving by sticking it in the center. The bread is ready when the toothpick comes out clean.

59. RED ROLLS

Prep & Cook Time: 45 minutes | Servings: 6

INGREDIENTS

7 cups of minced meat
1 small onion, diced
1 packet of spring roll sheets

2 oz. of Asian noodles
3 cloves of garlic, crushed
1 cup of mixed vegetables

1 tbsp. of sesame oil
2 tbsp. of water
1 tsp. of soy sauce

INSTRUCTIONS

1. Cook the noodles in hot water until they turn soft. Drain & cut to your desired length.
2. Grease the wok with sesame oil. Put it over a medium-high heat & fry the minced meat, mixed vegetables, garlic, & onion, stirring regularly to ensure the minced meat cooks through. The cooking time will vary depending on the pan you are using – allow 3-5 minutes if using a wok, & 7-10 if using a standard frying pan.
3. Drizzle in the soy sauce & add to the noodles, tossing well to allow the juices to spread & absorb evenly.
4. Spoon the stir-fry diagonally across a spring roll sheet & fold back the top point over the filling. Fold over the sides. Before folding back the bottom point, brush it with cold water, which will act as an adhesive.

5. Repeat until all the filling & sheets are used.
6. Pre-heat your Air Fryer at 360°F.
7. If desired, drizzle a small amount of oil over the top of the spring rolls to enhance the taste & ensure crispiness.
8. Cook the spring rolls in the Air Fryer for 8 minutes, in multiple batches if necessary. Serve & enjoy.

60. CHIA & OAT PORRIDGE

Prep & Cook Time: 15 minutes | Servings: 4

INGREDIENTS

4 cups of milk
2 tbsp. of peanut butter

2 cups of oats
1 cup of chia seeds

4 tbsp. of honey
1 tbsp. of butter, melted

INSTRUCTIONS

1. Pre-heat the Air Fryer to 390°F.
2. Put the peanut butter, honey, butter, & milk in a bowl & mix together using a whisk. Add in the oats & chia seeds & stir.
3. Transfer the mixture to an Air Fryer-proof bowl that is small enough to fit inside the Air Fryer & cook for 5 minutes. Give another stir before serving.

61. AMERICAN DONUTS

Prep & Cook Time: 1 hour 20 minutes | Servings: 6

INGREDIENTS

1 cup of flour
¼ cup of sugar
1 tsp. of baking powder

½ tsp. of salt
¼ tsp. of cinnamon
1 tbsp. of coconut oil, melted

2 tbsp. of liquid from canned chickpeas
¼ cup of milk

INSTRUCTIONS

1. Put the sugar, flour & baking powder in a bowl & combine. Mix in the salt & cinnamon.
2. In a separate bowl, combine the chickpea liquid, milk & coconut oil.
3. Slowly pour the dry ingredients into the wet ingredients & combine well to create a sticky dough.
4. Refrigerate for at least an hour.
5. Pre-heat your Air Fryer at 370°F.
6. Using your hands, shape the dough into several small balls & place each one inside the Air Fryer. Cook for 10 minutes, refraining from shaking the basket as they cook.
7. Lightly dust the balls with sugar & cinnamon & serve with a hot cup of coffee.

62. TOFU SCRAMBLE

Prep & Cook Time: 40 minutes | Servings: 3

INGREDIENTS

2 ½ cups red potato, chopped
1 tbsp. of olive oil
1 block of tofu, chopped finely
1tbsp. of olive oil

2 tbsp. of tamari
1 tsp. of turmeric powder
½ tsp. of onion powder
½ tsp. of garlic powder

½ cup of onion, chopped
4 cups of broccoli florets

INSTRUCTIONS

1. Pre-heat the Air Fryer at 400°F.
2. Toss together the potatoes & olive oil.
3. Cook the potatoes in a baking dish for 15 minutes, shaking once during the cooking time to ensure they fry evenly.
4. Combine the tofu, olive oil, turmeric, onion powder, tamari, & garlic powder together, before stirring in the onions, followed by the broccoli.
5. Top the potatoes with the tofu mixture & allow to cook for an additional 15 minutes. Serve warm.

63. SPINACH QUICHE

Prep & Cook Time: 1 hour 15 minutes | Servings: 4

INGREDIENTS

¾ cup of flour
½ cup of cold coconut oil
2 tbsp. of water
2 tbsp. of olive oil
1 onion, chopped

4 oz. of mushrooms, sliced
1 packet of firm tofu, pressed to remove excess water, then crumbled
1 lb. of spinach, washed & chopped
½ tbsp. of dried dill

2 tbsp. of yeast
Salt & pepper
Sprig of fresh parsley, chopped

INSTRUCTIONS

1. Pre-heat the Air Fryer at 375°F.
2. Firstly, prepare the pastry. Use a sieve to sift together the salt & flour into a bowl. Combine with the coconut oil to make the flour crumbly. Slowly pour in the water until a stiff dough is formed.
3. Wrap the dough in saran wrap & refrigerate for a half hour.
4. Sauté the onion in a skillet over medium heat for a minute. Add in the tofu & mushroom, followed by the spinach, yeast, & dill.
5. Sprinkle in salt & pepper as desired. Finally add in the parsley. Take the skillet off the heat.
6. Dust a flat surface with flour & roll out the dough until it is thin.

7. Grease a baking dish that is small enough to fit inside the Air Fryer. Place the dough in the tin & pour in the tofu mixture. Transfer the dish to the Air Fryer & cook for 30 minutes, ensuring the pastry crisps up.

64. MONKEY SALAD

Prep & Cook Time: 10 minutes | Servings: 1

INGREDIENTS

2 tbsp. of butter
1 cup of coconut flakes

1 cup of cashews
1 cup of almonds

1 cup of 90% dark chocolate shavings

INSTRUCTIONS

1. Inside your Air Fryer, melt the butter and add the coconut flakes.
2. Flash fry at 400°F/200°C for a few minutes.
3. Add the cashews & almonds & sauté for 3 minutes. Remove from the heat & sprinkle with dark chocolate shavings.
4. Serve!

65. JARLSBERG LUNCH OMELET

Prep & Cook Time: 10 minutes | Servings: 2

INGREDIENTS

4 medium mushrooms, sliced, 2 oz.
1 green onion, sliced

2 eggs, beaten
1 oz. of Jarlsberg or Swiss cheese,

1 oz. of ham, diced

INSTRUCTIONS

1. Add the mushrooms & green onion to a bowl and cook until tender inside your Air Fryer at 400°F/200°C.
2. Add the eggs & mix well.
3. Sprinkle with salt & top with the mushroom mixture, cheese & the ham.
4. When the egg is set, fold the plain side of the omelet on the filled side.
5. Cook for 1-2 more minutes & let it stand until the cheese has melted.
6. Serve!

66. MU SHU LUNCH PORK

Prep & Cook Time: 20 minutes | Servings: 2

INGREDIENTS

4 cups of coleslaw mix, with carrots
1 small onion, sliced thin

1 lb. of cooked pork, cut into ½" cubes
2 tbsp. of hoisin sauce

2 tbsp. of soy sauce

INSTRUCTIONS

1. In a bowl, add the oil. Toss in the cabbage, onions & pork. Mix.
2. Fry the 400°F/200°C inside your Air Fryer for 10 minutes.
3. Top with the hoisin & soy sauce. Fry for 2 more minutes.
4. Cook until browned.
5. Enjoy!

67. FIERY JALAPENO POPPERS

Prep & Cook Time: 40 minutes | Servings: 4

INGREDIENTS

5 oz. of cream cheese
¼ cup of mozzarella cheese

8 medium jalapeno peppers
½ tsp. of Mrs. Dash Table Blend

8 slices of bacon

INSTRUCTIONS

1. Preheat your Air Fryer to 400°F/200°C.
2. Cut the jalapenos in half.
3. Use a spoon to scrape out the insides of the peppers.
4. In a bowl, add together the cream cheese, mozzarella cheese & spices of your choice.
5. Pack the cream cheese mixture into the jalapenos & place the peppers on top.
6. Wrap each pepper in 1 slice of bacon, starting from the bottom & working up.
7. Bake for 30 minutes. Broil for an additional 3 minutes.
8. Serve!

68. BACON & CHICKEN PATTIES

Prep & Cook Time: 15 minutes | Servings: 2

INGREDIENTS

1 ½ oz. of chicken breast
4 slices of bacon

¼ cup of parmesan cheese
1 large egg

3 tbsp. of flour

INSTRUCTIONS

1. Cook the bacon inside your Air Fryer at 400°F/200°C until crispy.

2. Chop the chicken & bacon together in a food processor until fine.
3. Add in the parmesan, egg, flour & mix.
4. Make the patties by hand & fry on a medium heat in a pan with some oil.
5. Once browned, flip over, continue frying.
6. Serve!

69. CHEDDAR BACON BURST

Prep & Cook Time: 90 minutes | Servings: 8

INGREDIENTS

30 slices of bacon
2 ½ cups of cheddar cheese

4-5 cups of raw spinach
1-2 tbsp. of Southwest Seasoning

2 tsp. of Mrs. Dash Table Seasoning

INSTRUCTIONS

1. Preheat your Air Fryer to 375°F/190°C.
2. Weave the bacon into 15 vertical pieces & 12 horizontal pieces. Cut the extra 3 in half to fill in the rest, horizontally.
3. Season the bacon.
4. Add the cheese to the bacon.
5. Add the spinach & press down to compress.
6. Tightly roll up the woven bacon.
7. Line a baking sheet with kitchen foil & add plenty of salt to it.
8. Put the bacon on top of a cooling rack & put that on top of your baking sheet.
9. Bake for 60-70 minutes.
10. Let cool for 10-15 minutes before
11. Slice & enjoy!

70. GRILLED HAM & CHEESE

Prep & Cook Time: 30 minutes | Servings: 2

INGREDIENTS

3 buns
4 slices of medium-cut deli ham

1 tbsp. of salted butter
1 oz. of flour

3 slices of cheddar cheese
3 slices of muenster cheese

INSTRUCTIONS

Bread:
1. Preheat your Air Fryer to 350°F/175°C.
2. Mix the flour, salt & baking powder in a bowl. Put to the side.
3. Add in the butter & coconut oil to a skillet.
4. Melt for 20 seconds & pour into another bowl.
5. In this bowl, mix in the dough.
6. Scramble two eggs. Add to the dough.
7. Add ½ tbsp. of coconut flour to thicken, & place evenly into a cupcake tray. Fill about ¾ inch.
8. Bake for 20 minutes until browned.
9. Allow to cool for 15 minutes & cut each in half for the buns.
Sandwich:
1. Fry the deli meat in a skillet on a high heat.
2. Put the ham & cheese between the buns.
3. Heat the butter on medium high.
4. When brown, turn to low & add the dough to pan.
5. Press down with a weight until you smell burning, then flip to crisp both sides.
6. Enjoy!

71. MELTED PROSCIUTTO SPINACH SALAD

Prep & Cook Time: 5 minutes | Servings: 2

INGREDIENTS

2 cups of baby spinach
⅓ lb. of prosciutto

1 cantaloupe
1 avocado

¼ cup of diced red onion
handful of raw, of walnuts

INSTRUCTIONS

1. Put a cup of spinach on each plate.
2. Top with the diced prosciutto, cubes of balls of melon, slices of avocado, a handful of red onion & a few walnuts.
3. Add some freshly ground pepper, if you like.
4. Flash fry inside your Air Fryer at 400°F/200°C until the salad is crisp.
5. Serve!

72. RICED CAULIFLOWER & CURRY CHICKEN

Prep & Cook Time: 40 minutes | Servings: 6

INGREDIENTS

2 lb. of chicken (4 breasts) 3 tbsp. of butter 1 head cauliflower (around 1 kg)
1 packet of curry paste ½ cup of heavy cream

INSTRUCTIONS
1. Add the curry paste and chicken to a dish. Mix. Place inside your Air Fryer and cook at 400°F/200°C for 25 minutes.
2. Cut a cauliflower head into florets & blend in a food processor to make the riced cauliflower.
3. When the chicken is cooked, uncover, add the cream & cook for an additional 7 minutes.
4. Serve!

---

73. MASHED GARLIC TURNIPS

Prep & Cook Time: 10 minutes | Servings: 2

INGREDIENTS

3 cups of diced turnip ¼ cup of heavy cream Salt & pepper to season
2 cloves of garlic, minced 3 tbsp. of melted butter

INSTRUCTIONS
1. Fry the turnips inside your Air Fryer at 400°F/200°C until tender.
2. Drain & mash the turnips.
3. Add the cream, butter, salt, pepper & garlic. Combine well.
4. Serve!

---

74. LASAGNA SPAGHETTI SQUASH

Prep & Cook Time: 90 minutes | Servings: 6

INGREDIENTS

25 slices of mozzarella cheese 30 oz. of whole-milk ricotta cheese 4 lb. of ground beef
1 jar (40 oz.) of Marinara sauce 2 large spaghetti squash, cooked (44 oz.)

INSTRUCTIONS
1. Preheat your Air Fryer to 375°F/190°C.
2. Slice the spaghetti squash & place it face down inside a Air Fryer proof dish. Fill with water until covered.
3. Bake for 45 minutes until skin is soft.
4. Sear the meat until browned.
5. In a large skillet, heat the browned meat & marinara sauce. Set aside when warm.
6. Scrape the flesh off the cooked squash to resemble strands of spaghetti.
7. Layer the lasagna in a large, greased pan in alternating layers of spaghetti squash, meat sauce, mozzarella, ricotta. Repeat until all increased have been used.
8. Bake for 30 minutes & serve!

---

75. BLUE CHEESE CHICKEN WEDGES

Prep & Cook Time: 45 minutes | Servings: 4

INGREDIENTS

Blue cheese dressing 4 strips of bacon ¾ cup of your favorite buffalo sauce
2 tbsp. of crumbled blue cheese 2 chicken breasts (boneless)

INSTRUCTIONS
1. Cook the chicken & buffalo sauce inside your Air Fryer at 400°F/200°C for 35 minutes.
2. Add the blue cheese & buffalo pulled chicken. Top with the cooked bacon crumble.
3. Serve & enjoy.

---

76. 'OH SO GOOD' SALAD

Prep & Cook Time: 10 minutes | Servings: 2

INGREDIENTS

6 brussels sprouts 1 tsp. of olive/grapeseed oil 1 tbsp. of freshly grated parmesan
½ tsp. of apple cider vinegar 1 grind of salt

INSTRUCTIONS
1. Slice the clean brussels sprouts in half.
2. Cut thin slices in the opposite direction.
3. Once sliced, cut the roots off & discard.
4. Toss together with the apple cider, oil & salt.
5. Sprinkle with the parmesan cheese.
6. Flash fry in your Air Fryer at 400°F/200°C for 23 minutes until the cheese is melted and crisp. Take out and let cool. Serve!

---

77. 'I LOVE BACON'

Prep & Cook Time: 90 minutes | Servings: 4

INGREDIENTS

30 slices of thick-cut bacon

12 oz. of steak

10 oz. of pork sausage

4 oz. of cheddar cheese, shredded

INSTRUCTIONS

1. Lay out 5 x 6 slices of bacon in a woven pattern & bake inside your Air Fryer at 400°F/200°C for 20 minutes until crisp.
2. Combine the steak, bacon & sausage to form a meaty mixture.
3. Lay out the meat in a rectangle of similar size to the bacon strips. Season with salt/pepper.
4. Place the bacon weave on top of the meat mixture.
5. Place the cheese in the center of the bacon.
6. Roll the meat into a tight roll & refrigerate.
7. Make a 7 x 7 bacon weave & roll the bacon weave over the meat, diagonally.
8. Bake at 400°F/200°C for 60 minutes or 165°F/75°C internally.
9. Let rest for 5 minutes before serving.

---

78. LEMON DILL TROUT

Prep & Cook Time: 15 minutes | Servings: 1

INGREDIENTS

2 lb. of pan-dressed trout (or other small fish), fresh or frozen

1 ½ tsp. of salt

½ cup of butter or margarine

2 tbsp. of dill weed

3 tbsp. of lemon juice

INSTRUCTIONS

1. Cut the fish lengthwise & season the with pepper.
2. Prepare a skillet by melting the butter & dill weed.
3. Cook inside your air Fryer at 400°F/200°C, flesh side down, for 5 minutes per side.
4. Remove the fish. Add the lemon juice to the butter & dill to create a sauce.
5. Serve the fish with the sauce.

---

79. 'NO POTATO' SHEPHERD'S PIE

Prep & Cook Time: 70 minutes | Servings: 6

INGREDIENTS

1 lb. of lean ground beef

8 oz. of mushroom sauce mix

¼ cup of ketchup

1 lb. packet of frozen mixed vegetables

1 lb. of bake mix

INSTRUCTIONS

1. Preheat your Air Fryer to 375°F/190°C.
2. Prepare the bake mix according to packet instructions. Layer into the skillet base.
3. Cut the dough into triangles & roll them from base to tip. Set to the side.
4. Brown the ground beef with the salt. Stir in the mushroom sauce, ketchup & mixed vegetables.
5. Bring the mixture to the boil & reduce the heat to medium, cover & simmer until tender.
6. Put the dough triangles on top of the mixture, tips pointing towards the center.
7. Bake for 60 minutes until piping hot & serve!

---

80. EASY SLIDER

Prep & Cook Time: 70 minutes | Servings: 6

INGREDIENTS

1 lb. of Ground Beef

1 egg

Garlic/salt/pepper/onion powder to taste

Several dashes of Worcestershire sauce

8 oz. of cheddar cheese (½ oz. per patty)

INSTRUCTIONS

1. Mix the beef, eggs & spices together.
2. Divide the meat into 1.5 oz. patties.
3. Add a half-ounce of cheese to each patty & combine two patties to make one burger, like a sandwich.
4. Bake in a preheated 375°F/190°C Air Fryer for 40 minutes. Serve!

---

81. DIJON HALIBUT STEAK

Prep & Cook Time: 40 minutes | Servings: 1

INGREDIENTS

1 6-oz. fresh or thawed halibut steak

1 tbsp. of butter

1 tbsp. of lemon juice

½ tbsp. of Dijon mustard

1 tsp. of fresh basil

INSTRUCTIONS

1. Heat the butter, basil, lemon juice & mustard in a small saucepan to make a glaze.
2. Brush both sides of the halibut steak with the mixture.
3. Grill the fish in a preheated 375°F/190°C Air Fryer for 30 minutes. Serve!

---

82. CAST-IRON CHEESY CHICKEN

INGREDIENTS

4 chicken breasts

4 bacon strips

4 oz. of ranch dressing

2 green onions

4 oz. of cheddar cheese

INSTRUCTIONS

1. Pour the oil into a dish. Add the chicken breasts. Bake in a preheated 375°F/190°C Air Fryer for 20 minutes.
2. Fry the bacon in a skillet until brown. Dice the green onions.
3. Take the chicken out of the Air Fryer & top with soy sauce and onions.
4. Toss in the ranch, bacon, green onions & top with cheese.
5. Cook until the cheese is browned, for around 4 minutes.
6. Serve.

83. CAULIFLOWER RICE CHICKEN CURRY

Prep & Cook Time: 50 minutes | *Servings: 4*

INGREDIENTS

2 lb. of chicken (4 breasts)

1 packet of curry paste

3 tbsp. of butter

½ cup of heavy cream

1 head of cauliflower (around 1 kg/2.2 lb.)

INSTRUCTIONS

1. Melt the butter in a pot. Mix in the curry paste. Add the water and chicken. Mix.
2. Bake in a preheated 375°F/190°C Air Fryer for 40 minutes.
3. Shred the cauliflower florets in a food processor to resemble rice.
4. Once the chicken is cooked, uncover, & incorporate the cauliflower mix.
5. Cook for 5 minutes & serve.

84. BACON CHOPS

Prep & Cook Time: 40 minutes | *Servings: 2*

INGREDIENTS

2 pork chops (I prefer bone-in, but boneless chops work great as well)

1 bag of shredded brussels sprouts

4 slices of bacon

Worcestershire sauce

Lemon juice (optional)

INSTRUCTIONS

1. Place the pork chops on a baking sheet with the Worcestershire sauce.
2. Bake in a preheated 375°F/190°C Air Fryer for 30 minutes.
3. Turnover & cook for another 5 minutes. Put to the side when done.
4. Cook the chopped bacon in a large pan until browned. Add the shredded brussels sprouts & cook together.
5. Stir the brussels sprouts with the bacon & grease & cook for 5 minutes until the bacon is crisp.

85. CHICKEN IN A BLANKET

Prep & Cook Time: 60 minutes | *Servings:*

INGREDIENTS

3 boneless chicken breasts

1 packet of bacon

1 8-oz. of packet cream cheese

3 jalapeno peppers

Salt, pepper, garlic powder or other seasonings

INSTRUCTIONS

1. Cut the chicken breast in half lengthwise to create two pieces.
2. Cut the jalapenos in half lengthwise & remove the seeds.
3. Dress each breast with a half-inch slice of cream cheese & half a slice of jalapeno. Sprinkle with garlic powder, salt & pepper.
4. Roll the chicken & wrap 2 to 3 pieces of bacon around it—secure with toothpicks.
5. Bake in a preheated 375°F/190°C Air Fryer for 50 minutes.
6. Serve!

86. STUFFED CHICKEN ROLLS

Prep & Cook Time: 45 minutes | *Servings: 4*

INGREDIENTS

4 boneless, skinless chicken breasts

7 oz. of cream cheese

¼ cup of green onions, chopped

4 slices of bacon, partially cooked

INSTRUCTIONS

1. Partially cook your strips of bacon, about 5 minutes for each side & set aside.
2. Pound the chicken breasts to a quarter-inch thick.
3. Mix the cream cheese & green onions together. Spread 2 tbsp. of the mixture onto each breast. Roll & wrap them with the strip of bacon, then secure with a toothpick.
4. Place the chicken on a baking sheet & bake in a preheated Air Fryer at 375°F/190°C for 30 minutes.
5. Broil for 5 minutes to crisp the bacon.
6. Serve.

87. DUCK FAT RIBEYE

Prep & Cook Time: 20 minutes | Servings: 1

INGREDIENTS

One 16-oz. of ribeye steak (1 - 1 ¼ inch thick)
1 tbsp. of duck fat (or other high smoke point oil like peanut oil)
½ tbsp. of butter
½ tsp. of thyme, chopped
Salt & pepper

INSTRUCTIONS

1. Preheat a skillet in your Air Fryer at 400°F/200°C.
2. Season the steaks with the oil, salt & pepper. Remove the skillet from the Air Fryer once pre-heated.
3. Put the skillet on your stove top burner on a medium heat & drizzle in the oil.
4. Sear the steak for 1-4 minutes, depending on if you like it rare, medium or well done.
5. Turn over the steak & place in your Air Fryer for 6 minutes.
6. Take out the steak from your Air Fryer & place it back on the stove top on low heat.
7. Toss in the butter & thyme & cook for 3 minutes, basting as you go along.
8. Rest for 5 minutes & serve.

88. EASY ZOODLES & TURKEY BALLS

Prep & Cook Time: 35 minutes | Servings: 2

INGREDIENTS

1 zucchini, cut into spirals
1 can of vodka pasta sauce
1 packet of meatballs

INSTRUCTIONS

1. Cook the meatballs & sauce on a high heat in your Air Fryer for 25 minutes, shaking occasionally.
2. Wash the zucchini & put through a vegetable spiral maker.
3. Boil the water & blanch the raw zoodles for 60 seconds. Remove & drain.
4. Combine the zoodles & prepared saucy meatballs.
5. Serve!

89. SAUSAGE BALLS

Prep & Cook Time: 25 minutes | Servings: 6

INGREDIENTS

12 oz. of Jimmy Dean's Sausage
6 oz. of shredded cheddar cheese
10 cubes cheddar (optional)

INSTRUCTIONS

1. Mix the shredded cheese & sausage.
2. Divide the mixture into 12 equal parts to be stuffed.
3. Add a cube of cheese to the center of the sausage & roll into balls.
4. Air Fry at 375°F/190°C for 15 minutes until crisp.
5. Serve!

90. BACON SCALLOPS

Prep & Cook Time: 10 minutes | Servings: 6

INGREDIENTS

12 scallops
12 thin bacon slices
12 toothpicks
Salt & pepper
½ tbsp. of oil

INSTRUCTIONS

1. Wrap each scallop with a piece of thinly cut bacon—secure with a toothpick.
2. Air Fry at 375°F/190°C for 15 minutes until crisp.
3. Season to taste.
4. Cook for 3 minutes per side.
5. Serve!

91. BUFFALO CHICKEN SALAD

Prep & Cook Time: 40 minutes | Servings: 1

INGREDIENTS

3 cups of salad of your choice
1 chicken breast
½ cup of shredded cheese of your choice
Buffalo wing sauce of your choice
Ranch or blue cheese dressing

INSTRUCTIONS

1. Preheat your Air Fryer to 400°F/200°C.
2. Douse the chicken breast in the buffalo wing sauce & bake for 25 minutes. In the last 5 minutes, throw the cheese on the wings until it melts.
3. When cooked, remove from the Air Fryer & slice into pieces.
4. Place on a bed of lettuce.

5. Pour the salad dressing of your choice on top.
6. Serve!

---

92. MEATBALLS

Prep & Cook Time: 30 minutes | Servings: 6

INGREDIENTS

1 lb. of ground beef (or ½ lb. beef, ½ lb. pork)

½ cup of grated parmesan cheese
1 tbsp. of minced garlic (or paste)

½ cup of mozzarella cheese
1 tsp. of freshly ground pepper

INSTRUCTIONS

1. Preheat your Air Fryer to 400°F/200°C.
2. In a bowl, mix all the ingredients together.
3. Roll the meat mixture into 5 generous meatballs.
4. Bake inside your Air Fryer at 170°F/80°C for about 18 minutes.
5. Serve with sauce!

---

93. FAT BOMBS

Prep & Cook Time: 100 minutes | Servings: 2

INGREDIENTS

1 cup of coconut butter
1 cup of coconut milk (full fat, canned)

1 tsp. of vanilla extract
½ tsp. of nutmeg

½ cup of coconut shreds

INSTRUCTIONS

1. Add all the ingredients except the shredded coconut into your Air Fryer basket.
2. Cook at 400°F/200°C for 10 minutes. Stir & melt until they start melting.
3. Then, take them off of the heat.
4. Put the glass bowl into your refrigerator until the mix can be rolled into doughy balls. Usually this happens after around 30 minutes.
5. Roll the dough into 1-inch balls through the coconut shreds.
6. Place the balls on a plate & refrigerate for one hour.
7. Serve!

---

94. CABBAGE & BEEF CASSEROLE

Prep & Cook Time: 40 minutes | Servings: 6

INGREDIENTS

½ lb. of ground beef
½ cup of chopped onion

½ bag coleslaw mix
1-½ cups of tomato sauce

1 tbsp. of lemon juice

INSTRUCTIONS

1. In your Air Fryer, cook the ground beef at 400°F/200°C for 30 minutes until browned & to the side.
2. Mix in the onion & cabbage to the skillet & sauté until soft.
3. Add the ground beef back in along with the tomato sauce & lemon juice.
4. Bring the mixture to a boil, then cover & simmer for 30 minutes.
5. Enjoy!

---

95. ROAST BEEF LETTUCE WRAPS

Prep & Cook Time: 10 minutes | Servings: 4

INGREDIENTS

8 large iceberg lettuce leaves
8 oz. (8 slices) of rare roast beef

½ cup of homemade mayonnaise
8 slices of provolone cheese

1 cup of baby spinach

INSTRUCTIONS

1. Wash the lettuce leaves & sake them dry. Try not to rip them.
2. Place 1 slice of roast beef inside each wrap.
3. Smother 1 tbsp. of mayonnaise on top of each piece of roast beef.
4. Top the mayonnaise with 1 slice of provolone cheese & 1 cup of baby spinach.
5. Roll the lettuce up around the toppings. Crisp inside your at 400°F/200°C Air Fryer for 2 minutes until browned.
6. Serve & enjoy!

---

96. TURKEY AVOCADO ROLLS

Prep & Cook Time: 10 minutes | Servings: 6

INGREDIENTS

12 slices (12 oz.) of turkey breast
12 slices of Swiss cheese

2 cups of baby spinach
1 large avocado, cut into 12 slices

INSTRUCTIONS

1. Lay out the slices of turkey breast flat & place a slice of Swiss cheese on top of each one.

2. Top each slice with 1 cup baby spinach & 3 slices of avocado.
3. Sprinkle each "sandwich" with lemon pepper.
4. Roll up the sandwiches & secure with toothpicks.
5. Cook for a few minutes inside your Air Fryer on a low heat until crisp.
6. Serve & season immediately or refrigerate until ready to serve.

97. NEARLY PIZZA

Prep & Cook Time: 30 minutes | Servings: 4

INGREDIENTS

4 large portobello mushrooms
4 tsp. of olive oil

1 cup of marinara sauce
1 cup of shredded mozzarella cheese

10 slices of sugar-free pepperoni

INSTRUCTIONS

1. Preheat your Air Fryer to 375°F/190°C.
2. De-steam the 4 mushrooms & brush each cap with the olive oil, one spoon for each cap.
3. Place on a baking sheet & bake stem side down for 8 minutes.
4. Take out of the Air Fryer & fill each cap with 1 cup marinara sauce, 1 cup of mozzarella cheese & 3 slices of pepperoni.
5. Cook for another 10 minutes until browned.
6. Serve hot.

98. TACO STUFFED PEPPERS

Prep & Cook Time: 30 minutes | Servings: 4

INGREDIENTS

1 lb. of ground beef
1 tbsp. of taco seasoning mix

1 can of diced tomatoes & green chilis
4 green bell peppers

1 cup of shredded Monterey jack cheese, divided

INSTRUCTIONS

1. Set a skillet over a high heat & cook the ground beef for seven to ten minutes. Make sure it is cooked through & brown all over. Drain the fat.
2. Stir in the taco seasoning mix, as well as the diced tomatoes & green chilis. Allow the mixture to cook for a further three to five minutes.
3. In the meantime, slice the tops off the green peppers & remove the seeds & membranes.
4. When the meat mixture is fully cooked, spoon equal amounts of it into the peppers & top with the Monterey jack cheese. Then place the peppers into your Air Fryer.
5. Cook at 350°F for fifteen minutes.
6. The peppers are ready when they are soft, & the cheese is bubbling & brown. Serve warm & enjoy!

99. BEEF TENDERLOIN & PEPPERCORN CRUST

Prep & Cook Time: 45 minutes | Servings: 6

INGREDIENTS

2 lb. of beef tenderloin
2 tsp. of roasted garlic, minced

2 tbsp. of salted butter, melted
3 tbsp. of ground 4-peppercorn blender

INSTRUCTIONS

1. Remove any surplus fat from the beef tenderloin.
2. Combine the roasted garlic & melted butter to apply to your tenderloin with a brush.
3. On a plate, spread out the peppercorns & roll the tenderloin in them, making sure they are covering & clinging to the meat.
4. Cook the tenderloin in your Air Fryer for twenty-five minutes at 400°F, turning halfway through cooking.
5. Let the tenderloin rest for ten minutes before slicing & serving.

100. BRATWURSTS

Prep & Cook Time: 18 minutes | Servings: 4

INGREDIENTS

4 x 3-oz. beef bratwursts

INSTRUCTIONS

1. Place the beef bratwursts in the basket of your Air Fryer & cook for fifteen minutes at 375°F, turning once halfway through.
2. Enjoy with toppings & sides of your choice.

101. BACON-WRAPPED HOT DOG

Prep & Cook Time: 25 minutes | Servings: 4

INGREDIENTS

4 slices of sugar-free bacon
4 beef hot dogs

INSTRUCTIONS

1. Take a slice of bacon & wrap it around the hot dog, securing it with a toothpick. Repeat with the other pieces of bacon & hot dogs, placing each wrapped dog in the basket of your Air Fryer.

2. Cook at 370°F for ten minutes, turning halfway through to fry the other side.
3. Once hot & crispy, the hot dogs are ready to serve. Enjoy!

102. HERB SHREDDED BEEF

Prep & Cook Time: 25 minutes | Servings: 6

INGREDIENTS

1 tsp. of dried dill
1 tsp. of dried thyme

1 tsp. of garlic powder
2 lb. of beefsteak

3 tbsp. of butter

INSTRUCTIONS

1. Pre-heat your Air Fryer at 360°F.
2. Combine the dill, thyme, & garlic powder together, & massage into the steak.
3. Cook the steak in the Air Fryer for twenty minutes, then remove, shred, & return to the Air Fryer. Add the butter & cook for a further two minutes at 365°F. Make sure the beef is coated in the butter before serving.

103. HERBED BUTTER RIB EYE STEAK

Prep & Cook Time: 60 minutes | Servings: 4

INGREDIENTS

4 ribeye steaks
Olive oil

¾ tsp. of dry rub
½ cup of butter

1 tsp. of dried basil
3 tbsp. of lemon garlic seasoning

INSTRUCTIONS

1. Massage the olive oil into the steaks & your favorite dry rub. Leave aside to sit for thirty minutes.
2. In a bowl, combine the button, dried basil, & lemon garlic seasoning, then refrigerate.
3. Pre-heat the Air Fryer at 450°F & set a rack inside. Place the steaks on top of the rack & allow to cook for fifteen minutes.
4. Remove the steaks from the Air Fryer when cooked & serve with the herbed butter.

104. FLANK STEAK & AVOCADO BUTTER

Prep & Cook Time: 40 minutes | Servings: 1

INGREDIENTS

1 flank steak
Salt & pepper

2 avocados
2 tbsp. of butter, melted

½ cup of chimichurri sauce

INSTRUCTIONS

1. Rub the flank steak with salt & pepper to taste & leave to sit for twenty minutes.
2. Pre-heat the Air Fryer at 400°F & place a rack inside.
3. Halve the avocados & take out the pits. Spoon the flesh into a bowl & mash with a fork. Mix in the melted butter & chimichurri sauce, making sure everything is well combined.
4. Put the steak in the Air Fryer & cook for six minutes. Flip over & allow to cook for another six minutes.
5. Serve the steak with the avocado butter & enjoy!

105. MOZZARELLA BEEF

Prep & Cook Time: 30 minutes | Servings: 6

INGREDIENTS

12 oz. of beef brisket
2 tsp. of Italian herbs

2 tsp. of butter
1 onion, sliced

7 oz. of mozzarella cheese, sliced

INSTRUCTIONS

1. Pre-heat the Air Fryer at 365°F.
2. Cut up the brisket into four equal slices & season with the Italian herbs.
3. Allow the butter to melt in the Air Fryer. Place the slices of beef inside along with the onion. Put a piece of mozzarella on top of each piece of brisket & cook for twenty-five minutes.
4. Enjoy!

106. ROSEMARY RIB EYE STEAKS

Prep & Cook Time: 40 minutes | Servings: 2

INGREDIENTS

¼ cup of butter
1 clove minced garlic

Salt & pepper
1 ½ tbsp. of balsamic vinegar

¼ cup of rosemary, chopped
2 ribeye steaks

INSTRUCTIONS

1. Melt the butter in a skillet over medium heat. Add the garlic & fry until fragrant.
2. Remove the skillet from the heat & add in the salt, pepper, & vinegar. Allow it to cool.
3. Add the rosemary, then pour the whole mixture into a Ziploc bag.
4. Put the ribeye steaks in the bag & shake well, making sure to coat the meat well. Refrigerate for an hour, then allow to sit for a further twenty minutes.

5. Pre-heat the Air Fryer at 400°F & set the rack inside. Cook the ribeyes for fifteen minutes.
6. Take care when removing the steaks from the Air Fryer & plate up. Enjoy!

107. HERBED BUTTER BEEF LOIN

Prep & Cook Time: 25 minutes | Servings: 4

INGREDIENTS

1 tbsp. of butter, melted
¼ of dried thyme

1 tsp. of garlic salt
¼ tsp. of dried parsley

1 lb. of beef loin

INSTRUCTIONS

1. In a bowl, combine the melted butter, thyme, garlic salt, & parsley.
2. Cut the beef loin into slices & generously apply the seasoned butter using a brush.
3. Pre-heat your Air Fryer at 400°F & place a rack inside.
4. Cook the beef for fifteen minutes.
5. Take care when removing it & serve hot.

108. LAMB RIBS

Prep & Cook Time: 25 minutes | Servings: 4

INGREDIENTS

1 lb. of lamb ribs
2 tbsp. of mustard

1 tsp. of rosemary, chopped
Salt & pepper

¼ cup mint leaves, chopped
1 cup of Green yogurt

INSTRUCTIONS

1. Pre-heat the Air Fryer at 350°F.
2. Use a brush to apply the mustard to the lamb ribs, & season with rosemary, as well as salt & pepper as desired.
3. Cook the ribs in the Air Fryer for eighteen minutes.
4. Meanwhile, combine together the mint leaves & yogurt in a bowl.
5. Remove the lamb ribs from the Air Fryer when cooked & serve with the mint yogurt. Enjoy!

109. LAMB SATAY

Prep & Cook Time: 25 minutes | Servings: 2

INGREDIENTS

¼ tsp. of cumin
1 tsp. of ginger

½ tsp. of nutmeg
Salt & pepper

2 boneless lamb steaks
Olive oil cooking spray

INSTRUCTIONS

1. Combine the cumin, ginger, nutmeg, salt & pepper in a bowl.
2. Cube the lamb steaks & massage the spice mixture into each one.
3. Leave to marinate for ten minutes, then transfer onto metal skewers.
4. Pre-heat the Air Fryer at 400°F.
5. Spritz the skewers with the olive oil cooking spray, then cook them in the Air Fryer for eight minutes.
6. Take care when removing them from the Air Fryer & serve with sauce of your choice.

110. ITALIAN LAMB CHOPS

Prep & Cook Time: 20 minutes | Servings: 2

INGREDIENTS

2 lamp chops
2 tsp. of Italian herbs

2 avocados
½ cup of mayonnaise

1 tbsp. of lemon juice

INSTRUCTIONS

1. Season the lamb chops with the Italian herbs, then set aside for five minutes.
2. Pre-heat the Air Fryer at 400°F & place the rack inside.
3. Put the chops on the rack & allow to cook for twelve minutes.
4. In the meantime, halve the avocados & open to remove the pits. Spoon the flesh into a blender.
5. Add in the mayonnaise & lemon juice & pulse until a smooth consistency is achieved.
6. Take care when removing the chops from the Air Fryer, then plate up & serve with the avocado mayo.

111. BREADED PORK CHOPS

Prep & Cook Time: 25 minutes | Servings: 4

INGREDIENTS

1 tsp. of chili powder
½ tsp. of garlic powder

½ oz. of flour, finely ground
4 x 4-oz. of pork chops

1 tbsp. of coconut oil, melted

INSTRUCTIONS

1. Combine the chili powder, garlic powder, & flour.

2. Coat the pork chops with the coconut oil, followed by the flour mixture, taking care to cover them completely. Then place the chops in the basket of the Air Fryer.
3. Cook the chops for fifteen minutes at 400°F, turning halfway through.
4. Once they are browned, check the temperature has reached 145°F before serving with the sides of your choice.

112. JUICY MEXICAN PORK CHOPS

Prep & Cook Time: 25 minutes | Servings: 2

INGREDIENTS

¼ tsp. of dried oregano
1 ½ tsp. of taco seasoning mix

2 x 4-oz. of boneless pork chops
2 tbsp. of butter, divided

INSTRUCTIONS

1. Combine the dried oregano & taco seasoning to rub into the pork chops.
2. In your Air Fryer, cook the chops at 400°F for fifteen minutes, turning them over halfway through to cook on the other side.
3. When the chops are a brown color, check the internal temperature has reached 145°F & remove from the Air Fryer. Serve with a garnish of butter.

113. BABY BACK RIBS

Prep & Cook Time: 45 minutes | Servings: 2

INGREDIENTS

2 tsp. of red pepper flakes
¾ of ground ginger

3 cloves minced garlic
Salt & pepper

2 baby back ribs

INSTRUCTIONS

1. Pre-heat your Air Fryer at 350°F.
2. Combine the red pepper flakes, ginger, garlic, salt & pepper in a bowl, making sure to mix well. Massage the mixture into the baby back ribs.
3. Cook the ribs in the Air Fryer for thirty minutes.
4. Take care when taking the rubs out of the Air Fryer. Place them on a serving dish & enjoy with a barbecue sauce of your choosing.

114. PULLED PORK

Prep & Cook Time: 30 minutes | Servings: 1

INGREDIENTS

1 lb. of pork tenderloin
2 tbsp. of barbecue dry rub

⅓ cup of heavy cream
1 tsp. of butter

INSTRUCTIONS

1. Pre-heat your Air Fryer at 370°F.
2. Massage the dry rub of your choice into the tenderloin, coating it well.
3. Cook the tenderloin in the Air Fryer for twenty minutes. When cooked, shred with two forks.
4. Add the heavy cream & butter into the Air Fryer along with the shredded pork & stir well. Cook for a further four minutes.
5. Allow to cool a little, then serve & enjoy.

115. RIBS

Prep & Cook Time: 60 minutes | Servings: 4

INGREDIENTS

1 lb. of pork ribs
1 tbsp. of barbecue dry rub

1 tsp. of mustard
1 tbsp. of apple cider vinegar

1 tsp. of sesame oil

INSTRUCTIONS

1. Chop up the pork ribs.
2. Combine the dry rub, mustard, apple cider vinegar, & sesame oil, then coat the ribs with this mixture. Refrigerate the ribs for twenty minutes.
3. Preheat the Air Fryer at 360°F.
4. When the ribs are ready, place them in the Air Fryer & cook for 15 minutes. Flip them & cook on the other side for a further fifteen minutes. Then serve & enjoy!

116. PORK CHOPS

Prep & Cook Time: 15 minutes | Servings: 3

INGREDIENTS

3 pork chops
½ tsp. of dried rosemary

1 tsp. of garlic salt
1 tsp. of peppercorns

1 tbsp. of butter

INSTRUCTIONS

1. Pre-heat your Air Fryer to 365°F.
2. Combine the dried rosemary & garlic salt & rub into the pork chops.
3. Place the peppercorns & butter into the Air Fryer & allow the butter to melt.
4. Add in the pork chops & cook for six minutes. Flip them & cook for an additional five minutes before serving.

117. SRIRACHA CAULIFLOWER

Prep & Cook Time: 25 minutes | Servings: 4

INGREDIENTS

¼ cup of vegan butter, melted
¼ cup of sriracha sauce

4 cups of cauliflower florets
1 cup of breadcrumbs

1 tsp. of salt

INSTRUCTIONS

1. Mix together the sriracha & vegan butter in a bowl & pour this mixture over the cauliflower, taking care to cover each floret entirely.
2. In a separate bowl, combine the breadcrumbs & salt.
3. Dip the cauliflower florets in the breadcrumbs, coating each one well. Cook in the Air Fryer for 17 minutes in a 375°F pre-heated Air Fryer.

118. RATATOUILLE

Prep & Cook Time: 30 minutes | Servings: 4

INGREDIENTS

1 sprig of basil
1 sprig of flat-leaf parsley
1 sprig of mint
1 tbsp. of coriander powder
1 tsp. of capers
½ lemon, juiced

Salt & pepper
2 eggplants, sliced crosswise
2 red onions, chopped
4 cloves of garlic, minced
2 red peppers, sliced crosswise
1 fennel bulb., sliced crosswise

3 large zucchinis, sliced crosswise
5 tbsp. of olive oil
4 large tomatoes, chopped
2 tsp. of herbs de Provence

INSTRUCTIONS

1. Blend together the basil, parsley, coriander, mint, lemon juice & capers, with a little salt & pepper. Make sure all ingredients are well-incorporated.
2. Pre-heat the Air Fryer at 400°F.
3. Coat the eggplant, onions, garlic, peppers, fennel, & zucchini with olive oil.
4. Take a baking dish small enough to fit inside the Air Fryer. Transfer the vegetables into the dish & top with the tomatoes & herb puree. Sprinkle on some more salt & pepper if desired, as well as the herbs de Provence.
5. Fry for 25 minutes. Serve!

119. PESTO STUFFED BELLA MUSHROOMS

Prep & Cook Time: 25 minutes | Servings: 6

INGREDIENTS

1 cup of basil
½ cup of cashew nuts, soaked overnight
½ cup of yeast
1 tbsp. of lemon juice

2 cloves of garlic
1 tbsp. of olive oil
Salt

1 lb. of baby Bella mushroom, stems removed

INSTRUCTIONS

1. Pre-heat the Air Fryer at 400°F.
2. Prepare your pesto. In a food processor, blend together the basil, cashew nuts, yeast, lemon juice, garlic & olive oil to combine well. Sprinkle on salt as desired.
3. Turn the mushrooms cap-side down & spread the pesto on the underside of each cap.
4. Transfer to the Air Fryer & cook for 15 minutes. Serve!

120. VEG BURGER

Prep & Cook Time: 25 minutes | Servings: 8

INGREDIENTS

½ lb. of cauliflower, steamed & diced
2 tsp. of coconut oil melted
2 tsp. of garlic, minced
¼ cup of desiccated coconut
½ cup of oats

3 tbsp. of flour
1 flax egg [1 tbsp. flaxseed + 3 tbsp. of water]
1 tsp. of mustard powder
2 tsp. of thyme

2 tsp. of parsley
2 tsp. of chives
Salt & pepper
1 cup of breadcrumbs

INSTRUCTIONS

1. Pre-heat the Air Fryer at 390°F.
2. Drain any excess water out of the cauliflower on a kitchen towel.
3. Combine the cauliflower with all of ingredients bar the breadcrumbs, incorporating everything well.
4. Using your hands, shape 8 equal-sized amounts of the mixture into burger patties. Coat the patties in breadcrumbs before putting them in the basket of the Air Fryer in a single layer.
5. Cook for 10-15 minutes, ensuring the patties crisp up.

121. CHILI POTATO WEDGES

Prep & Cook Time: 50 minutes | Servings: 4

INGREDIENTS

1 lb. of fingerling potatoes, washed & cut into wedges
1 tsp. of olive oil

1 tsp. of salt
1 tsp. of black pepper
1 tsp. of cayenne pepper

1 tsp. of yeast
½ tsp. of garlic powder

INSTRUCTIONS

1. Pre-heat the Air Fryer at 400°F.
2. Coat the potatoes with the rest of the ingredients.
3. Transfer to the basket of your Air Fryer & allow to cook for 16 minutes, shaking the basket at the halfway point.

122. LOBSTER TAILS

Prep & Cook Time: 16minutes | Servings: 4

INGREDIENTS

2 lobster tails, shell cut from the top ½
1 cup of butter, melted

½ tsp. of ground paprika
Salt

White pepper, to taste
1 lemon, juiced

INSTRUCTIONS

1. Whack the lobster tails inside your Air Fryer.
2. Combine the remaining ingredients inside a mixing bowl & pour them over the lobster tails.
3. Switch your Air Fryer to 'broil' mode and cook for 15 minutes at 350°F.
4. Serve warm.

123. CHRISTMAS BRUSSELS SPROUTS

Prep & Cook Time: 20 minutes | Servings: 2

INGREDIENTS

2 cups of Brussels sprouts, halved
1 tbsp. of olive oil

1 tbsp. of balsamic vinegar
1 tbsp. of maple syrup

¼ tsp. of sea salt

INSTRUCTIONS

1. Pre-heat the Air Fryer at 375°F.
2. Evenly coat the Brussels sprouts with the olive oil, balsamic vinegar, maple syrup, & salt.
3. Transfer to the basket of your Air Fryer & cook for 5 minutes. Give the basket a good shake, turn the heat up to 400°F & continue to cook for another 8 minutes.

124. SUMMER ROLLS

Prep & Cook Time: 25 minutes | Servings: 4

INGREDIENTS

1 cup of shiitake mushroom, sliced thinly
1 celery stalk, chopped
1 medium carrot, shredded
½ tsp. of ginger, finely chopped

1 tsp. of sugar
1 tbsp. of soy sauce
1 tsp. of yeast
8 spring roll sheets

1 tsp. of corn starch
2 tbsp. of water

INSTRUCTIONS

1. In a bowl, combine the ginger, soy sauce, yeast, carrots, celery, & sugar.
2. Mix together the cornstarch & water to create an adhesive for your spring rolls.
3. Scoop a teaspoonful of the vegetable mixture into the middle of the spring roll sheets. Brush the edges of the sheets with the cornstarch adhesive & enclose around the filling to make spring rolls.
4. Pre-heat your Air Fryer at 400°F. When warm, place the rolls inside & cook for 15 minutes or until crisp.

125. RICE BOWL

Prep & Cook Time: 55 minutes | Servings: 4

INGREDIENTS

¼ cup of cucumber, sliced
1 tsp. of salt
1 tbsp. of sugar
7 tbsp. of Japanese rice vinegar

3 medium-sized eggplants, sliced
3 tbsp. of white miso paste
1 tbsp. of mirin rice wine
4 cups of sushi rice, cooked

4 spring onions
1 tbsp. of sesame seeds, toasted

INSTRUCTIONS

1. Coat the cucumber slices with the rice wine vinegar, salt, & sugar.
2. Place a dish on top of the bowl to weight it down completely.
3. Pre-heat the Air Fryer at 400°F.
4. In a bowl, mix together the eggplants, mirin rice wine, & miso paste. Allow to marinate for half an hour.
5. Cook the eggplant in the Air Fryer for 10 minutes.

6. Place the eggplant slices in the Air Fryer & cook for 10 minutes.
7. Fill the bottom of a serving bowl with rice & top with the eggplants & pickled cucumbers. Add the spring onions & sesame seeds for garnish.

126. ASIAN TOFU BITES

Prep & Cook Time: 20 minutes | Servings: 4

INGREDIENTS

1 packet of firm tofu, cubed & pressed to remove excess water
1 tbsp. of soy sauce
1 tbsp. of ketchup

1 tbsp. of maple syrup
½ tsp. of vinegar
1 tsp. of liquid smoke
1 tsp. of hot sauce

2 tbsp. of sesame seeds
1 tsp. of garlic powder
Salt & pepper

INSTRUCTIONS

1. Pre-heat the Air Fryer at 375°F.
2. Take a baking dish small enough to fit inside the Air Fryer & spritz it with cooking spray.
3. Combine all the ingredients to coat the tofu completely & allow the marinade to absorb for half an hour.
4. Transfer the tofu to the baking dish, then cook for 15 minutes. Flip the tofu over & cook for another 15 minutes on the other side.

127. CHICKPEAS

Prep & Cook Time: 20 minutes | Servings: 4

INGREDIENTS

One 15-oz. of can chickpeas, drained but
  not rinsed

2 tbsp. of olive oil
1 tsp. of salt

2 tbsp. of lemon juice

INSTRUCTIONS

1. Pre-heat the Air Fryer at 400°F.
2. Add all the ingredients together in a bowl & mix. Transfer this mixture to the basket of the Air Fryer.
3. Cook for 15 minutes, ensuring the chickpeas become nice & crispy.

128. CAULIFLOWER CHEESE TATER TOTS

Prep & Cook Time: 25 minutes | Servings: 12

INGREDIENTS

1 lb. of cauliflower, steamed & chopped
½ cup of yeast
1 tbsp. of oats
1 flax egg [1 tbsp. desiccated coconut +
3 tbsp. flaxseed meal

+ 3 tbsp. of water]
1 onion, chopped
1 tsp. of garlic, minced
1 tsp. of parsley, chopped
1 tsp. of oregano, chopped

1 tsp. of chives, chopped
Salt & pepper
½ cup of breadcrumbs

INSTRUCTIONS

1. Pre-heat the Air Fryer at 390°F.
2. Drain any excess water out of the cauliflower by wringing it with a paper towel.
3. In a bowl, combine the cauliflower with the remaining ingredients, save the breadcrumbs. Using your hands, shape the mixture into several small balls.
4. Coat the balls in the breadcrumbs & transfer to the basket of your Air Fryer. Allow to cook for 6 minutes, after which you should raise the temperature to 400°F & then leave to cook for an additional 10 minutes.

129. SWEET ONIONS & POTATOES

Prep & Cook Time: 30 minutes | Servings: 6

INGREDIENTS

2 sweet potatoes, peeled & cut into
chunks
2 sweet onions, cut into chunks

3 tbsp. of olive oil
1 tsp. of dried thyme
Salt & pepper

¼ cup almonds, sliced & toasted

INSTRUCTIONS

1. Pre-heat the Air Fryer at 425°F.
2. In a bowl, combine all of the ingredients, except for the sliced almonds.
3. Transfer the vegetables & dressing to a ramekin & cook in the Air Fryer for 20 minutes.
4. When ready to serve, add the almonds on top.

130. MUSHROOM PIZZA SQUARES

Prep & Cook Time: 20 minutes | Servings: 10

INGREDIENTS

1 vegan pizza dough
1 cup of oyster mushrooms, chopped

1 shallot, chopped
¼ red bell pepper, chopped

2 tbsp. of parsley
Salt & pepper

INSTRUCTIONS

1. Pre-heat the Air Fryer at 400°F.
2. Cut the vegan pizza dough into squares.
3. In a bowl, combine the oyster mushrooms, shallot, bell pepper & parsley. Sprinkle some salt & pepper as desired.
4. Spread this mixture on top of the pizza squares.
5. Cook in the Air Fryer for 10 minutes.

131. TOFU & SWEET POTATOES

Prep & Cook Time: 50 minutes | Servings: 8

INGREDIENTS

8 sweet potatoes, scrubbed
2 tbsp. of olive oil
1 large onion, chopped

2 green chilies, deseeded & chopped
½ lb. of tofu, crumbled
2 tbsp. of Cajun seasoning

cup of tomatoes
1 can of kidney beans, drained & rinsed
Salt & pepper

INSTRUCTIONS

1. Pre-heat the Air Fryer at 400°F.
2. With a knife, pierce the skin of the sweet potatoes in numerous places & cook in the Air Fryer for half an hour, making sure they become soft. Remove from the Air Fryer, halve each potato, & set to one side.
3. Over a medium heat, fry the onions & chilis in a little oil for 2 minutes until fragrant.
4. Add in the tofu & Cajun seasoning & allow to cook for a further 3 minutes before incorporating the kidney beans & tomatoes. Sprinkle some salt & pepper as desire.
5. Top each sweet potato halve with a spoonful of the tofu mixture & serve.

132. RISOTTO

Prep & Cook Time: 40 minutes | Servings: 2

INGREDIENTS

1 onion, diced
2 cups of chicken stock, boiling
½ cup of parmesan cheese or cheddar

cheese, grated
1 clove of garlic, minced
¾ cup of arborio rice

1 tbsp. of olive oil
1 tbsp. of butter

INSTRUCTIONS

1. Turn the Air Fryer to 390°F & set for 5 minutes to warm.
2. Grease a round baking tin with oil & stir in the butter, garlic, & onion.
3. Put the tin in the Air Fryer & allow to cook for 4 minutes.
4. Pour in the rice & cook for a further 4 minutes, stirring three times throughout the cooking time.
5. Turn the temperature down to 320°F.
6. Add the chicken stock & give the dish a gentle stir. Cook for 22 minutes, leaving the Air Fryer uncovered.
7. Pour in the cheese, stir once more & serve.

133. CHICKPEA & AVOCADO MASH

Prep & Cook Time: 30 minutes | Servings: 4

INGREDIENTS

1 medium-sized head of cauliflower, cut into florets
1 can of chickpeas, drained & rinsed

1 tbsp. of extra-virgin olive oil
2 tbsp. of lemon juice
Salt & pepper

4 flatbreads, toasted
2 ripe avocados, mashed

INSTRUCTIONS

1. Pre-heat the Air Fryer at 425°F.
2. In a bowl, mix together the chickpeas, cauliflower, lemon juice & olive oil. Sprinkle salt & pepper as desired.
3. Put inside the Air Fryer basket & cook for 25 minutes.
4. Spread on top of the flatbread along with the mashed avocado. Sprinkle on more pepper & salt as desired & enjoy with hot sauce.

134. FRIED POTATOES

Prep & Cook Time: 55 minutes | Servings: 1

INGREDIENTS

1 medium russet potato, scrubbed & peeled
1 tsp. of olive oil

¼ tsp. of onion powder
1/8 tsp. of salt
A dollop of vegan butter

A dollop of vegan cream cheese
1 tbsp. of Kalamata olives
1 tbsp. of chives, chopped

INSTRUCTIONS

1. Pre-heat the Air Fryer at 400°F.
2. In a bowl, coat the potatoes with the onion powder, salt, olive oil, & vegan butter.
3. Transfer to the Air Fryer & allow to cook for 40 minutes, turning the potatoes over at the halfway point.
4. Take care when removing the potatoes from the Air Fryer & enjoy with the vegan cream cheese, Kalamata olives & chives on top, plus any other vegan sides you desire.

135. FRENCH GREEN BEANS

Prep & Cook Time: 20 minutes | Servings: 4

INGREDIENTS

1 ½ lb. of French green beans, stems removed & blanched
1 tbsp. of salt

½ lb. of shallots, peeled & cut into quarters
½ tsp. of ground white pepper

2 tbsp. of olive oil
¼ cup of almonds, toasted

INSTRUCTIONS

1. Pre-heat the Air Fryer at 400°F.
2. Coat the vegetables with the rest of the ingredients in a bowl.
3. Transfer to the basket of your Air Fryer & cook for 10 minutes, making sure the green beans achieve a light brown color.

---

136. BLACK BEAN CHILI

Prep & Cook Time: 25 minutes | Servings: 6

INGREDIENTS

1 tbsp. of olive oil
1 medium onion, diced
3 cloves of garlic, minced
1 cup of vegetable broth

3 cans of black beans, drained & rinsed
2 cans of diced tomatoes
2 chipotle peppers, chopped
2 tsp. of cumin

2 tsp. of chili powder
1 tsp. of dried oregano
½ tsp. of salt

INSTRUCTIONS

1. Over a medium heat, fry the garlic & onions in a little oil for 3 minutes.
2. Add in the remaining ingredients, stirring constantly & scraping the bottom to prevent sticking.
3. Pre-heat your Air Fryer at 400°F.
4. Take a heat-resistant dish small enough to fit inside the Air Fryer & place the mixture inside. Put a sheet of aluminum foil on top.
5. Transfer to the Air Fryer & cook for 20 minutes.
6. When ready, plate up & serve with diced avocado, chopped cilantro, & chopped tomatoes.

---

137. CAULIFLOWER

Prep & Cook Time: 20 minutes | Servings: 4

INGREDIENTS

1 head of cauliflower, cut into florets
1 tbsp. of extra-virgin olive oil
2 scallions, chopped

5 cloves of garlic, sliced
1 ½ tbsp. of tamari
1 tbsp. of rice vinegar

½ tsp. of sugar
1 tbsp. of sriracha

INSTRUCTIONS

1. Pre-heat the Air Fryer to 400°F.
2. Put the cauliflower florets in the Air Fryer & drizzle some oil over them before cooking for 10 minutes.
3. Turn the cauliflower over, throw in the onions & garlic, & stir. Cook for another 10 minutes.
4. Mix together the rest of the ingredients in a bowl.
5. Remove the cooked cauliflower from the Air Fryer & coat it in the sauce.
6. Return to the Air Fryer & allow to cook for another 5 minutes. Enjoy with a side of rice.

---

138. TOFU BITES

Prep & Cook Time: 65 minutes | Servings: 3

INGREDIENTS

2 tbsp. of sesame oil
¼ cup of maple syrup
3 tbsp. of peanut butter
¼ cup of soy sauce
3t bsp. of chili garlic sauce

2 tbsp. of rice wine vinegar
2 cloves of garlic, minced
1-inch of fresh ginger, peeled & grated
1 tsp. of red pepper flakes
1 block of extra firm tofu, pressed to

remove excess water & cubed
Toasted peanuts, chopped
1 tsp. of sesame seeds
1 sprig of cilantro, chopped

INSTRUCTIONS

1. Whisk together the first 9 ingredients in a large bowl to well combine.
2. Transfer to an airtight bag along with the cubed tofu. Allow to marinate for a minimum of a half hour.
3. Pre-heat the Air Fryer to 425°F.
4. Put the tofu cubes in the Air Fryer, keep any excess marinade for the sauce. Cook for 15 minutes.
5. In the meantime, heat the marinade over a medium heat to reduce by half.
6. Plate up the cooked tofu with some cooked rice & serve with the sauce. Complete the dish with the sesame seeds, cilantro & peanuts.

---

139. FAUX RICE

Prep & Cook Time: 60 minutes | Servings: 8

INGREDIENTS

1 medium-to-large head of cauliflower
½ lemon, juiced

2 garlic cloves, minced
2 cans of mushrooms, 8 oz. each

1 can of water chestnuts, 8 oz.
¾ cup of peas

½ cup of egg substitute or 1 egg, beaten
4 tbsp. of soy sauce

1 tbsp. of peanut oil
1 tbsp. of sesame oil

1 tbsp. of ginger, fresh & minced
Cooking spray

INSTRUCTIONS
1. Mix together the peanut oil, soy sauce, sesame oil, minced ginger, lemon juice, & minced garlic to combine well.
2. Peel & wash the cauliflower head before cutting it into small florets.
3. In a food processor, pulse the florets in small batches to break them down to resemble rice grains.
4. Pour into your Air Fryer basket.
5. Drain the can of water chestnuts & roughly chop them. Pour into the basket.
6. Cook at 350°F for 20 minutes.
7. In the meantime, drain the mushrooms. When the 20 minutes are up, add the mushrooms & the peas to the Air Fryer & continue to cook for another 15 minutes.
8. Lightly spritz a frying pan with cooking spray. Prepare an omelet with the egg substitute or the beaten egg, ensuring it is firm. Lay on a cutting board & slice it up.
9. When the cauliflower is ready, throw in the omelet & cook for an additional 5 minutes. Serve hot.

140. POTATO CROQUETTES

Prep & Cook Time: 25 minutes | Servings: 10

INGREDIENTS
¼ cup of yeast
2 cups of boiled potatoes, mashed
1 flax egg [1 tbsp. flaxseed meal + 3 tbsp.

of water]
1 tbsp. of flour
2 tbsp. of chives, chopped

Salt & pepper
2 tbsp. of vegetable oil
¼ cup of breadcrumbs

INSTRUCTIONS
1. Pre-heat the Air Fryer to 400°F.
2. In a bowl, combine together the yeast, potatoes, flax eggs, flour, & chives. Sprinkle with salt & pepper as desired.
3. In separate bowl mix together the vegetable oil & breadcrumbs to achieve a crumbly consistency.
4. Use your hands to shape the potato mixture into small balls & dip each one into the breadcrumb mixture.
5. Place the croquettes inside the Air Fryer & cook for 15 minutes, ensuring the croquettes turn golden brown.

141. SWEET & SOUR TOFU

Prep & Cook Time: 55 minutes | Servings: 2

INGREDIENTS
2 tsp. of apple cider vinegar
1 tbsp. of sugar
1 tbsp. of soy sauce
3 tsp. of lime juice

1 tsp. of ground ginger
1 tsp. of garlic powder
½ block firm tofu, pressed to remove excess liquid & cut into cubes

1 tsp. of cornstarch
2 green onions, chopped
Toasted sesame seeds for garnish

INSTRUCTIONS
1. In a bowl, thoroughly combine the apple cider vinegar, sugar, soy sauce, lime juice, ground ginger, & garlic powder.
2. Cover the tofu with this mixture & leave to marinate for at least 30 minutes.
3. Transfer the tofu to the Air Fryer, keeping any excess marinade for the sauce. Cook at 400°F for 20 minutes or until crispy.
4. In the meantime, thicken the sauce with the cornstarch over a medium-low heat.
5. Serve the cooked tofu with the sauce, green onions, sesame seeds, & some rice.

142. VEGETABLE SALAD

Prep & Cook Time: 20 minutes | Servings: 4

INGREDIENTS
6 plum tomatoes, halved
2 large red onions, sliced
4 long red pepper, sliced
2 yellow pepper, sliced

6 cloves of garlic, crushed
1 tbsp. of extra-virgin olive oil
1 tsp. of paprika
½ lemon, juiced

Salt & pepper
1 tbsp. of baby capers

INSTRUCTIONS
1. Pre-heat the Air Fryer at 420°F.
2. Put the tomatoes, onions, peppers, & garlic in a large bowl & cover with the extra virgin olive oil, paprika, & lemon juice. Sprinkle with salt & pepper as desired.
3. Line the inside of your Air Fryer with aluminum foil. Place the vegetables inside & allow to cook for 10 minutes, ensuring the edges turn brown.
4. Serve in a salad bowl with the baby capers. Make sure all the ingredients are well combined.

143. MEDITERRANEAN VEGETABLES

Prep & Cook Time: 30 minutes | Servings: 4

INGREDIENTS
1 cup cherry tomatoes, halved
1 large zucchini, sliced
1 green pepper, sliced

1 parsnip, sliced
1 carrot, sliced
1 tsp. of mixed herbs

1 tsp. of mustard
1 tsp. of garlic puree
6 tbsp. of olive oil

Salt & pepper

INSTRUCTIONS

1. Pre-heat the Air Fryer at 400°F.
2. Combine all the ingredients in a bowl, making sure to coat the vegetables well.
3. Transfer to the Air Fryer & cook for 6 minutes, ensuring the vegetables are tender & browned.

144. SWEET POTATOES

Prep & Cook Time: 55 minutes | Servings: 4

INGREDIENTS

2 potatoes, peeled & cubed
4 carrots, cut into chunks
1 head of broccoli, cut into florets

4 zucchinis, sliced thickly
Salt & pepper
¼ cup of olive oil

1 tbsp. of dry onion powder

INSTRUCTIONS

1. Pre-heat the Air Fryer to 400°F.
2. In a baking dish small enough to fit inside the Air Fryer, add all the ingredients & combine well.
3. Cook for 45 minutes in the Air Fryer, ensuring the vegetables are soft & the sides have browned before serving.

145. SAGE CHICKEN ESCALLOPS

Prep & Cook Time: 45 minutes | Servings: 4

INGREDIENTS

4 skinless chicken breasts
2 eggs, beaten
½ cup of flour

6 sage leaves
¼ cup of breadcrumbs
¼ cup of parmesan cheese

Cooking spray

INSTRUCTIONS

1. Cut the chicken breasts into thin, flat slices.
2. In a bowl, combine the parmesan with the sage.
3. Add in the flour & eggs & sprinkle with salt & pepper as desired. Mix well.
4. Dip chicken in the flour-egg mixture.
5. Coat the chicken in the breadcrumbs.
6. Spritz the inside of the Air Fryer with cooking spray & set it to 390°F, allowing it to warm.
7. Cook the chicken for 20 minutes.
8. When golden, serve with fried rice.

146. FRIED PICKLES

Prep & Cook Time: 30 minutes | Servings: 4

INGREDIENTS

14 dill pickles, sliced
¼ cup of flour
1/8 tsp. of baking powder

Salt
2 tbsp. of cornstarch + 3 tbsp. of water
6 tbsp. of breadcrumbs

½ tsp. of paprika
Cooking spray

INSTRUCTIONS

1. Pre-heat your Air Fryer at 400°F.
2. Drain any excess moisture out of the dill pickles on a paper towel.
3. In a bowl, combine the flour, baking powder & salt.
4. Throw in the cornstarch & water mixture & combine well with a whisk.
5. Put the panko breadcrumbs in a shallow dish along with the paprika. Mix thoroughly.
6. Dip the pickles in the flour batter, before coating in the breadcrumbs. Spritz all the pickles with the cooking spray.
7. Transfer to the Air Fryer & cook for 15 minutes, until a golden-brown color is achieved.

147. CAULIFLOWER BITES

Prep & Cook Time: 30 minutes | Servings: 4

INGREDIENTS

1 cup of flour
⅓ cup of desiccated coconut
Salt & pepper
1 flax egg [1 tbsp. flaxseed meal + 3 tbsp.

of water]
1 small cauliflower, cut into florets
1 tsp. of mixed spice
½ tsp. of mustard powder

2 tbsp. of maple syrup
1 clove of garlic, minced
2 tbsp. of soy sauce

INSTRUCTIONS

1. Pre-heat the Air Fryer to 400°F.
2. In a bowl, mix together the oats, flour, & desiccated coconut, sprinkling with some salt & pepper as desired.
3. In a separate bowl, season the flax egg with a pinch of salt.
4. Coat the cauliflower with mixed spice & mustard powder.
5. Dip the florets into the flax egg, then into the flour mixture. Cook for 15 minutes in the Air Fryer.

6. In the meantime, place a saucepan over medium heat & add in the maple syrup, garlic, & soy sauce. Boil first, before reducing the heat to allow the sauce to thicken.
7. Remove the florets from the Air Fryer & transfer to the saucepan. Coat the florets in the sauce before returning to the Air Fryer & allowing to cook for an additional 5 minutes.

148. CHICKEN & VEGGIES

Prep & Cook Time: 30 minutes | Servings: 4

INGREDIENTS

8 chicken thighs
5 oz. of mushrooms, sliced
1 red onion, diced
Fresh black pepper, to taste
10 medium asparagus

½ cup of carrots, diced
¼ cup of balsamic vinegar
2 red bell peppers, diced
½ tsp. of sugar
2 tbsp. of extra-virgin olive oil

1 ½ tbsp. of fresh rosemary
2 cloves of garlic, chopped
½ tbsp. of dried oregano
1 tsp. of salt
2 fresh sage, chopped

INSTRUCTIONS

1. Pre-heat the Air Fryer to 400°F.
2. Grease the inside of a baking tray with the oil.
3. Season the chicken with salt & pepper.
4. Put all of the vegetables in a large bowl & throw in the oregano, garlic, sugar, mushrooms, vinegar, & sage. Combine everything well before transferring to the baking tray.
5. Put the chicken thighs in the baking tray. Cook in the Air Fryer for about 20 minutes.
6. Serve hot.

149. FALAFEL

Prep & Cook Time: 30 minutes | Servings: 8

INGREDIENTS

1 tsp. of cumin seeds
½ tsp. of coriander seeds
2 cups of chickpeas from can, drained
½ tsp. of red pepper flakes

3 cloves of garlic
¼ cup of parsley, chopped
¼ cup of coriander, chopped
½ onion, diced

1 tbsp. of lemon juice
3 tbsp. of flour
½ tsp. of salt cooking spray

INSTRUCTIONS

1. Fry the cumin & coriander seeds over medium heat until fragrant.
2. Grind using a mortar & pestle.
3. Put all of ingredients, except for the cooking spray, in a food processor & blend until a fine consistency is achieved.
4. Use your hands to mold the mixture into falafels & spritz with the cooking spray.
5. Preheat your Air Fryer at 400°F.
6. Transfer the falafels to the Air Fryer in one single layer.
7. Cook for 15 minutes, serving when they turn golden brown.

150. EASY ASPARAGUS

Prep & Cook Time: 10 minutes | Servings: 4

INGREDIENTS

1 lb. of fresh asparagus spears, trimmed

1 tbsp. of olive oil

Salt & pepper

INSTRUCTIONS

1. Pre-heat the Air Fryer at 375°F.
2. Combine all of the ingredients & transfer to the Air Fryer.
3. Cook for 5 minutes until soft.

151. CAULIFLOWER STEAK

Prep & Cook Time: 30 minutes | Servings: 2

INGREDIENTS

1 cauliflower, sliced into two
1 tbsp. of olive oil

2 tbsp. of onion, chopped
¼ tsp. of vegetable stock powder

¼ cup of milk
Salt & pepper

INSTRUCTIONS

1. Place the cauliflower in a bowl of salted water & allow to absorb for at least 2 hours.
2. Pre-heat the Air Fryer to 400°F.
3. Rinse off the cauliflower, put inside the Air Fryer & cook for 15 minutes.
4. In the meantime, fry the onions over medium heat, stirring constantly, until they turn translucent. Pour in the vegetable stock powder & milk. Bring to a boil & then lower the heat.
5. Let the sauce reduce & add in salt & pepper.
6. Plate up the cauliflower steak & top with the sauce.

152. ROCKET SALAD

Prep & Cook Time: 35 minutes | Servings: 4

INGREDIENTS

8 fresh figs, halved
1 ½ cups of chickpeas, cooked
1 tsp. of cumin seeds, crushed

4 tbsp. of balsamic vinegar
2 tbsp. of extra-virgin olive oil
Salt & pepper

3 cups of arugula rocket, washed & dried

INSTRUCTIONS

1. Pre-heat the Air Fryer to 375°F.
2. Cover the Air Fryer basket with aluminum foil & grease lightly with oil. Put the figs in the Air Fryer & allow to cook for 10 minutes.
3. In a bowl, combine the chickpeas & cumin seeds.
4. Remove the cooked figs from the Air Fryer & replace with chickpeas. Cook for 10 minutes. Leave to cool.
5. In the meantime, prepare the dressing. Mix together the balsamic vinegar, olive oil, salt & pepper.
6. In a salad bowl combine the arugula rocket with the cooled figs & chickpeas.
7. Toss with the sauce & serve right away.

153. VEGAN RAVIOLI

Prep & Cook Time: 15 minutes | Servings: 4

INGREDIENTS

½ cup of breadcrumbs
2 tsp. of yeast
1 tsp. of dried basil

1 tsp. of dried oregano
1 tsp. of garlic powder
Salt & pepper

¼ cup of aquafaba
8 oz. of vegan ravioli
Cooking spray

INSTRUCTIONS

1. Cover the Air Fryer basket with aluminum foil & coat with a light brushing of oil.
2. Pre-heat the Air Fryer to 400°F. Combine together the panko breadcrumbs, yeast, basil, oregano, & garlic powder. Sprinkle on salt & pepper to taste.
3. Put the aquafaba in a separate bowl. Dip the ravioli in the aquafaba before coating it in the panko mixture. Spritz with cooking spray & transfer to the Air Fryer.
4. Cook for 6 minutes ensuring to shake the Air Fryer basket halfway.

154. THANKSGIVING SPROUTS

Prep & Cook Time: 20 minutes | Servings: 6

INGREDIENTS

1 ½ lb. of Brussels sprouts, cleaned & trimmed

3 tbsp. of olive oil
1 tsp. of salt

1 tsp. of black pepper

INSTRUCTIONS

1. Pre-heat the Air Fryer to 375°F. Cover the basket with aluminum foil & coat with a light brushing of oil.
2. In a mixing bowl, combine all ingredients, coating the sprouts well.
3. Put in the Air Fryer basket & cook for 10 minutes. Shake the Air Fryer basket throughout the duration to ensure even cooking.

155. ROASTED GARLIC, BROCCOLI & LEMON

Prep & Cook Time: 25 minutes | Servings: 6

INGREDIENTS

2 heads of broccoli, cut into florets
2 tsp. of extra virgin olive oil

1 tsp. of salt
½ tsp. of black pepper

1 clove of garlic, minced
½ tsp. of lemon juice

INSTRUCTIONS

1. Cover the Air Fryer basket with aluminum foil & coat with a light brushing of oil.
2. Pre-heat the Air Fryer to 375°F.
3. In a bowl, combine all ingredients save for the lemon juice & transfer to the Air Fryer basket. Allow to cook for 15 minutes.
4. Serve with the lemon juice.

156. PEPPERONI PIZZA

Prep & Cook Time: 15 minutes | Servings: 3

INGREDIENTS

3 portobello mushroom caps, scooped
3 tbsp. of olive oil
3 tbsp. of tomato sauce

3 tbsp. of mozzarella, shredded
12 slices of pepperoni
Salt

1 pinch of dried Italian seasoning

INSTRUCTIONS

1. Pre-heat the Air Fryer to 330°F.
2. Season both sides of the portobello mushrooms with a drizzle of olive oil, then sprinkle salt & the Italian seasonings on the insides.
3. With a knife, spread the tomato sauce evenly over the mushroom, before adding the mozzarella on top.

4. Put the portobello in the cooking basket & place in the Air Fryer.
5. Cook for 1 minute, before taking the cooking basket out of the Air Fryer & putting the pepperoni slices on top.
6. Cook for another 3 to 5 minutes. Garnish with freshly grated parmesan cheese & crushed red pepper flakes & serve.

157. BABY CORN PAKODAS

Prep & Cook Time: 20 minutes | Servings: 5

INGREDIENTS

1 cup of flour
¼ tsp. of baking soda
¼ tsp. of salt

½ tsp. of curry powder
½ tsp. of red chili powder
¼ tsp. of turmeric powder

¼ cup of water
10 pc. Of baby corn, blanched

INSTRUCTIONS

1. Pre-heat the Air Fryer to 425°F.
2. Cover the Air Fryer basket with aluminum foil & coat with a light brushing of oil.
3. In a bowl, combine all ingredients save for the corn. Stir with a whisk until well combined.
4. Coat the corn in the batter & put inside the Air Fryer.
5. Cook for 8 minutes until a golden-brown color is achieved.

158. CHICKEN-MUSHROOM CASSEROLE

Prep & Cook Time: 30 minutes | Servings: 4

INGREDIENTS

4 chicken breasts
½ cup of shredded cheese
Salt

1 cup of coconut milk
1 cup of mushrooms
1 broccoli, cut into florets

1 tbsp. of curry powder

INSTRUCTIONS

1. Pre-heat your Air Fryer to 350°F. Spritz a casserole dish with some cooking spray.
2. Cube the chicken breasts & combine with curry powder & coconut milk in a bowl. Season with salt.
3. Add in the broccoli & mushroom & mix well.
4. Pour the mixture into the casserole dish. Top with the cheese.
5. Transfer to your Air Fryer & cook for about 20 minutes.
6. Serve warm.

159. PITA BREAD PIZZA

Prep & Cook Time: 15 minutes | Servings: 1

INGREDIENTS

1 pita bread
1 tbsp. of pizza sauce
6 pepperoni slices

¼ cup of grated mozzarella cheese
1 tsp. of olive oil
¼ tsp. of garlic powder

¼ tsp. of dried oregano

INSTRUCTIONS

1. Pre-heat your Air Fryer to 350°F.
2. Spread the pizza sauce on top of the pita bread. Place the pepperoni slices over the sauce, followed by the mozzarella cheese.
3. Season with garlic powder & oregano.
4. Put the pita pizza inside the Air Fryer & place a trivet on top.
5. Cook for 6 minutes & enjoy.

160. PAPRIKA TOFU

Prep & Cook Time: 25 minutes | Servings: 4

INGREDIENTS

2 block extra firm tofu, pressed to remove excess water & cubed

¼ cup of cornstarch
1 tbsp. of smoked paprika

Salt & pepper

INSTRUCTIONS

1. Cover the Air Fryer basket with aluminum foil & coat with a light brushing of oil.
2. Pre-heat the Air Fryer to 370°F.
3. Combine all ingredients in a bowl, coating the tofu well.
4. Put in the Air Fryer basket & allow to cook for 12 minutes. Serve!

161. MAC & CHEESE

Prep & Cook Time: 15 minutes | Servings: 2

INGREDIENTS

1 cup of cooked macaroni
½ cup of warm milk

1 tbsp. of parmesan cheese
1 cup of grated cheddar cheese

Salt & pepper, to taste

INSTRUCTIONS

1. Pre-heat the Air Fryer to 350°F.
2. In a baking dish, mix together all of the ingredients, except for Parmesan.
3. Put the dish inside the Air Fryer & allow to cook for 10 minutes.
4. Add the Parmesan cheese on top & serve.

162. PASTA SALAD

Prep & Cook Time: 2 hours 25 minutes | Servings: 8

INGREDIENTS

4 tomatoes, medium & cut in eighths
3 eggplants, small
3 zucchinis, medium sized
2 bell peppers, any color

4 cups of large pasta, uncooked in any
1 cup of cherry tomatoes, sliced
½ cup of Italian dressing, fat-free
8 tbsp. of parmesan, grated

2 tbsp. of extra virgin olive oil
2 tsp. of pink Himalayan salt
1 tsp. of basil, dried
High quality cooking spray

INSTRUCTIONS

1. Wash & dry the eggplant. Cut off the stem & throw it away. Do not peel the eggplant. Cut it into half-inch-thick round slices.
2. Coat the eggplant slices with 1 tbsp. of extra virgin olive oil, & transfer to the Air Fryer basket.
3. Cook the eggplant for 40 minutes at 350°F. Once it is tender & cooked through, remove from the Air Fryer & set to one side.
4. Wash & dry the zucchini. Cut off the stem & throw it away. Do not peel the zucchini. Cut the zucchini into half-inch-thick round slices.
5. Combine with the olive oil to coat & put it in the Air Fryer basket.
6. Cook the zucchini for about 25 minutes at 350°F. Once it is tender & cooked through, remove from the Air Fryer & set to one side.
7. Wash the tomatoes & cut them into eight equal slices. Transfer them to the Air Fryer basket & spritz lightly with high quality cooking spray. Cook the tomatoes for 30 minutes at 350°F. Once they have shrunk & are beginning to turn brown, set them to one side.
8. Cook the pasta & drain it. Rinse with cold water & set it aside to cool.
9. Wash, dry & halve the bell peppers. Remove the stems & seeds.
10. Wash & halve the cherry tomatoes.
11. In a large bowl, mix together the bell peppers & cherry tomatoes. Stir in the roasted vegetables, cooked pasta, pink Himalayan salt, dressing, chopped basil leaves, & grated parmesan, ensuring to incorporate everything well.
12. Let the salad cool & marinate in the refrigerator.
13. Serve the salad cold or at room temperature.

163. PROSCIUTTO & POTATO SALAD

Prep & Cook Time: 15 minutes | Servings: 8

INGREDIENTS

4 lb. of potatoes, boiled & cubed
15 slices of prosciutto, diced
15 oz. of sour cream

2 cups of shredded cheddar cheese
2 tbsp. of mayonnaise
1 tsp. of salt

1 tsp. of black pepper
1 tsp. of dried basil

INSTRUCTIONS

1. Pre-heat the Air Fryer to 350°F.
2. Place the potatoes, prosciutto, & cheddar in a baking dish. Put it in the Air Fryer & allow to cook for 7 minutes.
3. In a separate bowl, mix together the sour cream, mayonnaise, salt, pepper, & basil using a whisk.
4. Coat the salad with the dressing & serve.

164. CHICKEN QUESADILLAS

Prep & Cook Time: 20 minutes | Servings: 4

INGREDIENTS

2 soft taco shells
1 lb. of boneless chicken breasts
1 large green pepper, sliced

1 medium-sized onion, sliced
½ cup of Cheddar cheese, shredded
½ cup of salsa sauce

2 tbsp. of olive oil
Salt & pepper, to taste

INSTRUCTIONS

1. Pre-heat the Air Fryer to 370°F & drizzle the basket with 1 tbsp. of olive oil.
2. Lay one taco shell into the bottom of the Air Fryer & spread some salsa inside the taco. Slice the chicken breast into strips & put the strips into taco shell.
3. Top the chicken with the onions & peppers.
4. Season with salt & pepper. Add the shredded cheese & top with the second taco shell.
5. Drizzle with another tbsp. of olive oil. Put the rack over the taco to keep it in place.
6. Cook for 4 – 6 minutes, until it turns lightly brown & is cooked through. Serve either hot or cold.

165. MOZZARELLA BRUSCHETTA

Prep & Cook Time: 10 minutes | Servings: 1

INGREDIENTS

6 small loaf slices
½ cup of tomatoes, finely chopped

3 oz. of mozzarella cheese, grated
1 tbsp. of fresh basil, chopped

1 tbsp. of olive oil

INSTRUCTIONS

1. Pre-heat the Air Fryer to 350°F. Place the bread inside & cook for about 3 minutes.
2. Add the tomato, mozzarella, prosciutto, & a drizzle of olive oil on top.
3. Cook the bruschetta for an additional minute before serving.

166. SAUSAGE-CHICKEN CASSEROLE

Prep & Cook Time: 30 minutes | Servings: 8

INGREDIENTS

2 cloves of minced garlic
10 eggs
1 cup of broccoli, chopped
½ tbsp. of salt

1 cup of cheddar, shredded & divided
¼ tbsp. of pepper
¾ cup of whipping cream

1 x 12-oz. packet of cooked chicken
sausage

INSTRUCTIONS

1. Pre-heat the Air Fryer to 400°F.
2. In a large bowl, beat the eggs with a whisk. Pour in the whipping cream & cheese. Combine well.
3. In a separate bowl, mix together the garlic, broccoli, salt, pepper & cooked sausage.
4. Place the chicken sausage mix in a casserole dish. Top with the cheese mixture.
5. Transfer to the Air Fryer & cook for about 20 minutes.

167. CASHEW & CHICKEN MANCHURIAN

Prep & Cook Time: 30 minutes | Servings: 6

INGREDIENTS

1 cup chicken boneless
1 spring onions, chopped
1 onion, chopped
3 green chilis
6 cashew nuts

1 tsp. ginger, chopped
½ tsp. of garlic, chopped
1 Egg
2 tbsp. of flour
1 tbsp. of cornstarch

1 tsp. of soy sauce
2 tsp. of chili paste
1 tsp. of pepper
Pinch of MSG
1 tbsp. of oil

INSTRUCTIONS

1. Pre-heat your Air Fryer at 360°F
2. Toss together the chicken, egg, salt & pepper to coat well.
3. Combine the cornstarch & flour & use this to cover the chicken.
4. Cook in the Air Fryer for 10 minutes.
5. In the meantime, toast the nuts in a frying pan. Add in the onions & cook until they turn translucent. Combine with the remaining ingredients to create the sauce.
6. Finally, add in the chicken. When piping hot, garnish with the spring onions & serve.

168. CHEESE & BACON ROLLS

Prep & Cook Time: 25 minutes | Servings: 4

INGREDIENTS

8 oz. of refrigerated crescent roll dough
   [usually 1 can]

6 oz. of sharp cheddar cheese, grated
1 lb. of bacon, cooked & chopped

INSTRUCTIONS

1. Roll out the crescent dough flat & slice it into 1" x 1 ½" pieces.
2. In a bowl, mix together the cheese & bacon. Take about ¼ cup of this mixture & spread it across one slice of dough. Repeat with the rest of the mixture & dough.
3. Set your Air Fryer to 330°F & allow to warm.
4. Place the rolls on the Air Fry tray & transfer to the Air Fryer. Alternatively, you can put them in the food basket.
5. Bake for roughly 6 – 8 minutes until a golden-brown color is achieved. Watch them carefully to prevent burning, as they may cook very quickly.

169. KIDNEY BEANS OATMEAL

Prep & Cook Time: 25 minutes | Servings: 2 – 4

INGREDIENTS

2 large bell peppers, halved lengthwise,
deseeded
2 tbsp. of cooked kidney beans
2 tbsp. of cooked chickpeas

2 cups of oatmeal, cooked
1 tsp. of ground cumin
½ tsp. of paprika
½ tsp. of salt or to taste

¼ tsp. of black pepper powder
¼ cup yogurt

INSTRUCTIONS

1. Pre-heat the Air Fryer at 355°F.
2. Put the bell peppers, cut-side-down, in the Air Fryer. Allow to cook for 2 – 3 minutes.
3. Take the peppers out of the Air Fryer & let cool.
4. In a bowl, combine together the rest of the ingredients.
5. Divide the mixture evenly & use each portion to stuff a pepper.

6. Return to the Air Fryer & continue to air fry for 4 minutes. Serve hot.

170. CHICKEN FILLETS & BRIE

Prep & Cook Time: 40 minutes | Servings: 4

INGREDIENTS

4 slices of turkey, cured
2 large chicken fillets

4 slices of brie cheese
1 tbsp. of chives, chopped

Salt & pepper

INSTRUCTIONS

1. Pre-heat Air Fryer to 360°F. Slice each chicken fillet in half & sprinkle on salt & pepper. Coat with the brie & chives.
2. Wrap the turkey around the chicken & secure with toothpick.
3. Cook for 15 minutes until a brown color is achieved.

171. CHEESE & MACARONI BALLS

Prep & Cook Time: 25 minutes | Servings: 2

INGREDIENTS

2 cups of leftover macaroni
1 cup of cheddar cheese, shredded
3 large eggs

1 cup of milk
½ cup of flour
1 cup of breadcrumbs

½ tsp. of salt
¼ tsp. of black pepper

INSTRUCTIONS

1. In a bowl, combine the leftover macaroni & shredded cheese.
2. Pour the flour in a separate bowl. Put the breadcrumbs in a third bowl. Finally, in a fourth bowl, mix together the eggs & milk with a whisk.
3. With an ice-cream scoop, create balls from the macaroni mixture. Coat them the flour, then in the egg mixture, & lastly in the breadcrumbs.
4. Pre-heat the Air Fryer to 365°F & cook the balls for about 10 minutes, giving them an occasional stir. Ensure they crisp up nicely.
5. Serve with the sauce of your choice.

172. CHEESE PIZZA

Prep & Cook Time: 15 minutes | Servings: 4

INGREDIENTS

1 pc. of bread
½ lb. of mozzarella cheese

1 tbsp. of olive oil
2 tbsp. of ketchup

⅓ cup of sausage
1 tsp. of garlic powder

INSTRUCTIONS

1. Using a tbsp., spread the ketchup over the pita bread.
2. Top with the sausage & cheese. Season with the garlic powder & 1 tbsp. of olive oil.
3. Pre-heat the Air Fryer to 340°F.
4. Put the pizza in the Air Fryer basket & cook for 6 minutes. Enjoy!

173. PORTABELLA PIZZA

Prep & Cook Time: 15 minutes | Servings: 3

INGREDIENTS

3 tbsp. of olive oil
3 portobello mushroom caps, cleaned & scooped

3 tbsp. of mozzarella, shredded
3 tbsp. of tomato sauce
Salt

12 slices of pepperoni
Pinch of dried Italian seasonings

INSTRUCTIONS

1. Pre-heat the Air Fryer to 330°F.
2. Coat both sides of the mushroom cap with a drizzle of oil, before seasoning the inside with the Italian seasonings & salt. Evenly spread the tomato sauce over the mushroom & add the cheese on top.
3. Put the mushroom into the cooking basket of the Air Fryer. Place the slices of pepperoni on top of the portobello pizza after a minute of cooking & continue to cook for another 3-5 minutes. Serve!

174. AMERICAN HOT DOGS

Prep & Cook Time: 20 minutes | Servings: 4

INGREDIENTS

3 Brazilian sausages, cut into 3 equal pieces

9 bacon fillets, raw
Black pepper to taste

Salt

INSTRUCTIONS

1. Pre-heat the Air Fryer for 5 minutes at 355°F.
2. Take a slice of bacon & wrap it around each piece of sausage. Sprinkle with some salt & pepper as desired, as well as a half-tsp. of Italian herbs if you like.
3. Fry the sausages for 15 minutes & serve warm.

175. GARLIC BACON

Prep & Cook Time: 40 minutes | Servings: 4

INGREDIENTS

4 potatoes, peeled & cut into bite-size chunks

6 cloves garlic, unpeeled
4 strips of bacon, chopped

1 tbsp. of fresh rosemary, finely chopped

INSTRUCTIONS

1. In a large bowl, thoroughly combine the potatoes, garlic, bacon, & rosemary. Place the ingredients in a baking dish.
2. Set your Air Fryer to 350°F & briefly allow to warm.
3. Cook the potatoes for 25-30 minutes until a golden-brown color is achieved.

---

176. MEXICAN PIZZA

Prep & Cook Time: 15 minutes | Servings: 4

INGREDIENTS

¾ cup refried beans
1 cup salsa
12 frozen beef meatballs, pre-cooked

2 jalapeno peppers, sliced
6 slices of bread
1 cup of pepper Jack cheese, shredded

1 cup of Colby cheese, shredded

INSTRUCTIONS

1. Pre-heat the Air Fryer for 4 minutes at 370°F.
2. In a bowl, mix together the salsa, meatball, jalapeno pepper & beans.
3. Place a spoonful of this mixture on top of each pita bread, along with a topping of pepper Jack & Colby cheese.
4. Bake in the Air Fryer for 10 minutes. Serve hot.

---

177. PESTO GNOCCHI

Prep & Cook Time: 30 minutes | Servings: 4

INGREDIENTS

1 packet [16-oz.] of shelf-stable gnocchi
1 medium-sized onion, chopped
3 cloves of garlic, minced

1 jar [8 oz.] of pesto
⅓ cup of parmesan cheese, grated
1 tbsp. of extra virgin olive oil

Salt & black pepper to taste

INSTRUCTIONS

1. Pre-heat the Air Fryer to 340°F.
2. In a large bowl combine the onion, garlic, & gnocchi, & drizzle with the olive oil. Mix thoroughly.
3. Transfer the mixture to the Air Fryer & cook for 15 – 20 minutes, stirring occasionally, making sure the gnocchi become lightly brown & crispy.
4. Add in the pesto & Parmesan cheese & give everything a good stir before serving straightaway.

---

178. CHEESEBURGER SLIDERS

Prep & Cook Time: 20 minutes | Servings: 3

INGREDIENTS

1 lb. of ground beef
6 slices of cheddar cheese

6 dinner rolls
Salt & pepper

INSTRUCTIONS

1. Pre-heat the Air Fryer to 390°F.
2. With your hands, shape the ground beef into 6 x 2.5-oz. patties. Sprinkle on some salt & pepper to taste.
3. Place the burgers in the cooking basket & cook for 10 minutes. Take care when removing them from the Air Fryer.
4. Top the patties with the cheese. Put them back in the Air Fryer & allow to cook for another minute before serving.

---

179. LOW-CARB PIZZA CRUST

Prep & Cook Time: 20 minutes | Servings: 4

INGREDIENTS

1 tbsp. of full-fat cream cheese
½ cup of whole milk

mozzarella cheese, grated
2 tbsp. of flour

1 egg white

INSTRUCTIONS

1. In a microwave-safe bowl, combine the cream cheese, mozzarella, & flour & heat in the microwave for half a minute. Mix well to create a smooth consistency. Add in the egg white & stir to form a soft ball of dough.
2. With slightly wet hands, press the dough into a pizza crust about six inches in diameter.
3. Place a sheet of parchment paper in the bottom of your Air Fryer & lay the crust on top. Cook for ten minutes at 350°F, turning the crust over halfway through the cooking time.
4. Top the pizza base with the toppings of your choice & enjoy!

---

180. BACON-WRAPPED ONION RINGS

INGREDIENTS

1 large onion, peeled   8 slices of sugar-free bacon   1 tbsp. of sriracha

INSTRUCTIONS

1. Chop up the onion into slices a quarter-inch thick. Gently pull apart the rings. Take a slice of bacon & wrap it around an onion ring. Repeat with the rest of the ingredients. Place each onion ring in your Air Fryer.
2. Cut the onion rings at 350°F for ten minutes, turning them halfway through to ensure the bacon crisps up.
3. Serve hot with the sriracha.

---

181. SMOKED BBQ TOAST

Prep & Cook Time: 10 minutes | Servings: 1

INGREDIENTS

2 tsp. of coconut oil, melted   1 tsp. of chili powder   2 slices of bread
¼ tsp. of smoked paprika   ¼ tsp. cumin

INSTRUCTIONS

1. Mix the melted coconut oil with the paprika, chili powder, & cumin. Place the bread slices in a large bowl & pour the coconut oil over them, tossing them to cover them evenly.
2. Place the slices in the basket of your Air Fryer & spread them out across the base.
3. Cook for six minutes at 320°F, giving the basket an occasional shake to make sure everything is cooked evenly.
4. Leave to cool & serve.

---

182. ROASTED EGGPLANT

Prep & Cook Time: 20 minutes | Servings: 1

INGREDIENTS

1 large eggplant   ¼ tsp. of salt
2 tbsp. of olive oil   ½ tsp. of garlic powder

INSTRUCTIONS

1. Prepare the eggplant by slicing off the top & bottom & cutting it into slices around a quarter-inch thick.
2. Apply olive oil to the slices with a brush, coating both sides. Season each side with sprinklings of salt & garlic powder.
3. Place the slices in the Air Fryer & cook for fifteen minutes at 390°F.
4. Serve right away.

---

183. LOW-CARB PITA CHIPS

Prep & Cook Time: 15 minutes | Servings: 1

INGREDIENTS

1 cup of mozzarella cheese, shredded   ¼ cup of blanched finely ground flour
1 egg   ½ oz. of flour

INSTRUCTIONS

1. Melt the mozzarella in the microwave. Add the egg & flour, combine together to form a smooth paste. Microwave the cheese again if it begins to set.
2. Put the dough between two sheets of parchment paper & use a rolling pin to flatten it out into a rectangle. The thickness is up to you. With a sharp knife, cut into the dough to form triangles. It may be necessary to complete this step-in multiple batches.
3. Place the chips in the Air Fryer & cook for five minutes at 350°F. Turn them over & cook on the other side for another five minutes, or until the chips are golden & firm.
4. Allow the chips to cool & harden further. They can be stored in an airtight container.

---

184. FLATBREAD

Prep & Cook Time: 20 minutes | Servings: 1

INGREDIENTS

1 cup of mozzarella cheese, shredded   ¼ cup of blanched finely ground flour   1 oz. of full-fat cream cheese, softened

INSTRUCTIONS

1. Microwave the mozzarella for half a minute until melted. Combine with the flour to achieve a smooth consistency, before adding the cream cheese. Keep mixing to create a dough, microwaving the mixture again if the cheese begins to harden.
2. Divide the dough into two equal pieces. Between two sheets of parchment paper, roll out the dough until it is about a quarter-inch thick. Cover the bottom of your Air Fryer with another sheet of parchment.
3. Transfer the dough into the Air Fryer & cook at 320°F for seven minutes. You may need to complete this step in two batches. Make sure to turn the flatbread halfway through cooking. Take care when removing it from the Air Fryer & serve warm.

---

185. BUFFALO CAULIFLOWER

Prep & Cook Time: 10 minutes | Servings: 1

INGREDIENTS

½ packet of dry ranch seasoning
2 tbsp. of salted butter, melted

Cauliflower florets
¼ cup of buffalo sauce

INSTRUCTIONS

1. In a bowl, combine the dry ranch seasoning & butter. Toss with the cauliflower florets to coat & transfer them to the Air Fryer.
2. Cook at 400°F for five minutes, shaking the basket occasionally to ensure the florets cook evenly.
3. Remove the cauliflower from the Air Fryer, pour the buffalo sauce over it, & enjoy.

186. BRUSSELS SPROUT CHIPS

Prep & Cook Time: 15 minutes | Servings: 1

INGREDIENTS

1 lb. of Brussels sprouts

1 tbsp. of coconut oil, melted

1 tbsp. of butter, melted

INSTRUCTIONS

1. Prepare the Brussels sprouts by halving them, discarding any loose leaves.
2. Combine with the melted coconut oil & transfer to your Air Fryer.
3. Cook at 400°F for ten minutes, giving the basket a good shake throughout the cooking time to brown them up if desired.
4. The sprouts are ready when they are partially caramelized. Remove them from the Air Fryer & serve with a topping of melted butter before serving.

187. CAULIFLOWER TOTS

Prep & Cook Time: 20 minutes | Servings: 8

INGREDIENTS

1 large head of cauliflower
½ cup of parmesan cheese, grated

1 cup of mozzarella cheese, shredded
1 tsp. of seasoned salt

1 egg

INSTRUCTIONS

1. Place a steamer basket over a pot of boiling water, ensuring the water is not high enough to enter the basket.
2. Cut up the cauliflower into florets & transfer to the steamer basket. Cover the pot with a lid & leave to steam for seven minutes, making sure the cauliflower softens.
3. Place the florets on a cheesecloth & leave to cool. Remove as much moisture as possible. This is crucial as it ensures the cauliflower will harden.
4. In a bowl, break up the cauliflower with a fork.
5. Stir in the parmesan, mozzarella, seasoned salt, & egg, incorporating the cauliflower well with all of the other ingredients. Make sure the mixture is firm enough to be moldable.
6. Using your hand, mold about two tbsp. of the mixture into tots & repeat until you have used up all of the mixture. Put each tot into your Air Fryer basket. They may need to be cooked in multiple batches.
7. Cook at 320°F for twelve minutes, turning them halfway through. Ensure they are brown in color before serving.

188. HERBED GARLIC RADISHES

Prep & Cook Time: 15 minutes | Servings: 2

INGREDIENTS

1 lb. of radishes
2 tbsp. of butter, melted

¼ tsp. of dried oregano
½ tsp. of dried parsley

½ tsp. of garlic powder

INSTRUCTIONS

1. Prepare the radishes by cutting off their tops & bottoms & quartering them.
2. In a bowl, combine the butter, dried oregano, dried parsley, & garlic powder. Toss with the radishes to coat.
3. Transfer the radishes to your Air Fryer & cook at 350°F for ten minutes, shaking the basket at the halfway point to ensure the radishes cook evenly through. The radishes are ready when they begin to turn brown.

189. JICAMA FRIES

Prep & Cook Time: 25 minutes | Servings: 1

INGREDIENTS

1 small jicama, peeled
¼ tsp. of onion powder

¾ tsp. of chili powder
¼ tsp. of garlic powder

¼ tsp. of ground black pepper

INSTRUCTIONS

1. To make the fries, cut the jicama into matchsticks of your desired thickness.
2. In a bowl, toss them with the onion powder, chili powder, garlic powder, & black pepper to coat. Transfer the fries into the basket of your Air Fryer.
3. Cook at 350°F for twenty minutes, giving the basket an occasional shake throughout the cooking process. The fries are ready when they are hot & golden in color. Enjoy!

190. ZESTY SALMON JERKY

INGREDIENTS

1 lb. of boneless skinless salmon

½ tsp. of liquid smoke

½ tsp. of ground ginger

¼ cup of soy sauce

¼ tsp. of red pepper flakes

INSTRUCTIONS

1. Cut the salmon into strips about four inches long & a quarter-inch thick.
2. Put the salmon in an airtight container or bag along with the liquid smoke, ginger, soy sauce, & red pepper flakes, combining everything to coat the salmon completely. Leave the salmon in the refrigerator for at least two hours.
3. Transfer the salmon slices in the Air Fryer, taking care not to overlap any pieces. This step may need to be completed in multiple batches.
4. Cook at 140°F for four hours.
5. Take care when removing the salmon from the Air Fryer & leave it to cool. This jerky makes a good snack & can be stored in an airtight container.

191. ZUCCHINI BITES

Prep & Cook Time: 15 minutes | Servings: 4

INGREDIENTS

4 zucchinis

1 egg

½ cup of parmesan cheese, grated

1 tbsp. of Italian herbs

1 cup of coconut, grated

INSTRUCTIONS

1. Thinly grate the zucchini & dry with a cheesecloth, ensuring to remove all of the moisture.
2. In a bowl, combine the zucchini with the egg, parmesan, Italian herbs, & grated coconut, mixing well to incorporate everything. Using your hands, mold the mixture into balls.
3. Pre-heat the Air Fryer at 400°F & place a rack inside. Lay the zucchini balls on the rack & cook for ten minutes. Serve hot.

192. POP CORN BROCCOLI

Prep & Cook Time: 10 minutes | Servings: 1

INGREDIENTS

4 egg yolks

¼ cup of butter, melted

2 cups of coconut flower

Salt & pepper

2 cups of broccoli florets

INSTRUCTIONS

1. In a bowl, whisk the egg yolks & melted butter together. Throw in the coconut flour, salt & pepper, then stir again to combine well.
2. Pre-heat the Air Fryer at 400°F.
3. Dip each broccoli floret into the mixture & place in the Air Fryer. Cook for six minutes, in multiple batches if necessary. Take care when removing them from the Air Fryer & enjoy!

193. ROSEMARY GREEN BEANS

Prep & Cook Time: 10 minutes | Servings: 1

INGREDIENTS

1 tbsp. of butter, melted

2 tbsp. of rosemary

½ tsp. of salt

3 cloves garlic, minced

¾ cup of green beans, chopped

INSTRUCTIONS

1. Pre-heat your Air Fryer at 390°F.
2. Combine the melted butter with the rosemary, salt, & minced garlic. Toss in the green beans, making sure to coat them well.
3. Cook in the Air Fryer for five minutes.

194. CARROT CROQUETTES

Prep & Cook Time: 10 minutes | Servings: 4

INGREDIENTS

2 medium-sized carrots, trimmed & grated

2 medium-sized celery stalks, trimmed & grated

½ cup of leek, finely chopped

1 tbsp. of garlic paste

¼ tsp. of freshly cracked black pepper

1 tsp. of sea salt

1 tbsp. of fresh dill, finely chopped

1 egg, lightly whisked

¼ cup of flour

¼ tsp. of baking powder

½ cup of breadcrumbs [seasoned or regular]

Chive mayo to serve

INSTRUCTIONS

1. Drain any excess liquid from the carrots & celery by placing them on a paper towel.
2. Stir together the vegetables with all of the other ingredients, save for the breadcrumbs & chive mayo.
3. Use your hands to mold 1 tbsp. of the vegetable mixture into a ball & repeat until all of the mixture has been used up. Press down on each ball with your hand or a palette knife. Cover completely with breadcrumbs. Spritz the croquettes with a non-stick cooking spray.
4. Arrange the croquettes in a single layer in your Air Fryer & fry for 6 minutes at 360°F.
5. Serve warm with the chive mayo on the side.

195. PEPPERED PUFF PASTRY

Prep & Cook Time: 25 minutes | Servings: 4

INGREDIENTS

1 ½ tbsp. of sesame oil
1 cup of white mushrooms, sliced
2 cloves garlic, minced
1 bell pepper, seeded & chopped

¼ tsp. of sea salt
¼ tsp. of dried rosemary
½ tsp. of ground black pepper
11 oz. of puff pastry sheets

½ cup of crème fraiche
1 egg, well whisked
½ cup of parmesan cheese, preferably freshly grated

INSTRUCTIONS

1. Pre-heat your Air Fryer to 400°F.
2. In a skillet, heat the sesame oil over a moderate heat & fry the mushrooms, garlic, & pepper until soft & fragrant.
3. Sprinkle on the salt, rosemary, & pepper.
4. In the meantime, unroll the puff pastry & slice it into 4-inch squares.
5. Spread the crème fraiche across each square.
6. Spoon equal amounts of the vegetables into the puff pastry squares. Enclose each square around the filling in a triangle shape, pressing the edges with your fingertips.
7. Brush each triangle with some whisked egg & cover with grated Parmesan.
8. Cook for 22-25 minutes.

---

196. SAUTÉED GREEN BEANS

Prep & Cook Time: 12 minutes | Servings: 4

INGREDIENTS

¾ lb. of green beans, cleaned
1 tbsp. of balsamic vinegar
¼ tsp. of salt

½ tsp. of mixed peppercorns, freshly cracked
1 tbsp. of butter

Sesame seeds to serve

INSTRUCTIONS

1. Pre-heat your Air Fryer at 390°F.
2. Combine the green beans with the rest of the ingredients, except for the sesame seeds. Transfer to the Air Fryer & cook for 10 minutes.
3. In the meantime, heat the sesame seeds in a small skillet to toast all over, stirring constantly to prevent burning.
4. Serve the green beans accompanied by the toasted sesame seeds.

---

197. HORSERADISH MAYO & GORGONZOLA MUSHROOMS

Prep & Cook Time: 15 minutes | Servings: 5

INGREDIENTS

½ cup of breadcrumbs
2 cloves garlic, pressed
2 tbsp. of fresh coriander, chopped
⅓ tsp. of salt

½ tsp. of crushed red pepper flakes
1 ½ tbsp. of olive oil
20 medium-sized mushrooms
½ cup of Gorgonzola cheese, grated

¼ cup of low-fat mayonnaise
1 tsp. of prepared horseradish
1 tbsp. of fresh parsley, finely chopped

INSTRUCTIONS

1. Combine the breadcrumbs together with the garlic, coriander, salt, red pepper, & the olive oil.
2. Take equal-sized amounts of the bread crumb mixture & use them to stuff the mushroom caps. Add the grated Gorgonzola on top of each.
3. Put the mushrooms in the Air Fryer grill pan & transfer to the Air Fryer.
4. Grill them at 380°F for 8-12 minutes, ensuring the stuffing is warm throughout.
5. In the meantime, prepare the horseradish mayo. Mix together the mayonnaise, horseradish & parsley.
6. When the mushrooms are ready, serve with the mayo.

---

198. SCALLION & RICOTTA POTATOES

Prep & Cook Time: 15 minutes | Servings: 4

INGREDIENTS

4 baking potatoes
2 tbsp. of olive oil
½ cup of Ricotta cheese
2 tbsp. of scallions, chopped

1 heaped tbsp. of fresh parsley, roughly chopped
1 heaped tbsp. of coriander, minced
2 oz. of Cheddar cheese, grated

1 tsp. of celery seeds
½ tsp. of salt
½ tsp. of garlic pepper

INSTRUCTIONS

1. Pierce the skin of the potatoes with a knife.
2. Cook in the Air Fryer basket for roughly 13 minutes at 350°F. If they are not cooked through by this time, leave for 2 – 3 minutes longer.
3. In the meantime, make the stuffing by combining all the other ingredients.
4. Cut halfway into the cooked potatoes to open them.
5. Spoon equal amounts of the stuffing into each potato & serve hot.

---

199. CRUMBED BEANS

Prep & Cook Time: 10 minutes | Servings: 4

INGREDIENTS

½ cup of flour
1 tsp. of smoky chipotle powder
½ tsp. of ground black pepper

1 tsp. of sea salt flakes
2 eggs, beaten
½ cup of crushed saltines

10 oz. of wax beans

INSTRUCTIONS

1. Combine the flour, chipotle powder, black pepper, & salt in a bowl. Put the eggs in a second bowl. Place the crushed saltines in a third bowl.
2. Wash the beans with cold water & discard any tough strings.
3. Coat the beans with the flour mixture, before dipping them into the beaten egg. Lastly cover them with the crushed saltines.
4. Spritz the beans with a cooking spray.
5. Air-fry at 360°F for 4 minutes. Give the cooking basket a good shake & continue to cook for 3 minutes. Serve hot.

200. COLBY POTATO PATTIES

Prep & Cook Time: 15 minutes | Servings: 8

INGREDIENTS

2 lb. of white potatoes, peeled & grated
½ cup of scallions, finely chopped
½ tsp. of freshly ground black pepper, or
  more to taste

1tbsp. of sea salt
½ tsp. of hot paprika
2 cups of Colby cheese, shredded
¼ cup of canola oil

1 cup crushed crackers

INSTRUCTIONS

1. Boil the potatoes until soft. Dry them off & peel them before mashing thoroughly, leaving no lumps.
2. Combine the mashed potatoes with scallions, pepper, salt, paprika, & cheese.
3. Mold the mixture into balls with your hands & press with your palm to flatten them into patties.
4. In a shallow dish, combine the canola oil & crushed crackers. Coat the patties in the crumb mixture.
5. Cook the patties inside your Air Fryer at 360°F for about 10 minutes, in multiple batches if necessary.
6. Serve with tabasco mayo or the sauce of your choice.

201. TURKEY GARLIC POTATOES

Prep & Cook Time: 45 minutes | Servings: 2

INGREDIENTS

3 unsmoked turkey strips
6 small potatoes

1 tsp. of garlic, minced
2 tsp. of olive oil

Salt
Pepper

INSTRUCTIONS

1. Peel the potatoes & cube them finely.
2. Coat in 1 tsp. of oil & cook in the Air Fryer for 10 minutes at 350°F.
3. In a separate bowl, slice the turkey finely & combine with the garlic, oil, salt & pepper. Pour the potatoes into the bowl & mix well.
4. Lay the mixture on some silver aluminum foil, transfer to the Air Fryer & cook for about 10 minutes.
5. Serve with raita.

202. CROUTONS

Prep & Cook Time: 25 minutes | Servings: 4

INGREDIENTS

2 slices of bread
1 tbsp. of olive oil

INSTRUCTIONS

1. Cut the slices of bread into medium-size chunks.
2. Coat the inside of the Air Fryer with the oil. Set it to 390°F & allow it to heat up.
3. Place the chunks inside & shallow fry for at least 8 minutes.
4. Serve with hot soup.

203. GARLIC STUFFED MUSHROOMS

Prep & Cook Time: 25 minutes | Servings: 4

INGREDIENTS

6 small mushrooms
1 oz. of onion, peeled & diced
1 tbsp. of breadcrumbs

1 tbsp. of olive oil
1 tsp. of garlic, pureed
1 tsp. of parsley

Salt & pepper

INSTRUCTIONS

1. Combine the breadcrumbs, oil, onion, parsley, salt, pepper & garlic in a bowl. Cut out the mushrooms' stalks & stuff each cap with the crumb mixture.
2. Cook in the Air Fryer for 10 minutes at 350°F.
3. Serve with a side of mayo dip.

204. ZUCCHINI SWEET POTATOES

Prep & Cook Time: 20 minutes | Servings: 4

INGREDIENTS

2 large-sized sweet potatoes, peeled & quartered
1 medium-sized zucchini, sliced
1 Serrano pepper, deveined & thinly sliced
1 bell pepper, deveined & thinly sliced

1 – 2 carrots, cut into matchsticks
¼ cup olive oil
1 ½ tbsp. of maple syrup
½ tsp. of porcini powder
¼ tsp. of mustard powder
½ tsp. of fennel seeds

1 tbsp. of garlic powder
½ tsp. of fine sea salt
¼ tsp. of ground black pepper
Tomato ketchup to serve

INSTRUCTIONS

1. Put the sweet potatoes, zucchini, peppers, & the carrot into the basket of your Air Fryer. Coat with a drizzling of olive oil.
2. Pre-heat the Air Fryer at 350°F.
3. Cook the vegetables for 15 minutes.
4. In the meantime, prepare the sauce by vigorously combining the other ingredients, save for the tomato ketchup, with a whisk.
5. Lightly grease a baking dish small enough to fit inside your Air Fryer.
6. Move the cooked vegetables to the baking dish, pour over the sauce & make sure to coat the vegetables well.
7. Raise the temperature to 390°F & cook the vegetables for an additional 5 minutes.
8. Serve warm with a side of ketchup.

---

205. CHEESE LINGS

Prep & Cook Time: 25 minutes | Servings: 6

INGREDIENTS

1 cup of flour
small cubes cheese, grated

¼ tsp. of chili powder
1 tsp. of butter

Salt
1 tsp. of baking powder

INSTRUCTIONS

1. Combine all the ingredients to form a dough, along with a small amount water as necessary.
2. Divide the dough into equal portions & roll each one into a ball.
3. Pre-heat Air Fryer at 360°F.
4. Transfer the balls to the Air Fryer & air fry for 5 minutes, stirring periodically.

---

206. POTATO SIDE DISH

Prep & Cook Time: 30 minutes | Servings: 2

INGREDIENTS

2 medium potatoes
1 tsp. of butter

3 tbsp. of sour cream
1 tsp. of chives

1 ½ tbsp. of cheese, grated
Salt & pepper

INSTRUCTIONS

1. Pierce the potatoes with a fork & boil them in water until they are cooked.
2. Transfer to the Air Fryer & cook for 15 minutes at 350°F.
3. In the meantime, combine the sour cream, cheese & chives in a bowl. Cut the potatoes halfway to open them up & fill with the butter & toppings.
4. Serve with salad.

---

207. ROASTED POTATOES & CHEESE

Prep & Cook Time: 55 minutes | Servings: 4

INGREDIENTS

4 medium potatoes
1 asparagus bunch

⅓ cup of cottage cheese
⅓ cup of low-fat crème fraiche

1 tbsp. of wholegrain mustard

INSTRUCTIONS

1. Pour some oil into your Air Fryer & pre-heat to 390°F.
2. Cook potatoes for 20 minutes.
3. Boil the asparagus in salted water for 3 minutes.
4. Remove the potatoes & mash them with rest of ingredients. Sprinkle on salt & pepper.
5. Serve with rice.

---

208. VEGETABLE & CHEESE OMELET

Prep & Cook Time: 15 minutes | Servings: 2

INGREDIENTS

3 tbsp. of milk
4 eggs, whisked
1 tsp. of melted butter
Salt & ground black pepper, to taste

1 red bell pepper, deveined & chopped
1 green bell pepper, deveined & chopped
1 white onion, finely chopped

½ cup of baby spinach leaves, roughly chopped
½ cup of Halloumi cheese, shaved

INSTRUCTIONS
1. Grease the Air Fryer baking pan with some canola oil.
2. Place all of the ingredients in the baking pan & stir well.
3. Transfer to the Air Fryer & cook at 350°F for 13 minutes.
4. Serve warm.

209. SCRAMBLED EGGS

Prep & Cook Time: 15 minutes | Servings: 2

INGREDIENTS
2 tbsp. of olive oil, melted
4 eggs, whisked
5 oz. of fresh spinach, chopped

1 medium-sized tomato, chopped
1 tsp. of fresh lemon juice
½ tsp. of coarse salt

½ tsp. of ground black pepper
½ cup of fresh basil, roughly chopped

INSTRUCTIONS
1. Grease the Air Fryer baking pan with the oil, tilting it to spread the oil around. Pre-heat the Air Fryer at 280°F.
2. Mix the remaining ingredients, apart from the basil leaves, whisking well until everything is completely combined.
3. Cook in the Air Fryer for 8 - 12 minutes.
4. Top with fresh basil leaves before serving with a little sour cream if desired.

210. SWEET CORN FRITTERS

Prep & Cook Time: 20 minutes | Servings: 4

INGREDIENTS
1 medium-sized carrot, grated
1 yellow onion, finely chopped
4 oz. canned sweet corn kernels, drained
1 tsp. of sea salt flakes

1 heaping tbsp. of fresh cilantro, chopped
1 medium-sized egg, whisked
2 tbsp. of plain milk
1 cup of Parmesan cheese, grated

¼ cup of flour
⅓ tsp. of baking powder
⅓ tsp. of sugar

INSTRUCTIONS
1. Place the grated carrot in a colander & press down to squeeze out any excess moisture. Dry it with a paper towel.
2. Combine the carrots with the remaining ingredients.
3. Mold 1 tbsp. of the mixture into a ball & press it down with your hand or a spoon to flatten it. Repeat until the rest of the mixture is used up.
4. Spritz the balls with cooking spray.
5. Arrange in the basket of your Air Fryer, taking care not to overlap any balls. Cook at 350°F for 8 to 11 minutes or until they're firm.
6. Serve warm.

211. ROSEMARY CORNBREAD

Prep & Cook Time: 1 hr. | Servings: 6

INGREDIENTS
1 cup of cornmeal
1 ½ cups of flour
½ tsp. of baking soda
½ tsp. of baking powder

¼ tsp. of salt
1 tsp. of dried rosemary
¼ tsp. of garlic powder
2 tbsp. of sugar

2 eggs
¼ cup of melted butter
1 cup of buttermilk
½ cup of corn kernels

INSTRUCTIONS
1. In a bowl, combine all the dry ingredients. In a separate bowl, mix together all the wet ingredients. Combine the two.
2. Fold in the corn kernels & stir vigorously.
3. Pour the batter into a lightly greased round loaf pan that is lightly greased.
4. Cook inside your Air Fryer for 1 hour at 380°F.

212. VEGGIE ROLLS

Prep & Cook Time: 30 minutes | Servings: 6

INGREDIENTS
2 potatoes, mashed
¼ cup of peas
¼ cup of carrots, mashed
1 small cabbage, sliced
¼ beans
2 tbsp. of sweetcorn

1 small onion, chopped
1 tsp. of capsicum
1 tsp. of coriander
2 tbsp. of butter
Ginger
Garlic to taste

½ tsp. of masala powder
½ tsp. of chili powder
½ cup of breadcrumbs
1 packet of spring roll sheets
½ cup of cornstarch slurry

INSTRUCTIONS
1. Boil all the vegetables in water over a low heat. Rinse & allow to dry.
2. Unroll the spring roll sheets & spoon equal amounts of vegetable onto the center of each one. Fold into spring rolls & coat each one with the slurry & breadcrumbs.
3. Pre-heat the Air Fryer to 390°F. Cook the rolls for 10 minutes.
4. Serve with a side of boiled rice.

213. GRILLED CHEESE

Prep & Cook Time: 25 minutes | Servings: 2

INGREDIENTS

4 slices of bread   ½ cup of sharp cheddar cheese   ¼ cup of butter, melted

INSTRUCTIONS

1. Pre-heat the Air Fryer at 360°F.
2. Put cheese & butter in separate bowls.
3. Apply the butter to each side of the bread slices with a brush.
4. Spread the cheese across two of the slices of bread & make two sandwiches. Transfer both to the Air Fryer.
5. Cook for 5 – 7 minutes or until a golden-brown color is achieved & the cheese is melted.

---

214. POTATO GRATIN

Prep & Cook Time: 55 minutes | Servings: 6

INGREDIENTS

½ cup of milk   1 tsp. of black pepper   ½ cup of semi-mature cheese, grated
7 medium russet potatoes, peeled   ½ cup of cream   ½ tsp. of nutmeg

INSTRUCTIONS

1. Pre-heat the Air Fryer to 390°F.
2. Cut the potatoes into wafer-thin slices.
3. In a bowl, combine the milk & cream & sprinkle with salt, pepper, & nutmeg as desired.
4. Use the milk mixture to coat the slices of potatoes. Place in an 8" heat-resistant baking dish. Top the potatoes with the rest of the cream mixture.
5. Put the baking dish into the basket of the Air Fryer & cook for 25 minutes.
6. Pour the cheese over the potatoes.
7. Cook for an additional 10 minutes, ensuring the top is nicely browned before serving.

---

215. ROASTED VEGETABLES

Prep & Cook Time: 30 minutes | Servings: 6

INGREDIENTS

1 ⅓ cup of small parsnips   1 ⅓ cup of small butternut squash   Salt & pepper
1 ⅓ cup of celery [3 – 4 stalks]   1 tbsp. of fresh thyme needles
2 red onions   1 tbsp. of olive oil

INSTRUCTIONS

1. Pre-heat the Air Fryer to 390°F.
2. Peel the parsnips & onions & cut them into 2-cm cubes. Slice the onions into wedges.
3. Do not peel the butternut squash. Cut it in half, de-seed it, & cube.
4. Combine the cut vegetables with the thyme, olive oil, salt & pepper.
5. Put the vegetables in the basket & transfer the basket to the Air Fryer.
6. Cook for 20 minutes, stirring once throughout the cooking time, until the vegetables are nicely browned & cooked through.

---

216. SWEET POTATO CURRY FRIES

Prep & Cook Time: 55 minutes | Servings: 4

INGREDIENTS

2.2 lb. of sweet potatoes   2 tbsp. of olive oil
1 tsp. of curry powder   Salt

INSTRUCTIONS

1. Pre-heat Air Fryer to 390°F.
2. Wash the sweet potatoes before slicing them into matchsticks.
3. Drizzle the oil in the pan, place the fries inside & bake for 25 minutes.
4. Sprinkle with curry & salt before serving with ketchup if desired.

---

217. CRAB LEGS

Prep & Cook Time: 20 minutes | Servings: 3

INGREDIENTS

3 lb. of crab legs
¼ cup of salted butter, melted & divided   ½ lemon, juiced   ¼ tsp. of garlic powder

INSTRUCTIONS

1. In a bowl, toss the crab legs & two tbsp. of the melted butter together. Place the crab legs in the basket of the Air Fryer.
2. Cook at 400°F for fifteen minutes, giving the basket a good shake halfway through.
3. Combine the remaining butter with the lemon juice & garlic powder.
4. Crack open the cooked crab legs & remove the meat. Serve with the butter dip on the side & enjoy!

---

218. CRUSTY PESTO SALMON

Prep & Cook Time: 15 minutes | Servings: 2

INGREDIENTS

¼ cup of spinach, roughly chopped
¼ cup of pesto

2 x 4-oz. of salmon fillets
2 tbsp. of butter, melted

INSTRUCTIONS

1. Mix the spinach & pesto together.
2. Place the salmon fillets in a round baking dish, roughly six inches in diameter.
3. Brush the fillets with butter, followed by the pesto mixture, ensuring to coat both the top & bottom. Put the baking dish inside the Air Fryer.
4. Cook for twelve minutes at 390°F.
5. The salmon is ready when it flakes easily when prodded with a fork. Serve warm.

219. BUTTERY COD

Prep & Cook Time: 12 minutes | Servings: 2

INGREDIENTS

2 x 4-oz. of cod fillets
2 tbsp. of salted butter, melted

1 tsp. of Old Bay seasoning
½ medium lemon, sliced

INSTRUCTIONS

1. Place the cod fillets in a baking dish.
2. Brush with melted butter, season with Old Bay, & top with some lemon slices.
3. Wrap the fish in aluminum foil & put into your Air Fryer.
4. Cook for eight minutes at 350°F.
5. The cod is ready when it flakes easily. Serve hot.

220. SESAME TUNA STEAK

Prep & Cook Time: 12 minutes | Servings: 2

INGREDIENTS

1 tbsp. of coconut oil, melted
2 x 6-oz. of tuna steaks

½ tsp. of garlic powder
2 tsp. of black sesame seeds

2 tsp. of white sesame seeds

INSTRUCTIONS

1. Apply the coconut oil to the tuna steaks with a brunch, then season with garlic powder.
2. Combine the black & white sesame seeds. Embed them in the tuna steaks, covering the fish all over. Place the tuna into your Air Fryer.
3. Cook for eight minutes at 400°F, turning the fish halfway through.
4. The tuna steaks are ready when they have reached a temperature of 145°F. Serve straightaway.

221. LEMON GARLIC SHRIMP

Prep & Cook Time: 15 minutes | Servings: 2

INGREDIENTS

1 medium lemon
½ lb. of medium shrimp, deveined

½ tsp. of Old Bay seasoning
2 tbsp. of butter, melted

½ tsp. of minced garlic

INSTRUCTIONS

1. Grate the rind of the lemon into a bowl. Cut the lemon in half & juice it over the same bowl. Toss in the shrimp, Old Bay, & butter, mixing everything to make sure the shrimp is completely covered.
2. Transfer to a round baking dish roughly six inches wide, then place this dish in your Air Fryer.
3. Cook at 400°F for six minutes. The shrimp is cooked when it turns a bright pink color.
4. Serve hot, drizzling any leftover sauce over the shrimp.

222. FOIL PACKET SALMON

Prep & Cook Time: 15 minutes | Servings: 2

INGREDIENTS

2 x 4-oz. skinless salmon fillets
2 tbsp. of butter, melted

½ tsp. of garlic powder
1 medium lemon

½ tsp. of dried dill

INSTRUCTIONS

1. Take a sheet of aluminum foil & cut into two squares measuring roughly 5" x 5". Lay each of the salmon fillets at the center of each piece. Brush both fillets with a tbsp. of bullet & season with a quarter tsp. of garlic powder.
2. Halve the lemon & grate the skin of one half over the fish. Cut four half-slices of lemon, using two to top each fillet. Season each fillet with a quarter tsp. of dill.
3. Fold the tops & sides of the aluminum foil over the fish to create a kind of packet. Place each one in the Air Fryer.
4. Cook for twelve minutes at 400°F.
5. The salmon is ready when it flakes easily. Serve hot.

223. FOIL PACKET LOBSTER TAIL

Prep & Cook Time: 15 minutes | Servings: 2

INGREDIENTS

2 x 6-oz. lobster tail halves
2 tbsp. of salted butter, melted

½ medium lemon, juiced
½ tsp. of Old Bay seasoning

1 tsp. of dried parsley

INSTRUCTIONS

1. Lay each lobster on a sheet of aluminum foil. Pour a light drizzle of melted butter & lemon juice over each one, & season with Old Bay.
2. Fold down the sides & ends of the foil to seal the lobster. Place each one in the Air Fryer.
3. Cook at 375°F for twelve minutes.
4. Just before serving, top the lobster with dried parsley.

224. AVOCADO SHRIMP

Prep & Cook Time: 20 minutes | Servings: 2

INGREDIENTS

½ cup of onion, chopped
2 lb. of shrimp

1 tbsp. of seasoned salt
1 avocado

½ cup of pecans, chopped

INSTRUCTIONS

1. Pre-heat the Air Fryer at 400°F.
2. Put the chopped onion in the basket of the Air Fryer & spritz with some cooking spray. Leave to cook for five minutes.
3. Add the shrimp & set the timer for a further five minutes. Sprinkle with some seasoned salt, then allow to cook for an additional five minutes.
4. During these last five minutes, halve your avocado & remove the pit. Cube each half, then scoop out the flesh.
5. Take care when removing the shrimp from the Air Fryer. Place it on a dish & top with the avocado & the chopped pecans.

225. LEMON BUTTER SCALLOPS

Prep & Cook Time: 30 minutes | Servings: 1

INGREDIENTS

1 lemon
1 lb. of scallops

½ cup of butter
¼ cup of parsley, chopped

INSTRUCTIONS

1. Juice the lemon into a Ziploc bag.
2. Wash your scallops, dry them, & season to taste. Put them in the bag with the lemon juice. Refrigerate for an hour.
3. Remove the bag from the refrigerator & leave for about twenty minutes until it returns to room temperature. Transfer the scallops into a foil pan that is small enough to be placed inside the Air Fryer.
4. Pre-heat the Air Fryer at 400°F & put the rack inside.
5. Place the foil pan on the rack & cook for five minutes.
6. In the meantime, melt the butter in a saucepan over a medium heat. Zest the lemon over the saucepan, then add in the chopped parsley. Mix well.
7. Take care when removing the pan from the Air Fryer. Transfer the contents to a plate & drizzle with the lemon-butter mixture. Serve hot.

226. CHEESY LEMON HALIBUT

Prep & Cook Time: 20 minutes | Servings: 2

INGREDIENTS

1 lb. of halibut fillet
½ cup of butter

2 ½ tbsp. of mayonnaise
2 ½ tbsp. of lemon juice

¾ cup of parmesan cheese, grated

INSTRUCTIONS

1. Pre-heat your Air Fryer at 375°F.
2. Spritz the halibut fillets with cooking spray & season as desired.
3. Put the halibut in the Air Fryer & cook for twelve minutes.
4. In the meantime, combine the butter, mayonnaise, & lemon juice in a bowl with a hand mixer. Ensure a creamy texture is achieved.
5. Stir in the grated parmesan.
6. When the halibut is ready, open the drawer & spread the butter over the fish with a butter knife. Allow to cook for a further two minutes, then serve hot.

227. SPICY MACKEREL

Prep & Cook Time: 20 minutes | Servings: 2

INGREDIENTS

2 mackerel fillets
2 tbsp. of red chili flakes

2 tsp. of garlic, minced
1 tsp. of lemon juice

INSTRUCTIONS

1. Season the mackerel fillets with the red pepper flakes, minced garlic, & a drizzle of lemon juice. Allow to sit for five minutes.
2. Preheat your Air Fryer at 350°F.

3. Cook the mackerel for five minutes, before opening the drawer, flipping the fillets, & allowing to cook on the other side for another five minutes.
4. Plate the fillets, making sure to spoon any remaining juice over them before serving.

228. THYME SCALLOPS

Prep & Cook Time: 12 minutes | Servings: 1

INGREDIENTS

1 lb. of scallops
Salt & pepper

½ tbsp. of butter
½ cup thyme, chopped

INSTRUCTIONS

1. Wash the scallops & dry them completely. Season with pepper & salt, then set aside while you prepare the pan.
2. Grease a foil pan in several spots with the butter & cover the bottom with the thyme. Place the scallops on top.
3. Pre-heat the Air Fryer at 400°F & set the rack inside.
4. Place the foil pan on the rack & allow to cook for seven minutes.
5. Take care when removing the pan from the Air Fryer & transfer the scallops to a serving dish. Spoon any remaining butter in the pan over the fish & enjoy.

229. CRISPY CALAMARI

Prep & Cook Time: 15 minutes | Servings: 4

INGREDIENTS

1 lb. of fresh squid
Salt & pepper

2 cups of flour
1 cup of water

2 cloves garlic, minced
½ cup of mayonnaise

INSTRUCTIONS

1. Remove the skin from the squid & discard any ink. Slice the squid into rings & season with some salt & pepper.
2. Put the flour & water in separate bowls. Dip the squid firstly in the flour, then into the water, then into the flour again, ensuring that it is entirely covered with flour.
3. Pre-heat the Air Fryer at 400°F. Put the squid inside & cook for six minutes.
4. In the meantime, prepare the aioli by combining the garlic with the mayonnaise in a bowl.
5. Once the squid is ready, plate up & serve with the aioli.

230. FILIPINO BISTEK

Prep & Cook Time: 10 minutes + marinating time | Servings: 4

INGREDIENTS

2 milkfish bellies, sliced into four portions
¾ tsp. of salt
¼ tsp. of ground black pepper
¼ tsp. of cumin powder
2 tbsp. of calamansi juice

2 lemongrasses, trimmed & cut crosswise
   into small pieces
½ cup of tamari sauce
2 tbsp. of fish sauce [Patis]
2 tbsp. of sugar

1 tsp. of garlic powder
½ cup of chicken broth
2 tbsp. of olive oil

INSTRUCTIONS

1. Dry the fish using some paper towels.
2. Put the fish in a large bowl & coat with the rest of the ingredients. Allow to marinate for 3 hours in the refrigerator.
3. Cook the fish steaks on an Air Fryer grill basket at 340°F for 5 minutes.
4. Turn the steaks over & allow to grill for an additional 4 minutes. Cook until medium brown.
5. Serve with steamed white rice.

231. SALTINE FISH FILLETS

Prep & Cook Time: 15 minutes | Servings: 4

INGREDIENTS

1 cup of crushed saltines
¼ cup of extra-virgin olive oil
1 tsp. of garlic powder

½ tsp. of shallot powder
1 egg, well whisked
4 white fish fillets

Salt & ground black pepper to taste
Fresh Italian parsley to serve

INSTRUCTIONS

1. In a shallow bowl, combine the crushed saltines & olive oil.
2. In a separate bowl, mix together the garlic powder, shallot powder, & the beaten egg.
3. Sprinkle a good amount of salt & pepper over the fish, before dipping each fillet into the egg mixture.
4. Coat the fillets with the crumb mixture.
5. Air fry the fish at 370°F for 10 - 12 minutes.
6. Serve with fresh parsley.

232. COD NUGGETS

Prep & Cook Time: 25 minutes | Servings: 4

INGREDIENTS

| 1 lb. of cod fillet, cut into chunks | 1 cup of cracker crumbs | ½ cup of flour |
| 1 tbsp. of olive oil | 1 tbsp. of egg & water | Salt & pepper |

INSTRUCTIONS

1. Place the cracker crumbs & oil in food processor & pulse together. Sprinkle the cod pieces with salt & pepper.
2. Roll the cod pieces in the flour before dredging them in egg & coating them in the cracker crumbs.
3. Pre-heat the Air Fryer to 350°F.
4. Put the fish in the basket & air fry to 350°F for 15 minutes or until a light golden-brown color is achieved.
5. Serve hot.

---

233. SWEET POTATOES & SALMON

Prep & Cook Time: 45 minutes | Servings: 4

INGREDIENTS

For the Salmon Fillets:

4 x 6-oz. of skin-on salmon fillets
1 tbsp. of extra-virgin olive oil
1 tsp. of celery salt
¼ tsp. of ground black pepper, or more to taste

2 tbsp. of capers
Pinch of dry mustard
Pinch of ground mace
1 tsp. of smoked cayenne pepper

For the Potatoes:

4 sweet potatoes, peeled & cut into wedges
1 tbsp. of sesame oil
Kosher salt & pepper, to taste

INSTRUCTIONS

1. Coat all sides of the salmon filets with a brushing of oil. Cover with all the seasonings for the fillets.
2. Air fry at 360°F for 5 minutes, flip them over, & proceed to cook for 5 more minutes.
3. In the meantime, coat the sweet potatoes with the sesame oil, salt, & pepper.
4. Cook the potatoes at 380°F for 15 minutes.
5. Turn the potatoes over & cook for another 15 - 20 minutes.
6. Serve the potatoes & salmon together.

---

234. GRILLED SHRIMP

Prep & Cook Time: 35 minutes | Servings: 4

INGREDIENTS

18 shrimps, shelled & deveined
2 tbsp. of freshly squeezed lemon juice
½ tsp. of hot paprika
½ tsp. of salt

1 tsp. of lemon-pepper seasoning
2 tbsp. of extra-virgin olive oil
2 garlic cloves, peeled & minced
1 tsp. of onion powder

¼ tsp. of cumin powder
½ cup of fresh parsley, coarsely chopped

INSTRUCTIONS

1. Put all the ingredients in a bowl, making sure to coat the shrimp well. Refrigerate for 30 minutes.
2. Pre-heat the Air Fryer at 400°F
3. Air-fry the shrimp for 5 minutes, ensuring that the shrimps turn pink.
4. Serve with pasta or rice.

---

235. HOMEMADE COD FILLETS

Prep & Cook Time: 15 minutes | Servings: 4

INGREDIENTS

4 cod fillets
¼ tsp. of fine sea salt
¼ tsp. of ground black pepper, or more to taste

1 tsp. of cayenne pepper
½ cup of non-dairy milk
½ cup of fresh Italian parsley, coarsely chopped

1 tsp. of dried basil
½ tsp. of dried oregano
1 Italian pepper, chopped
4 garlic cloves, minced

INSTRUCTIONS

1. Lightly grease a baking dish with some vegetable oil.
2. Coat the cod fillets with salt, pepper, & cayenne pepper.
3. Blend the rest of the ingredients in a food processor. Cover the fish fillets in this mixture.
4. Transfer the fillets to the Air Fryer & cook at 380°F for 10 to 12 minutes, ensure the cod is flaky before serving.

---

236. CHRISTMAS FLOUNDER

Prep & Cook Time: 15 minutes + marinating time | Servings: 4

INGREDIENTS

4 flounder fillets
Sea salt & freshly cracked mixed peppercorns, to taste
1 ½ tbsp. of dark sesame oil

2 tbsp. of sake
¼ cup of soy sauce
1 tbsp. of grated lemon rind
2 garlic cloves, minced

1 tsp. of sugar
Fresh chopped chives, to serve

INSTRUCTIONS

1. Put all of the ingredients, except for the chives, in a large bowl. Coat the fillets well with the seasoning.
2. Refrigerate for 2 hours to let it marinate.

3. Place the fish fillets in the Air Fryer cooking basket & cook at 360°F for 10 to 12 minutes, turning once during the cooking time.
4. Simmer the rest of the marinade over a medium-to-low heat, stirring constantly, allowing it to thicken.
5. Plate up the flounder & add the glaze on top. Serve with fresh chives.

237. COCONUT PRAWNS

Prep & Cook Time: 10 minutes | Servings: 4

INGREDIENTS

12 prawns, cleaned & deveined
Salt & ground black pepper, to taste
½ tsp. of cumin powder
1 tsp. of fresh lemon juice

1 medium egg, whisked
⅓ cup of beer
½ cup of flour
1 tsp. of baking powder

1 tbsp. of curry powder
½ tsp. of grated fresh ginger
1 cup of flaked coconut

INSTRUCTIONS

1. Coat the prawns in the salt, pepper, cumin powder, & lemon juice.
2. In a bowl, combine together the whisked egg, beer, a quarter-cup of the flour, baking powder, curry, & ginger.
3. In a second bowl, put the remaining quarter-cup of flour, & in a third bowl, the flaked coconut.
4. Dredge the prawns in the flour, before coating them in the beer mixture. Finally, coat your prawns in the flaked coconut.
5. Air-fry at 360°F for 5 minutes. Flip them & allow to cook on the other side for another 2 to 3 minutes before serving.

238. CAJUN SHRIMP

Prep & Cook Time: 25 minutes | Servings: 4

INGREDIENTS

¼ tsp. of cayenne pepper
¼ tsp. of smoked paprika

½ tsp. of old bay seasoning
1 tbsp. of olive oil

Salt
1 ¼ lb. of tiger shrimp

INSTRUCTIONS

1. Pre-heat your Air Fryer to 390°F.
2. In a large bowl, combine together all the ingredients, ensuring to coat the shrimps well.
3. Transfer to the Air Fryer & cook for 5 minutes.
4. Serve over boiled rice.

239. CATFISH

Prep & Cook Time: 30 minutes | Servings: 4

INGREDIENTS

2 catfish fillets [catfish]
1 medium egg, beaten
1 cup of breadcrumbs

1 cup of tortilla chips
1 lemon, juiced & peeled
1 tsp. of parsley

Salt & pepper

INSTRUCTIONS

1. Slice up the catfish fillets neatly & drizzle lightly with the lemon juice.
2. In a separate bowl, combine the breadcrumbs with the lemon rind, parsley, tortillas, salt & pepper. Pour into your food processor & pulse.
3. Put the fillets in a tray & spread it evenly across the base. Pour the mixture over the fish to cover well.
4. Transfer to your Air Fryer & cook at 350°F for 15 minutes. Serve with chips & a refreshing drink.

240. FISH FILLETS

Prep & Cook Time: 25 minutes | Servings: 4

INGREDIENTS

4 fish fillets
1 egg, beaten

1 cup of breadcrumbs
4 tbsp. of olive oil

Salt & pepper

INSTRUCTIONS

1. Pre-heat the Air Fryer at 350°F.
2. In a shallow dish, combine together the breadcrumbs, oil, pepper, & salt.
3. Pour the beaten egg into a second dish.
4. Dredge each fish fillet in the egg before rolling them in the breadcrumbs. Place in the Air Fryer basket.
5. Allow to cook in the Air Fryer for 12 minutes.

241. BEAN BURRITOS

Prep & Cook Time: 15 minutes | Servings: 4

INGREDIENTS

4 tortillas
1 can of beans
1 cup of cheddar cheese, grated

¼ tsp. of paprika
¼ tsp. of chili powder
¼ tsp. of garlic powder

Salt & pepper

INSTRUCTIONS

1. Pre-heat the Air Fryer to 350°F.
2. In a bowl, mix together the paprika, chili powder, garlic powder, salt & pepper.
3. Fill each tortilla with an equal portion of beans before adding the spice mixture & the cheddar cheese. Roll the tortilla wraps into burritos.
4. Cover the base of a baking dish with parchment paper.
5. Transfer the burritos to the baking dish.
6. Put in the Air Fryer & cook for roughly 5 minutes. Serve hot.

242. FISHMAN CAKES

Prep & Cook Time: 35 minutes | Servings: 4

INGREDIENTS

2 cups of white fish
1 cup of potatoes, mashed
1 tsp. of mix herbs
1 tsp. of mix spice

1 tsp. of coriander
1 tsp. of Worcestershire sauce
2 tsp. of chili powder
1 tsp. of milk

1 tsp. of butter
1 small onion, diced
¼ cup of breadcrumbs
Salt & pepper

INSTRUCTIONS

1. Place all of the ingredients in a bowl & combine.
2. Using your hands, mold equal portions of the mixture into small patties & refrigerate for 2 hours.
3. Put the fish cakes in the Air Fryer basket & cook at 400°F for 15 minutes. Serve hot.

243. SUNDAY'S SALMON

Prep & Cook Time: 20 minutes | Servings: 3

INGREDIENTS

½ lb. of salmon fillet, chopped
2 egg whites
2 tbsp. of chives, chopped
2 tbsp. of garlic, minced

½ cup of onion, chopped
⅔ cup of carrots, grated
⅔ cup of potato, grated
½ cup of breadcrumbs

¼ cup of flour
Pepper & salt

INSTRUCTIONS

1. In a shallow dish, combine the breadcrumbs with the pepper & salt.
2. Pour the flour into another dish.
3. In a third dish, add the egg whites.
4. Put all of the other ingredients in a large mixing bowl & stir together to combine.
5. Using your hands, shape equal amounts of the mixture into small balls. Roll each ball in the flour before dredging it in the egg & lastly covering it with breadcrumbs. Transfer all the coated croquettes to the Air Fryer basket & air fry at 320°F for 6 minutes.
6. Increase the heat to 350°F & allow to cook for another 4 minutes.
7. Serve hot.

244. WHITEFISH CAKES

Prep & Cook Time: 1 hr. 20 minutes | Servings: 4

INGREDIENTS

1 ½ cups of whitefish fillets, minced
1 ½ cups of green beans, finely chopped
½ cup of scallions, chopped
1 chili pepper, deveined & minced
1 tbsp. of red curry paste

1 tsp. of sugar
1 tbsp. of fish sauce
2 tbsp. of apple cider vinegar
1 tsp. of water
Sea salt flakes, to taste

½ tsp. of cracked black peppercorns
1 ½ tsp. of butter, at room temperature
1 lemon

INSTRUCTIONS

1. Place all of the ingredients a bowl, following the order in which they are listed.
2. Combine well with a spatula or your hands.
3. Mold the mixture into several small cakes & refrigerate for 1 hour.
4. Put a piece of aluminum foil in the cooking basket & lay the cakes on top.
5. Cook inside your Air Fyer at 390°F for 10 minutes. Turn each fish cake over before air-frying for another 5 minutes.
6. Serve the fish cakes with a side of cucumber relish.

245. MARINATED SARDINES

Prep & Cook Time: 1 hr. 15 minutes | Servings: 4

INGREDIENTS

¾ lb. of sardines, cleaned & rinsed
Salt & ground black pepper, to taste
For the Potatoes:
8 medium Russet potatoes, peeled & quartered

1 tsp. of smoked cayenne pepper
1 tbsp. of lemon juice

½ stick of melted butter
Salt & pepper, to taste

1 tbsp. of soy sauce
2 tbsp. of olive oil

1 tsp. of granulated garlic

INSTRUCTIONS

1. Dry the sardines with a paper towel.
2. Cover the sardines in the salt, black pepper, cayenne pepper, lemon juice, soy sauce, & olive oil, & leave to marinate for half an hour.
3. Air-fry the sardines at 350°F for roughly 5 minutes.
4. Raise the heat to 385°F & cook for an additional 7 - 8 minutes. Remove the sardines & plate up.
5. Wipe the cooking basket clean & pour in the potatoes, butter, salt, pepper, & garlic.
6. Roast at 390°F for 30 minutes. Serve the vegetables & the sardines together.

246. HALIBUT STEAKS

Prep & Cook Time: 15 minutes | Servings: 4

INGREDIENTS

1 lb. of halibut steaks
Salt & pepper
1 tsp. of dried basil
2 tbsp. of honey

¼ cup of vegetable oil
2 ½ tbsp. of Worcester sauce
1 tbsp. of freshly squeezed lemon juice
2 tbsp. of vermouth

1 tbsp. of fresh parsley leaves, coarsely chopped

INSTRUCTIONS

1. Put all of the ingredients in a large bowl. Combine & cover the fish completely with the seasoning.
2. Transfer to your Air Fryer & cook at 390°F for 5 minutes.
3. Turn the fish over & allow to cook for a further 5 minutes.
4. Ensure the fish is cooked through, leaving it in the Air Fryer for a few more minutes if necessary.
5. Serve with a side of potato salad.

247. FISHERMAN'S FISH FINGERS

Prep & Cook Time: 40 minutes | Servings: 4

INGREDIENTS

¾ lb. of fish, cut into fingers
1 cup of breadcrumbs
2 tsp. of mixed herbs
¼ tsp. of baking soda
2 eggs, beaten

3 tsp. of flour
2 tbsp. of Maida
1 tsp. of garlic ginger puree
½ tsp. of black pepper
2 tsp. of garlic powder

½ tsp. of red chili flakes
½ tsp. of turmeric powder
2 tbsp. of lemon juice
½ tsp. of salt

INSTRUCTIONS

1. Put the fish, garlic ginger puree, garlic powder, red chili flakes, turmeric powder, lemon juice, 1 tsp. of the mixed herbs, & salt in a bowl & combine well.
2. In a separate bowl, combine the flour, Maida, & baking soda.
3. In a third bowl pour in the beaten eggs.
4. In a fourth bowl, stir together the breadcrumbs, black pepper, & another tsp. of mixed herbs.
5. Pre-heat the Air Fryer to 350°F.
6. Coat the fish fingers in the flour. Dredge in the egg, then roll in the breadcrumb mixture.
7. Put the fish fingers in the Air Fryer's basket & allow to cook for 10 minutes, ensuring they crisp up nicely.

248. FISH TACO

Prep & Cook Time: 30 minutes | Servings: 4

INGREDIENTS

12 oz. of cod filet
1 cup of breadcrumbs
4 – 6 flour tortillas
1 cup of tempura butter

½ cup of salsa
½ cup of guacamole
2 tbsp. of freshly chopped cilantro
½ tsp. of salt

¼ tsp. of black pepper
Lemon wedges for garnish

INSTRUCTIONS

1. Slice the cod filets lengthwise & sprinkle salt & pepper on all sides.
2. Put the tempura butter in a bowl & coat each cod piece in it. Dip the fillets into the breadcrumbs.
3. Pre-heat the Air Fryer to 340°F.
4. Fry the cod sticks for about 10 – 13 minutes in the Air Fryer. Flip each one once while cooking.
5. In the meantime, coat one side of each tortilla with an even spreading of guacamole.
6. Put a cod stick in each tortilla & add the chopped cilantro & salsa on top. Lightly drizzle over the lemon juice. Fold into tacos.

249. CRISPY FISH FILLET

Prep & Cook Time: 15 minutes | Servings: 4

INGREDIENTS

2 fish fillets, each sliced into 4 pieces
1 tbsp. of lemon juice
1 tsp. of chili powder

4 tbsp. of mayonnaise
3 tbsp. of cornmeal
¼ tsp. of black pepper

4 tbsp. of flour
¼ tsp. of salt

INSTRUCTIONS

1. Pre-heat the Air Fryer at 400°F.

2. Combine together the flour, pepper, cornmeal, salt, & chili powder.
3. In a shallow bowl, stir together the lemon juice & mayonnaise.
4. Coat the fillets in the mayonnaise mixture, before covering with the flour mixture.
5. Put the coated fish into the Air Fryer's basket & cook for 5 minutes, ensuring they crisp up nicely. Serve hot.

250. CRISPY SHRIMP

Prep & Cook Time: 20 minutes | Servings: 8

INGREDIENTS

2 lb. of shrimp, peeled & deveined
4 egg whites
2 tbsp. of olive oil

1 cup of flour
½ tsp. of cayenne pepper
1 cup of breadcrumbs

Salt & pepper

INSTRUCTIONS

1. Combine together the flour, pepper, & salt in a shallow bowl.
2. In a separate bowl mix the egg whites using a whisk.
3. In a third bowl, combine the breadcrumbs, cayenne pepper, & salt.
4. Pre-heat your Air Fryer to 400°F.
5. Cover the shrimp with the flour mixture before dipping it in the egg white & lastly rolling in the breadcrumbs.
6. Put the coated shrimp in the Air Fryer's basket & top with a light drizzle of olive oil. Air fry the shrimp at 400°F for 8 minutes, in multiple batches if necessary.

251. FISH STICKS

Prep & Cook Time: 20 minutes | Servings: 4

INGREDIENTS

1 lb. of tilapia fillets, cut into strips
1 large egg, beaten

2 tsp. of Old Bay seasoning
1 tbsp. of olive oil

1 cup of breadcrumbs

INSTRUCTIONS

1. Pre-heat the Air Fryer at 400°F.
2. In a shallow dish, combine together the breadcrumbs, Old Bay, & oil. Put the egg in a small bowl.
3. Dredge the fish sticks in the egg. Cover them with breadcrumbs & put them in the Air Fryer's basket.
4. Cook the fish for 10 minutes or until they turn golden brown.
5. Serve hot.

252. CRAB HERB CROQUETTES

Prep & Cook Time: 30 minutes | Servings: 6

INGREDIENTS

1 lb. of crab meat
1 cup of breadcrumbs
2 egg whites
½ tsp. of parsley
¼ tsp. of chives

¼ tsp. of tarragon
2 tbsp. of celery, chopped
¼ cup of red pepper, chopped
1 tsp. of olive oil
½ tsp. of lime juice

4 tbsp. of sour cream
4 tbsp. of mayonnaise
¼ cup of onion, chopped
¼ tsp. of salt

INSTRUCTIONS

1. Put the breadcrumbs & salt in a bowl.
2. Pour the egg whites in a separate bowl.
3. Place the rest of the ingredients in a third bowl & combine thoroughly.
4. Using your hands, shape equal amounts of the mixture into small balls & dredge each ball in the egg white before coating with the breadcrumbs.
5. Put the croquettes in the Air Fryer basket & cook at 400°F for 18 minutes. Serve hot.

253. BROILED TILAPIA

Prep & Cook Time: 10 minutes | Servings: 4

INGREDIENTS

1 lb. of tilapia fillets

½ tsp. of lemon pepper

Salt

INSTRUCTIONS

1. Spritz the Air Fryer basket with some cooking spray.
2. Put the tilapia fillets in basket & sprinkle on the lemon pepper & salt.
3. Cook at 400°F for 7 minutes.
4. Serve with a side of vegetables.

254. SALMON PATTIES

Prep & Cook Time: 20 minutes | Servings: 4

INGREDIENTS

1 egg

14 oz. of canned salmon, drained

4 tbsp. of flour

| 4 tbsp. of cup cornmeal | ½ tsp. of garlic powder | Salt & pepper |
| 4 tbsp. of onion, minced | 2 tbsp. of mayonnaise | |

INSTRUCTIONS

1. Flake apart the salmon with a fork.
2. Put the flakes in a bowl & combine with the garlic powder, mayonnaise, flour, cornmeal, egg, onion, pepper, & salt.
3. Use your hands to shape equal portions of the mixture into small patties & put each one in the Air Fryer basket.
4. Air fry the salmon patties at 350°F for 15 minutes. Serve hot.

255. LEMON FISH

Prep & Cook Time: 25 minutes | Servings: 2

INGREDIENTS

2 tsp. of green chili sauce	1 tsp. of red chili sauce	¼ cup of sugar
2 tsp. of oil	2 – 3 lettuce leaves	4 fish fillets
2 egg whites	4 tsp. of flour	
Salt	2 lemons	

INSTRUCTIONS

1. Slice up one of the lemons & set aside.
2. Boil a half-cup of water in a saucepan. Stir in the sugar, ensuring it dissolves completely.
3. Put 1 cup of the flour, salt, green chili sauce, 2 teaspoons of oil & the egg white in a bowl & combine well.
4. Add 3 tbsp. of water & mix with a whisk until a smooth, thick consistency is achieved. Evenly spread the refined flour across a plate.
5. Dredge the fish fillets in the batter & cover with the refined flour.
6. Coat the Air Fryer's basket with a brushing of oil. Put the fish fillets in the basket & cook at 180°F for 10 – 15 minutes.
7. Add salt to the saucepan & combine well. Pour in the corn flour slurry & mix once more.
8. Add in the red chili sauce & stir.
9. Add the lemon slices. Squeeze the juice of the other lemon into the saucepan. Continue to cook, ensuring the sauce thickens well, stirring all the time.
10. Take the fish out of the Air Fryer, coat with a light brushing of oil & return to the Air Fryer basket.
11. Allow to cook for 5 additional minutes.
12. Shred up the lettuce leaves with your hands & arrange them on a serving platter.
13. Serve the fish over the lettuce & with the lemon sauce drizzled on top.

256. JUMBO SHRIMP

Prep & Cook Time: 10 minutes | Servings: 4

INGREDIENTS

12 jumbo shrimps	***For the Sauce:***	1 tsp. of chipotle powder
½ tsp. of garlic salt	1 tsp. of Dijon mustard	½ tsp. of cumin powder
¼ tsp. of freshly cracked mixed	4 tbsp. of mayonnaise	
peppercorns	1 tsp. of lemon zest	

INSTRUCTIONS

1. Sprinkle the garlic salt over the shrimp & coat with the cracked peppercorns.
2. Fry the shrimp in your Air Fryer at 395°F for 5 minutes.
3. Turn the shrimp over & allow to cook for a further 2 minutes.
4. In the meantime, mix together all ingredients for the sauce with a whisk.
5. Serve over the shrimp.

257. COD

Prep & Cook Time: 20 minutes | Servings: 5

INGREDIENTS

1 lb. of cod	2 cups of breadcrumbs	¼ tsp. of salt
3 tbsp. of milk	2 large eggs, beaten	
1 cup of oatmeal	½ tsp. of pepper	

INSTRUCTIONS

1. Combine together the milk & eggs in a bowl.
2. In a shallow dish, stir together breadcrumbs, pepper, & salt.
3. Pour the oatmeal into a second shallow dish.
4. Coat the cod sticks with the meal before dipping each one in the egg & rolling in breadcrumbs.
5. Put the fish sticks in the Air Fryer basket. Cook at 350°F for 12 minutes, shaking the basket halfway through cooking.

258. CHEESE TILAPIA

Prep & Cook Time: 20 minutes | Servings: 4

INGREDIENTS

| 1 lb. of tilapia fillets | ¾ cup of parmesan cheese, grated | 1 tbsp. of parsley, chopped |

| 2 tsp. of paprika | 1 tbsp. of olive oil | Salt & pepper |

INSTRUCTIONS
1. Pre-heat the Air Fryer to 400°F.
2. In a shallow dish, combine together the paprika, grated cheese, pepper, salt & parsley.
3. Pour a light drizzle of olive oil over the tilapia fillets. Cover the fillets with the paprika & cheese mixture.
4. Lay the fillets on a sheet of aluminum foil & transfer to the Air Fryer basket. Fry for 10 minutes. Serve hot.

259. CHEESE CRUST SALMON

Prep & Cook Time: 20 minutes | Servings: 5

INGREDIENTS

| 2 lb. of salmon fillet | ¼ cup of fresh parsley, chopped | Salt & pepper |
| 2 garlic cloves, minced | ½ cup of parmesan cheese, grated | |

INSTRUCTIONS
1. Pre-heat the Air Fryer to 350°F.
2. Lay the salmon, skin-side-down, on a sheet of aluminum foil. Place another sheet of foil on top.
3. Transfer the salmon to the Air Fryer & cook for 10 minutes.
4. Remove the salmon from the Air Fryer. Take off the top layer of foil & add the minced garlic, parmesan cheese, pepper, salt & parsley on top of the fish.
5. Return the salmon to the Air Fryer & resume cooking for another minute.

260. PARMESAN CRUSTED TILAPIA

Prep & Cook Time: 15 minutes | Servings: 4

INGREDIENTS

| ¾ cup of grated parmesan cheese | 1 tbsp. of olive oil | 2 tsp. of paprika |
| 4 tilapia fillets | 1 tbsp. of chopped parsley | Pinch of garlic powder |

INSTRUCTIONS
1. Pre-heat your Air Fryer at 350°F.
2. Coat each of the tilapia fillets with a light brushing of olive oil.
3. Combine all of the other ingredients together in a bowl.
4. Cover the fillets with the parmesan mixture.
5. Line the base of a baking dish with a sheet of parchment paper & place the fillets in the dish.
6. Transfer to the Air Fryer & cook for 5 minutes. Serve hot.

261. SALMON CROQUETTES

Prep & Cook Time: 15 minutes | Servings: 4

INGREDIENTS

| 1 lb. of can red salmon, mashed | 2 eggs, beaten | ½ bunch of parsley, chopped |
| ⅓ cup of olive oil | 1 cup of breadcrumbs | |

INSTRUCTIONS
1. Pre-heat the Air Fryer to 400°F.
2. In a mixing bowl, combine together the drained salmon, eggs, & parsley.
3. In a shallow dish, stir together the breadcrumbs & oil to combine well.
4. Mold equal-sized amounts of the mixture into small balls & coat each one with breadcrumbs.
5. Put the croquettes in the Air Fryer's basket & air fry for 7 minutes.

262. CREAMY SALMON

Prep & Cook Time: 20 minutes | Servings: 2

INGREDIENTS

| ¾ lb. of salmon, cut into 6 pieces | 1 tbsp. of olive oil | 3 tbsp. of sour cream |
| ¼ cup of yogurt | 1 tbsp. of dill, chopped | Salt |

INSTRUCTIONS
1. Sprinkle some salt on the salmon.
2. Put the salmon slices in the Air Fryer basket & add in a drizzle of olive oil.
3. Air fry the salmon at 285°F for 10 minutes.
4. In the meantime, combine together the cream, dill, yogurt, & salt.
5. Plate up the salmon & pour the creamy sauce over it. Serve hot.

263. FRIED CAJUN SHRIMP

Prep & Cook Time: 10 minutes | Servings: 4

INGREDIENTS

1 ¼ lb. of shrimp, peeled & deveined   ¼ tsp. of cayenne pepper   ½ tsp. of paprika
½ tsp. of old bay seasoning   1 tbsp. of olive oil   ¼ tsp. of salt

INSTRUCTIONS

1. Pre-heat the Air Fryer to 400°F.
2. Place all of the ingredients in a bowl & mix well to coat the shrimp evenly.
3. Put the seasoned shrimp in the Air Fryer's basket & air fry for 5 minutes. Serve hot.

264. GRILLED SALMON FILLETS

Prep & Cook Time: 20 minutes | Servings: 2

INGREDIENTS

2 salmon fillets   ⅓ cup of sugar   Garlic powder [optional]
⅓ cup of water   2 tbsp. of olive oil
⅓ cup of light soy sauce   Black pepper & salt to taste

INSTRUCTIONS

1. Sprinkle some salt & pepper on top of the salmon fillets. Season with some garlic powder if desired.
2. In a medium bowl, mix together the remaining ingredients with a whisk & use this mixture to coat the salmon fillets. Leave to marinate for 2 hours.
3. Pre-heat the Air Fryer at 355°F.
4. Remove any excess liquid from the salmon fillets & transfer to the Air Fryer. Cook for 8 minutes before serving warm.

265. PRAWNS

Prep & Cook Time: 30 minutes | Servings: 4

INGREDIENTS

1 lb. of prawns, peeled
1 lb. of bacon slices

INSTRUCTIONS

1. Pre-heat the Air Fryer to 400°F.
2. Wrap the bacon slices around the prawns & put them in Air Fryer's basket.
3. Air fry for 5 minutes & serve hot.

266. CHUNKY FISH

Prep & Cook Time: 10 minutes + chilling time | Servings: 4

INGREDIENTS

2 cans of canned fish   1 tsp. of whole-grain mustard   1 tsp. of paprika
2 celery stalks, trimmed & finely chopped   ½ tsp. of sea salt
1 egg, whisked   ¼ tsp. of freshly cracked black
1 cup of breadcrumbs   peppercorns

INSTRUCTIONS

1. Combine all of the ingredients in the order in which they appear. Mold the mixture into four equal-sized cakes. Leave to chill in the refrigerator for 50 minutes.
2. Put on an Air Fryer grill pan. Spritz all sides of each cake with cooking spray.
3. Grill at 360°F for 5 minutes. Turn the cakes over & resume cooking for an additional 3 minutes.
4. Serve with mashed potatoes if desired.

267. GLAZED HALIBUT STEAK

Prep & Cook Time: 70 minutes | Servings: 3

INGREDIENTS

1 lb. of halibut steak   2 tbsp. of lime juice   ¼ cup of orange juice
⅔ cup of low-sodium soy sauce   ¼ cup of sugar   1 garlic clove, smashed
½ cup of mirin   ¼ tsp. of crushed red pepper flakes   ¼ tsp. of ginger, ground

INSTRUCTIONS

1. Make the teriyaki glaze by mixing together all of the ingredients except for the halibut in a saucepan.
2. Bring it to a boil & lower the heat, stirring constantly until the mixture reduces by half. Remove from the heat & leave to cool.
3. Pour half of the cooled glaze into a Ziploc bag. Add in the halibut, making sure to coat it well in the sauce. Place in the refrigerator for 30 minutes.
4. Pre-heat the Air Fryer to 390°F.
5. Put the marinated halibut in the Air Fryer & allow to cook for 10 – 12 minutes.
6. Use any the remaining glaze to lightly brush the halibut steak with.
7. Serve with white rice or shredded vegetables.

268. BREADCRUMBED FISH

Prep & Cook Time: 25 minutes | Servings: 2 – 4

INGREDIENTS

4 tbsp. of vegetable oil
5 oz. of breadcrumbs

1 egg
4 medium fish fillets

INSTRUCTIONS

1   Pre-heat your Air Fryer to 350°F.
2   In a bowl, combine the breadcrumbs & oil.
3   In a separate bowl, stir the egg with a whisk. Dredge each fish fillet in the egg before coating it in the crumbs mixture. Put them in Air Fryer basket.
4   Cook for 12 minutes & serve hot.

269. CAJUN LEMON SALMON

Prep & Cook Time: 15 minutes | Servings: 1

INGREDIENTS

1 salmon fillet
1 tsp. of Cajun seasoning

½ lemon, juiced
¼ tsp. of sugar

2 lemon wedges, for serving

INSTRUCTIONS

1   Pre-heat the Air Fryer to 350°F.
2   Combine the lemon juice & sugar.
3   Cover the salmon with the sugar mixture.
4   Coat the salmon with the Cajun seasoning.
5   Line the base of your Air Fryer with a sheet of parchment paper.
6   Transfer the salmon to the Air Fryer & allow to cook for 7 minutes.

270. BREADED SALMON

Prep & Cook Time: 25 minutes | Servings: 4

INGREDIENTS

2 cups of breadcrumbs
4 fillets of salmon

1 cup of Swiss cheese, shredded
2 eggs, beaten

INSTRUCTIONS

1   Pre-heat your Air Fryer to 390°F.
2   Dredge the salmon fillets into the eggs. Add the Swiss cheese on top of each fillet.
3   Coat all sides of the fish with breadcrumbs. Put in an oven safe dish, transfer to the Air Fryer, & cook for 20 minutes.

271. ASIAN STYLE FISH

Prep & Cook Time: 35 minutes | Servings: 2

INGREDIENTS

1 medium sea bass, halibut or fish cutlet
    [11 – 12 oz.]
1 tomato, cut into quarters
1 lime, cut thinly

1 stalk of green onion, chopped
3 slices of ginger, julienned
2 garlic cloves, minced
1 chili, sliced

2 tbsp. cooking wine
1 tbsp. of olive oil
Steamed rice [optional]

INSTRUCTIONS

1   Fry the ginger & garlic in the oil until they turn golden brown.
2   Pre-heat the Air Fryer to 360°F.
3   Wash & dry the fish. Halve it, ensuring each half is small enough to fit inside the Air Fryer.
4   Put the fish in the basket of the Air Fryer. Pour in a drizzle of the cooking wine.
5   Place the tomato & lime slices on top of the fish slices.
6   Add the garlic ginger oil mixture on top, followed by the green onion & chili slices.
7   Top with a sheet of aluminum foil. Cook for 15 minutes, or longer if necessary.
8   Serve hot with a side of steamed rice if desired.

272. SEAFOOD FRITTERS

Prep & Cook Time: 50 minutes | Servings: 2 – 4

INGREDIENTS

2 cups of clam meat
1 cup of shredded carrot
½ cup of shredded zucchini

1 cup of flour, combined with ¾ cup of
water to make a batter
2 tbsp. of olive oil

¼ tsp. of pepper

INSTRUCTIONS

1　Pre-heat your Air Fryer to 390°F.
2　Combine the clam meat with the olive oil, shredded carrot, pepper & zucchini.
3　Using your hands, shape equal portions of the mixture into balls & roll each ball in the chickpea mixture.
4　Put the balls in the Air Fryer & cook for 30 minutes, ensuring they turn nice & crispy before serving.

273. CALAMARI

Prep & Cook Time: 25 minutes | Servings: 2

INGREDIENTS

1 cup of club soda
½ lb. of calamari tubes [or tentacles], about ¼ inch wide, rinsed & dried

½ cup of honey
1 – 2 tbsp. of sriracha
1 cup of flour

Sea salt to taste
Red pepper & black pepper to taste
Red pepper flakes to taste

INSTRUCTIONS

1　In a bowl, cover the calamari rings with club soda & mix well. Leave to sit for 10 minutes.
2　In another bowl, combine the   flour, salt, red & black pepper.
3　In a third bowl mix together the honey, pepper flakes, & Sriracha to create the sauce.
4　Remove any excess liquid from the calamari & coat each one with the flour mixture.
5　Spritz the Air Fryer basket with the cooking spray.
6　Arrange the calamari in the basket, well-spaced out & in a single layer.
7　Cook at 380°F for 11 minutes, shaking the basket at least two times during the cooking time.
8　Take the calamari out of the Air Fryer, coat it with half of the sauce & return to the Air Fryer. Cook for an additional 2 minutes.
9　Plate up the calamari & pour the rest of the sauce over it.

274. SALMON & DILL SAUCE

Prep & Cook Time: 45 minutes | Servings: 4

INGREDIENTS

For the Salmon:
1 ½ lb. of salmon
1 tsp. of olive oil

For the Dill Sauce:
½ cup of non-fat Greek yogurt
½ cup of sour cream

Salt
2 tbsp. of dill, finely chopped

INSTRUCTIONS

1　Pre-heat the Air Fryer to 270°F.
2　Slice the salmon into four 6-oz. pieces & pour a light drizzling of olive oil over each slice. Sprinkle on the salt.
3　Put the salmon in the cooking basket & allow to cook for 20 - 23 minutes.
4　Prepare the dill sauce by mixing together the yogurt, sour cream, chopped dill & salt.
5　Pour the sauce over the salmon & top with another sprinkling of chopped dill before serving.

275. BLACK COD

Prep & Cook Time: 30 minutes | Servings: 2

INGREDIENTS

2 [6- to 8-oz.] fillets of black cod
Salt
Freshly ground black pepper
Olive oil

1 cup of grapes, halved
1 small bulb. fennel, sliced ¼-inch thick
½ cup of pecans
3 cups of shredded kale

2 tsp. of white balsamic vinegar
2 tbsp. of extra-virgin olive oil

INSTRUCTIONS

1　Pre-heat the Air Fryer to 400°F.
2　Sprinkle the cod fillets with salt & pepper & drizzle some olive oil over the fish.
3　Put the fish skin-side-down in the Air Fryer basket. Air fry for 10 minutes. Transfer the fillets to a side plate & loosely cover with aluminum foil.
4　Coat the grapes, fennel & pecans with a drizzle of olive oil & sprinkle on some salt & pepper.
5　Place the grapes, fennel & pecans in the Air Fryer's basket & cook for 5 minutes at 400°F. Shake the basket occasionally throughout the cooking time.
6　Put the grapes, fennel & pecans in a bowl & add the kale.
7　Pour over the balsamic vinegar & olive oil & sprinkle with salt & pepper as desired. Serve with the fish & enjoy.

276. TILAPIA FILLETS

Prep & Cook Time: 25 minutes | Servings: 3

INGREDIENTS

1 lb. of tilapia fillets, sliced
4 wheat buns
2 egg yolks

1 tbsp. of fish sauce
2 tbsp. of mayonnaise
3 sweet pickle relish

1 tbsp. of hot sauce
1 tbsp. of nectar

INSTRUCTIONS

1　In a bowl, mix together the egg yolks & fish sauce.
2　Throw in the mayonnaise, sweet pickle relish, hot sauce & nectar.
3　Transfer the mixture to a round baking tray.

4   Put it in the Air Fryer & line the sides with the tilapia fillets. Cook for 15 minutes at 300°F.
5   Remove & serve on hamburger buns if desired.

277. SALMON MIXED EGGS

Prep & Cook Time: 25 minutes | Servings: 2

INGREDIENTS

1 lb. of salmon, cooked
2 eggs

1 onion, chopped
1 cup of celery, chopped

1 tbsp. of oil
Salt & pepper

INSTRUCTIONS

1   In a bowl, mix the eggs with a whisk. Stir in the celery, onion, salt & pepper.
2   Grease a round baking tray with the oil. Transfer the egg mixture to the tray. Cook in the Air Fryer on 300°F for 10 minutes.
3   Serve with cooked salmon.

278. CAJUN SALMON

Prep & Cook Time: 20 minutes | Servings: 1

INGREDIENTS

1 salmon fillet
Cajun seasoning

Light sprinkle of sugar
¼ lemon, juiced, to serve

INSTRUCTIONS

1   Pre-heat Air Fryer to 355°F.
2   Lightly cover all sides of the salmon with Cajun seasoning. Sprinkle conservatively with sugar.
3   For a salmon fillet about three-quarters of an inch thick, cook in the Air Fryer for 7 minutes, skin-side-up on the grill pan.
4   Serve with the lemon juice.

279. FISH FINGERS

Prep & Cook Time: 40 minutes | Servings: 2

INGREDIENTS

2 eggs
10 oz. of cod cut into fingers
½ tsp. of Turmeric Powder
½ Lemon, juiced
1 + 1 tsp. of mixed dried herbs
1 + 1 tsp. of Garlic Powder, separately

½ tsp. of Red Chili Flakes
1 cup of breadcrumbs
2 tbsp. of Maida
3 tsp. of flour
¼ tsp. of baking soda
1 tsp. of ginger garlic paste

½ tsp. of black pepper
½ tsp. of sea salt
1 – 2 tbsp. of olive oil
Ketchup or tartar sauce [optional]

INSTRUCTIONS

1   Put the fish fingers in a bowl. Cover with 1 tsp. of mixed herbs, 1 tsp. of garlic powder, salt, red chili flakes, turmeric powder, black pepper, ginger garlic paste, & lemon juice. Leave to absorb for at least 10 minutes.
2   In a separate bowl, mix together the   flour & baking soda. Crack the eggs in the mixture & stir again.
3   Throw in the marinated fish & set aside again for at least 10 minutes.
4   Combine the breadcrumbs & the remaining tsp. of mixed herbs & tsp. of garlic powder.
5   Roll the fish sticks with the bread crumb & herb mixture.
6   Pre-heat the Air Fryer at 360°F.
7   Line the basket of the Air Fryer with a sheet of aluminum foil. Place the fish fingers inside the Air Fryer & pour over a drizzle of the olive oil.
8   Cook for 10 minutes, ensuring the fish is brown & crispy before serving. Enjoy with ketchup or tartar sauce if desired

280. MEDITERRANEAN SALAD

Prep & Cook Time: 15 minutes | Servings: 2

INGREDIENTS

1 cup of cooked quinoa
1 red bell pepper, chopped
2 prosciutto slices, chopped

¼ cup of chopped kalamata olives
½ cup of crumbled feta cheese
1 tsp. of olive oil

1 tsp. of dried oregano
6 cherry tomatoes, halved
Salt & pepper, to taste

INSTRUCTIONS

1   Pre-heat your Air Fryer to 350°F.
2   Drizzle the inside of the Air Fryer with the olive oil. Place the red bell pepper inside & allow to cook for roughly 2 minutes. Put the prosciutto slices in the Air Fryer & cook for an additional 3 minutes.
3   Put the ham & pepper in an oven-proof bowl & remove any excess grease. Combine with the remaining ingredients, save for the tomatoes.
4   Finally, stir in the cherry tomato halves.

281. CURLY'S CAULIFLOWER

Prep & Cook Time: 30 minutes | Servings: 4

INGREDIENTS

4 cups of bite-sized cauliflower florets

1 cup of breadcrumbs, mixed with 1 tsp. of salt
¼ cup of melted butter [vegan/other]

¼ cup of buffalo sauce [vegan/other]
Mayo [vegan/other] or creamy dressing for dipping

INSTRUCTIONS

1 In a bowl, combine the butter & buffalo sauce to create a creamy paste.
2 Completely cover each floret with the sauce.
3 Coat the florets with the bread crumb mixture. Cook the florets in the Air Fryer for approximately 15 minutes at 350°F, shaking the basket occasionally.
4 Serve with a raw vegetable salad, mayo or creamy dressing.

282. FRIED MUSHROOMS

Prep & Cook Time: 40 minutes | Servings: 4

INGREDIENTS

2 lb. of button mushrooms
3 tbsp. of white or French vermouth [optional]

1 tbsp. of coconut oil
2 tsp. of herbs of your choice
½ tsp. of garlic powder

INSTRUCTIONS

1 Wash & dry the mushrooms. Slice them into quarters.
2 Pre-heat your Air Fryer at 320°F & add the coconut oil, garlic powder, & herbs to the basket.
3 Briefly cook the ingredients for 2 minutes & give them a stir. Put the mushrooms in the Air Fryer & cook for 25 minutes, stirring occasionally throughout.
4 Pour in the white vermouth & mix. Cook for an additional 5 minutes.
5 Serve hot.

283. CHEESY GARLIC BREAD

Prep & Cook Time: 20 minutes | Servings: 2

INGREDIENTS

1 baguette
4 tsp. of butter, melted

3 chopped garlic cloves
5 tsp. of sundried tomato pesto

1 cup of mozzarella cheese, grated

INSTRUCTIONS

1 Cut your baguette into 5 thick round slices.
2 Add the garlic cloves to the melted butter & brush onto each slice of bread.
3 Spread a tsp. of sun-dried tomato pesto onto each slice.
4 Top each slice with the grated mozzarella.
5 Transfer the bread slices to the Air Fryer & cook them at 180°F for 6 – 8 minutes.
6 Top with some freshly chopped basil leaves, chili flakes & oregano if desired.

284. STUFFED MUSHROOMS

Prep & Cook Time: 25 minutes | Servings: 4

INGREDIENTS

6 small mushrooms
1 tbsp. of onion, peeled & diced
1 tbsp. of breadcrumbs

1 tbsp. of olive oil
1 tsp. of garlic, pureed
1 tsp. of parsley

Salt & pepper

INSTRUCTIONS

1 Combine the breadcrumbs, oil, onion, parsley, salt, pepper & garlic in a bowl.
2 Scoop the stalks out of the mushrooms & spoon equal portions of the crumb mixture in the caps. Transfer to the Air Fryer & cook for 10 minutes at 350°F.
3 Serve with mayo dip if desired.

285. GRILLED TOMATOES

Prep & Cook Time: 25 minutes | Servings: 2

INGREDIENTS

2 tomatoes, medium to large
Herbs of your choice, to taste

Pepper
Cooking spray

INSTRUCTIONS

1 Wash & dry the tomatoes, before chopping them in half.
2 Lightly spritz them all over with cooking spray.
3 Season each half with herbs (oregano, basil, parsley, rosemary, thyme, sage, etc.) as desired & black pepper.
4 Put the halves in the tray of your Air Fryer. Cook for 20 minutes at 320°F, or longer if necessary. Larger tomatoes will take longer to cook.

286. CARROTS & RHUBARB

INGREDIENTS

1 lb. of heritage carrots
1 lb. of rhubarb

1 medium orange
½ cup of walnuts, halved

2 tsp. of walnut oil
½ tsp. of sugar

INSTRUCTIONS

1 Rinse the carrots to wash. Dry & chop them into 1-inch pieces.
2 Transfer them to the Air Fryer basket & drizzle over the walnut oil.
3 Cook at 320°F for about 20 minutes.
4 In the meantime, wash the rhubarb & chop it into ½-inch pieces.
5 Coarsely dice the walnuts.
6 Wash the orange & grate its skin into a small bowl. Peel the rest of the orange & cut it up into wedges.
7 Place the rhubarb, walnuts & sugar in the Air Fryer & allow to cook for an additional 5 minutes.
8 Add in 2 tbsp. of the orange zest, along with the orange wedges. Serve immediately.

287. BROCCOLI

Prep & Cook Time: 30 minutes | Servings: 4

INGREDIENTS

1 large head of broccoli
½ lemon, juiced
3 cloves garlic, minced

1 tbsp. of coconut oil
1 tbsp. of white sesame seeds

2 tsp. of Maggi sauce or other seasonings
  to taste

INSTRUCTIONS

1 Wash & dry the broccoli. Chop it up into small florets.
2 Place the minced garlic in your Air Fryer basket, along with the coconut oil, lemon juice & Maggi sauce.
3 Heat for 2 minutes at 320°F & give it a stir. Put the garlic & broccoli in the basket & cook for another 13 minutes.
4 Top the broccoli with the white sesame seeds & resume cooking for 5 more minutes, ensuring the seeds become nice & toasty.

288. MAPLE GLAZED BEETS

Prep & Cook Time: 60 minutes | Servings: 8

INGREDIENTS

3 ½ lb. of beetroots

4 tbsp. of maple syrup

1 tbsp. of coconut oil

INSTRUCTIONS

1 Wash & peel the beets. Cut them up into 1-inch pieces.
2 Put the coconut oil in the Air Fryer & melt for 1 minute at 320°F.
3 Place the beet cubes to the Air Fryer Basket & allow to cook for 40 minutes. Coat the beetroots in two tbsp. of the maple syrup & cook for another 10 minutes, ensuring the beets become soft.
4 Toss the cooked beets with the remaining two tbsp. of maple syrup & serve right away.

289. ENDIVE MARINATED IN CURRIED YOGURT

Prep & Cook Time: 20 minutes | Servings: 6

INGREDIENTS

6 heads of endive
½ cup plain & fat-free yogurt
3 tbsp. of lemon juice

1 tsp. of garlic powder [or 2 minced
cloves of garlic]
½ tsp. of curry powder

Salt & ground black pepper to taste

INSTRUCTIONS

1 Wash the endives & slice them in half lengthwise.
2 In a bowl, mix together the yogurt, lemon juice, garlic powder [or minced garlic], curry powder, salt & pepper. If you would like you marinade to be thinner, add some more lemon juice.
3 Brush the endive halves with the marinade, coating them completely. Allow to sit for a minimum of a half-hour & a maximum of one day.
4 Pre-heat Air Fryer to 320°F. Allow the endives to cook for 10 minutes & serve hot.

290. TASTY TOFU

Prep & Cook Time: 35 minutes | Servings: 4

INGREDIENTS

1x 12 oz. of packet low-fat & firm tofu
2 tbsp. of low-sodium soy sauce
2 tbsp. of fish sauce

1 tbsp. of coriander paste
1 tsp. of sesame oil
1 tsp. of duck fat or coconut oil

1 tsp. of Maggi sauce

INSTRUCTIONS

1 Remove the liquid from the packet of tofu & chop the tofu into 1-inch cubes. Line a plate with paper towels & spread the tofu out on top in one layer. Place another paper towel on top, followed by another plate, weighting it down with a heavier object if necessary. This is to dry the tofu out completely. Leave for a minimum of 30 minutes or a maximum of 24 hours, replacing the paper towels once or twice throughout the duration.
2 In a medium bowl, mix together the sesame oil, Maggi sauce, coriander paste, fish sauce, & soy sauce. Stir to combine fully.

3   Coat the tofu cubes with this mixture & allow to marinate for at least a half-hour, tossing the cubes a few times throughout to ensure even coating. Add another few drops of fish sauce or soy sauce to thin out the marinade if necessary.
4   Melt the duck fat/coconut oil in your Air Fryer at 350°F for about 2 minutes. Place the tofu cubes in the basket & cook for about 20 minutes or longer to achieve a crispier texture. Flip the tofu over or shake the basket every 10 minutes.
5   Serve hot with the dipping sauce of your choosing.

291. ROASTED PEPPERS

Prep & Cook Time: 40 minutes | Servings: 4

INGREDIENTS

12 medium bell peppers
1 sweet onion, small

1 tbsp. of Maggi sauce
1 tbsp. of extra virgin olive oil

INSTRUCTIONS

1   Warm up the olive oil & Maggi sauce in Air Fryer at 320°F.
2   Peel the onion, slice it into 1-inch pieces, & add it to the Air Fryer.
3   Wash & de-stem the peppers. Slice them into 1-inch pieces & remove all the seeds, with water if necessary [ensuring to dry the peppers afterwards].
4   Place the peppers in the Air Fryer.
5   Cook for about 25 minutes, or longer if desired. Serve hot.

292. ROASTED PARSNIP

Prep & Cook Time: 55 minutes | Servings: 5

INGREDIENTS

2 lb. of parsnips [about 6 large parsnips]
2 tbsp. of maple syrup

1 tbsp. of coconut oil
1 tbsp. of parsley, dried flakes

INSTRUCTIONS

1   Melt the duck fat or coconut oil in your Air Fryer for 2 minutes at 320°F.
2   Rinse the parsnips to clean them & dry them. Chop into 1-inch cubes. Transfer to the Air Fryer.
3   Cook the parsnip cubes in the fat/oil for 35 minutes, tossing them regularly.
4   Season the parsnips with parsley & maple syrup & allow to cook for another 5 minutes or longer to achieve a soft texture throughout. Serve straightaway.

293. CHEESE BOATS

Prep & Cook Time: 30 minutes | Servings: 2

INGREDIENTS

1 cup of ground chicken
1 zucchini
1 ½ cups of crushed tomatoes

½ tsp. of salt
¼ tsp. of pepper
½ tsp. of garlic powder

2 tbsp. of butter or olive oil
½ cup of cheese, grated
¼ tsp. of dried oregano

INSTRUCTIONS

1   Peel & halve the zucchini. Use a spoon to scoop out the flesh.
2   In a bowl, combine the ground chicken, tomato, garlic powder, butter, cheese, oregano, salt, & pepper. Fill in the hollowed-out zucchini with this mixture.
3   Transfer to the Air Fryer & bake for about 10 minutes at 400°F. Serve warm.

294. EGGPLANT

Prep & Cook Time: 45 minutes | Servings: 6

INGREDIENTS

3 eggplants, medium
½ lemon, juiced
1 tbsp. of duck fat, or coconut oil
1 tbsp. of Maggi sauce

3 tsp. of za'atar
1 tsp. of sumac
1 tsp. of garlic powder
1 tsp. of onion powder

1 tsp. of extra virgin olive oil
2 bay leaves

INSTRUCTIONS

1   Wash, dry & destem the eggplants. Chop them into 1-inch cubes.
2   In the Air Fryer basket, combine duck fat [or coconut oil], maggi sauce, za'atar, onion powder, garlic powder, sumac & bay leaves.
3   Melt the ingredients for 2 minutes at 320°F, stirring well.
4   Place the eggplant in the Air Fryer basket & allow to cook for 25 minutes.
5   In a large bowl, mix together the lemon juice & extra virgin olive oil. Add the cooked eggplant & stir to coat evenly.
6   Serve immediately with grated parmesan or fresh chopped basil if desired.

295. SWEET POTATO FRIES

Prep & Cook Time: 35 minutes | Servings: 5

INGREDIENTS

2 large, sweet potatoes
1 tbsp. of extra virgin olive oil

INSTRUCTIONS

1   Wash the sweet potatoes. Dry & peel them before chopping them into shoestring fries. In a bowl, toss the fries with the olive oil to coat well.
2   Set your Air Fryer to 320°F & briefly allow to warm. Put the sweet potatoes in the Air Fryer basket & fry for 15 minutes, stirring them at the halfway point.
3   Once done, toss again to make sure no fries are sticking to each other.
4   Turn the heat to 350°F & cook for a further 10 minutes, again giving them a good stir halfway through the cooking time.
5   Serve your fries straightaway.

296. CHICKEN, MUSHROOM & SPINACH PIZZA

Prep & Cook Time: 25 minutes | Servings: 4

INGREDIENTS

10 ½ oz. of minced chicken
1 tsp. of garlic powder

1 tsp. of black pepper
2 tbsp. of tomato basil sauce

5 button mushrooms, sliced thinly
Handful of spinach

INSTRUCTIONS

1   Pre-heat your Air Fryer at 450°F.
2   Add parchment paper onto your baking tray.
3   In a large bowl add the chicken with the black pepper & garlic powder.
4   Add one spoonful of the chicken mix onto your baking tray.
5   Flatten them into 7-inch rounds.
6   Bake in the Air Fryer for about 10 minutes.
7   Take out off the Air Fryer & add the tomato basil sauce onto each round.
8   Add the mushroom on top. Bake again for 5 minutes.
9   Serve immediately.

297. TURKEY SAUSAGE PATTIES

Prep & Cook Time: 20 minutes | Servings: 6

INGREDIENTS

1 lb. of lean ground turkey
1 tsp. of olive oil
1 tbsp. of chopped chives
1 small onion, diced

1 large garlic clove, chopped
¾ tsp. of paprika
Kosher salt & pepper to taste
Pinch of raw sugar

1 tbsp. of vinegar
1 tsp. of fennel seed
Pinch of nutmeg

INSTRUCTIONS

1   Pre-heat the Air Fryer to 375°F.
2   Add a half-tsp. of the oil to the Air Fryer, along with the onion & garlic. Air fry for 30 seconds before adding in the fennel. Place everything on a plate.
3   In a bowl, combine the ground turkey with the sugar, paprika, nutmeg, vinegar, chives & the onion mixture. Divide into equal portions & shape each one into a patty.
4   Add another tsp. of oil to the Air Fryer. Put the patties in the Air Fryer & cook for roughly 3 minutes.
5   Serve with salad or on hamburger buns.

298. BACON FRIES

Prep & Cook Time: 60 minutes | Servings: 2 – 4

INGREDIENTS

2 large russet potatoes, peeled & cut into
    ½ inch sticks
5 slices of bacon, diced
2 tbsp. of vegetable oil

2 ½ cups of cheddar cheese, shredded
3 oz. of cream cheese, melted
Salt & freshly ground black pepper
¼ cup of chopped scallions

Ranch dressing

INSTRUCTIONS

1   Boil a large pot of salted water.
2   Briefly cook the potato sticks in the boiling water for 4 minutes.
3   Drain the potatoes & run some cold water over them in order to wash off the starch. Pat them dry with a kitchen towel.
4   Pre-heat the Air Fryer to 400°F.
5   Put the chopped bacon in the Air Fryer & air-fry for 4 minutes. Shake the basket at the halfway point.
6   Place the bacon on paper towels to drain any excess fat & remove the grease from the Air Fryer drawer.
7   Coat the dried potatoes with oil & put them in the Air Fryer basket. Air-fry at 360°F for 25 minutes, giving the basket the occasional shake throughout the cooking time & sprinkling the fries with salt & freshly ground black pepper at the halfway point.
8   Take a casserole dish or baking pan that is small enough to fit inside your Air Fryer & place the fries inside.
9   Mix together the 2 cups of the Cheddar cheese & the melted cream cheese.
10 Pour the cheese mixture over the fries & top them with the rest of the Cheddar cheese & the cooked bacon crumbles.
11 Take absolute care when placing the baking pan inside the cooker. Use a foil sling [a sheet of aluminum foil folded into a strip about 2 inches wide by 24 inches long].

12 Cook the fries at 340°F for 5 minutes, ensuring the cheese melts.
13 Garnish the fries with the chopped scallions & serve straight from in the baking dish with some ranch dressing.

299. TOASTED PUMPKIN SEEDS

Prep & Cook Time: 25 minutes | Servings: 4

INGREDIENTS

1 ½ cups of pumpkin seeds [cut a whole pumpkin & scrape out the insides]

1 tsp. of smoked paprika
1 ½ tsp. of salt

Olive oil

INSTRUCTIONS

1 Run the pumpkin seeds under some cold water.
2 Over a medium heat, boil two quarts of salted water in a pot.
3 Add in the pumpkin seeds & cook in the water for 8 to 10 minutes.
4 Dump the contents of the pot into a sieve to drain the seeds. Place them on paper towels & allow them to dry for at least 20 minutes.
5 Pre-heat your Air Fryer to 350°F.
6 In a medium bowl coat the pumpkin seeds with olive oil, smoked paprika & salt.
7 Put them in the Air Fryer's basket & air fry for at least 30 minutes until slightly browned & crispy. Shake the basket a few times during the cooking time.
8 Allow the seeds to cool. Serve with a salad or keep in an airtight container for snacking.

300. BANANA PEPPERS

Prep & Cook Time: 20 minutes | Servings: 8

INGREDIENTS:

1 cup of full-fat cream cheese
Cooking spray

16 avocado slices
16 slices of salami

Salt & pepper
16 banana peppers

INSTRUCTIONS

1 Pre-heat the Air Fryer to 400°F.
2 Spritz a baking tray with cooking spray.
3 Remove the stems from the banana peppers with a knife.
4 Cut a slit into one side of each banana pepper.
5 Season the cream cheese with the salt & pepper & combine well.
6 Fill each pepper with one spoonful of the cream cheese, followed by one slice of avocado.
7 Wrap the banana peppers in the slices of salami & secure with a toothpick.
8 Place the banana peppers in the baking tray & transfer it to the Air Fryer. Bake for roughly 8 - 10 minutes.

301. BARBECUE SAUCE

Prep & Cook Time: 20 minutes | Servings: 6

INGREDIENTS

For the Sauce:
1 tbsp. of yellow mustard
1 tbsp. of apple cider vinegar
1 tbsp. of olive oil
¼ cup of unsulfured blackstrap molasses
¼ cup of ketchup

2 tbsp. of sugar
1 garlic clove, minced
Salt & ground black pepper, to taste
1/8 tsp. of ground allspice
¼ cup of water

For the Wings
2 lb. of chicken wings
¼ tsp. of celery salt
¼ cup of habanero hot sauce
Chopped fresh parsley, or garnish

INSTRUCTIONS:

1 Put all the ingredients for the sauce in a pan over a medium-to-high heat & bring the mixture to a boil.
2 Lower the heat & allow to simmer & thicken.
3 In the meantime, pre-heat your Air Fryer to 400°F.
4 Place the chicken wings in the Air Fryer & cook for 6 minutes.
5 Turn the wings & cook for another 6 minutes on the other side. Sprinkle some celery salt over them.
6 Serve the chicken wings with the prepared sauce, along with habanero sauce or any other accompaniment of your choice.

302. COCONUT SHRIMP

Prep & Cook Time: 20 minutes | Servings: 16

INGREDIENTS

½ tsp. of salt
1 lb. of large shrimp [about 16 to 20 peeled/de-veined]
½ cup of flour

2 egg whites
½ cup of breadcrumbs
½ cup of coconut, shredded
Zest of 1 lime

¼ tsp. of cayenne pepper
Spray can of vegetable or canola oil
Sweet chili sauce or duck sauce, to serve

INSTRUCTIONS

1 In a shallow dish, beat the eggs with a whisk.
2 Combine the breadcrumbs, coconut, lime zest, salt & cayenne pepper in a separate dish.
3 Pre-heat the Air Fryer to 400°F.

4   Coat the shrimp in the flour. Dip the shrimp into the egg mixture, & then into the breadcrumb coconut mixture, ensuring to coat the shrimp all over.
5   Place the shrimp on a plate & spritz with oil. Move the shrimp to the basket of your Air Fryer, taking care not to overlap the fish.
6   Air fry the shrimp for 5 - 6 minutes, ensuring that each shrimp is cooked through & firm before serving.

303. TORTILLA CHIPS

Prep & Cook Time: 5 minutes | Servings: 2

INGREDIENTS

8 corn tortillas   Salt   1 tbsp. of olive oil

INSTRUCTIONS

1   Pre-heat your Air Fryer to 390°F.
2   Slice the corn tortillas into triangles. Coat with a light brushing of olive oil.
3   Put the tortilla pieces in the wire basket & air fry for 3 minutes. You may need to do this in multiple batches.
4   Season with salt before serving.

304. NAAN BREAD DIPPERS

Prep & Cook Time: 50 minutes | Servings: 10

INGREDIENTS

4 naan bread, cut into 2-inch strips   2 cups of cooked chicken, shredded   Salt & freshly ground black pepper
3 tbsp. of butter, melted   4 scallions, minced   ½ cup of sliced almonds
12 oz. of light cream cheese, softened   ⅓ cup of golden raisins   ½ cup Major Grey's Chutney
1 cup of plain yogurt   6 oz. of cheese, grated [about 2 cups]
2 tsp. of curry powder   ¼ cup of fresh cilantro, chopped

INSTRUCTIONS

1   Pre-heat Air Fryer to 400°F.
2   Slice up the naan in thirds lengthwise before cutting crosswise into 2-inch strips. In a bowl, toss the strips with the melted butter.
3   Move the naan strips to Air Fryer basket. Toast for 5 minutes, shaking the basket halfway through. You will have to do this in two batches.
4   Mix together the softened cream cheese & yogurt with a hand mixer or in a food processor. Add in the curry powder & combine evenly.
5   Fold in the shredded chicken, scallions, golden raisins, Monterey Jack cheese & chopped cilantro.
6   Sprinkle with salt & freshly ground black pepper as desired.
7   Pour the mixture into a 1-quart baking dish & spread out evenly. Arrange the sliced almonds on top. Air-fry at 300°F for 25 minutes.
8   Put a dollop of Major Grey's chutney in the center of the dip & scatter the scallions on top.
9   Serve the naan dippers with the hot dip.

305. SNACK MIX

Prep & Cook Time: 30 minutes | Servings: 10

INGREDIENTS

½ cup of honey   2 cups of sesame sticks   1 cup of cashews
3 tbsp. of butter, melted   2 cups of pepitas [pumpkin seeds]   2 cups of crispy corn puff cereal
1 tsp. of salt   2 cups of granola   2 cups of mini pretzel crisps

INSTRUCTIONS

1   In a bowl, combine the honey, butter, & salt.
2   In another bowl, mix together the sesame sticks, pepitas, granola, cashews, corn puff cereal, & pretzel crisps.
3   Combine the contents of the two bowls.
4   Pre-heat your Air Fryer to 370°F.
5   Put the mixture in the Air Fryer basket & air-fry for 10 - 12 minutes to toast the snack mixture, shaking the basket frequently. You will have to do this in two batches.
6   Place the snack mix on a cookie sheet & allow it to cool fully.
7   Store in an airtight container for up to one week. Makes a great holiday gift!

306. FETA TRIANGLES

Prep & Cook Time: 55 minutes | Servings: 5

INGREDIENTS

1 egg yolk, beaten   1 scallion, finely chopped   2 tbsp. of olive oil ground black pepper to
4 oz. of feta cheese   2 sheets of frozen filo pastry, defrosted   taste
2 tbsp. of flat-leafed parsley, chopped

INSTRUCTIONS

1   In a bowl, combine the beaten egg yolk with the feta, parsley & scallion. Sprinkle on some pepper to taste.
2   Slice each sheet of filo dough into three strips.
3   Place a teaspoonful of the feta mixture on each strip of pastry.
4   Pinch the tip of the pastry & fold it up to enclose the filling & create a triangle. Continue folding the strip in zigzags until the filling is wrapped in a triangle. Repeat with all of the strips of pastry.

5   Pre-heat the Air Fryer to 390°F.
6   Coat the pastry with a light coating of oil & arrange in the cooking basket.
7   Place the basket in the Air Fryer & cook for 3 minutes.
8   Lower the heat to 360°F & cook for a further 2 minutes or until a golden-brown color is achieved

307. SAGE & ONION STUFFING

Prep & Cook Time: 35 minutes | Servings: 6

INGREDIENTS

2 lb. of sausage meat
½ onion
½ tsp. of garlic puree

1 tsp. of sage
3 tbsp. of breadcrumbs
Salt

Black pepper

INSTRUCTIONS

1   Combine all of the ingredients in a large bowl.
2   Take equal portions of the mixture, mold them into medium sized balls & put them in the Air Fryer.
3   Cook at 355°F for 15 minutes.

308. PUPPY POPPERS

Prep & Cook Time: 25 minutes | Servings: 50 treats

INGREDIENTS

½ cup of unsweetened applesauce
1 cup of peanut butter

2 cups of oats
1 cup of flour

1 tsp. of baking powder

INSTRUCTIONS

1   Combine the applesauce & peanut butter in a bowl to create a smooth consistency.
2   Pour in the oats, flour & baking powder. Continue mixing to form a soft dough.
3   Shape a half-tsp. of dough into a ball & continue with the rest of the dough.
4   Pre-heat the Air Fryer to 350°F.
5   Grease the bottom of the basket with oil.
6   Place the poppers in the Air Fryer & cook for 8 minutes, flipping the balls at the halfway point. You may need to cook the poppers in batches.
7   Let the poppers cool & serve immediately or keep in an airtight container for up to 2 weeks.

309. MASALA CASHEW

Prep & Cook Time: 20 minutes | Servings: 3

INGREDIENTS

½ lb. of cashew nuts
½ tsp. of garam masala powder
1 tsp. of coriander powder

1 tsp. of butter
1 tsp. of red chili powder
½ tsp. of black pepper

2 tsp. of dry mango powder
1 tsp. of sea salt

INSTRUCTIONS

1   Put all the ingredients in a large bowl & toss together well.
2   Arrange the cashew nuts in the basket of your Air Fryer.
3   Cook at 250°F for 15 minutes until the nuts are brown & crispy.
4   Let the nuts cool before serving or transferring to an airtight container to be stored for up to 2 weeks.

310. BACON WRAPPED SHRIMP

Prep & Cook Time: 50 minutes | Servings: 4

INGREDIENTS

1 ¼ lb. of tiger shrimp, peeled & deveined
    [16 pieces]

1 lb. of bacon, thinly sliced, room
    temperature [16 slices]

INSTRUCTIONS

1   Wrap each bacon slice around a piece of shrimp, from the head to the tail. Refrigerate for 20 minutes.
2   Pre-heat the Air Fryer to 390°F.
3   Place the shrimp in the Air Fryer's basket & cook for 5 – 7 minutes.
4   Allow to dry on a paper towel before serving.

311. TOMATO & AVOCADO EGG ROLLS

Prep & Cook Time: 20 minutes | Servings: 5

INGREDIENTS

10 egg roll wrappers
3 avocados, peeled & pitted

1 tomato, diced
Salt & pepper, to taste

INSTRUCTIONS

1   Pre-heat your Air Fryer to 350°F.

2   Put the tomato & avocados in a bowl. Sprinkle on some salt & pepper & mash together with a fork until a smooth consistency is achieved.
3   Spoon equal amounts of the mixture onto the wrappers. Roll the wrappers around the filling, enclosing them entirely.
4   Transfer the rolls to a lined baking dish & cook for 5 minutes.

312. MEATBALLS IN TOMATO SAUCE

Prep & Cook Time: 35 minutes | Servings: 4

INGREDIENTS

1 small onion, finely chopped
¾ lb. [12 oz.] of ground beef
1 tbsp. of chopped fresh parsley

½ tbsp. of chopped fresh thyme leaves
1 egg
3 tbsp. of breadcrumbs

Salt & pepper
10 oz. of favorite tomato sauce if desired

INSTRUCTIONS

1   Put all the ingredients in a bowl & combine well. Use your hands to mold the mixture into 10 - 12 balls.
2   Pre-heat the Air Fryer to 390°F.
3   Put the meatballs in the Air Fryer basket & place the basket in the Air Fryer.
4   Cook the meatballs for 8 minutes.
5   Put the meatballs in an oven dish, pour in the tomato sauce & set the dish in the basket of the Air Fryer.
6   Reduce the temperature to 330°F & warm the meatballs for 5 minutes.

313. AMAZING BLOOMING ONION

Prep & Cook Time: 40 minutes | Servings: 4

INGREDIENTS

4 medium/small onions

1 tbsp. of olive oil

4 dollops of butter

INSTRUCTIONS

1   Peel the onion. Cut off the top & bottom.
2   To make it bloom, cut as deeply as possible without slicing through it completely. 4 cuts [i.e. 8 segments] should do it.
3   Place the onions in a bowl of salted water & allow to absorb for 4 hours to help eliminate the sharp taste & induce the blooming process.
4   Pre-heat your Air Fryer to 355°F.
5   Transfer the onions to the Air Fryer. Pour over a light drizzle of olive oil & place a dollop of butter on top of each onion.
6   Cook or roast for 30 minutes. Remove the outer layer before serving if it is too brown.

314. CRAB CROQUETTES

Prep & Cook Time: 5 minutes | Servings: 6

INGREDIENTS

For the Filling:
1 lb. of lump crab meat
2 egg whites, beaten
1 tbsp. of olive oil
¼ cup of red onion, finely chopped
¼ red bell pepper, finely chopped
2 tbsp. of celery, finely chopped

¼ tsp. of tarragon, finely chopped
¼ tsp. of chives, finely chopped
½ tsp. of parsley, finely chopped
½ tsp. of cayenne pepper
¼ cup of mayonnaise
¼ cup of sour cream

For the Breading
3 eggs, beaten
1 cup of flour
1 cup of breadcrumbs
1 tsp. of olive oil
½ tsp. of salt

INSTRUCTIONS

1   Sauté the olive oil, onions, peppers, & celery over a medium heat, allowing to sweat until the vegetables turn translucent. This should take about 4 – 5 minutes.
2   Take off the heat & allow to cool.
3   In a food processor, pulse the breadcrumbs, olive oil & salt to form a fine crumb.
4   Place the eggs, panko mixture & flour in three separate bowls.
5   Combine the crabmeat, egg whites, mayonnaise, sour cream, spices & vegetables in a large bowl.
6   Pre-heat the Air Fryer to 390°F.
7   Take equal amounts of the crab mixture & shape into golf balls. Coat the balls in the flour, before dipping them in the eggs & finally in the panko, making sure the breadcrumbs stick well.
8   Put croquettes in the Air Fryer basket in a single layer & well-spaced.
9   Cook the croquettes for 8 – 10 minutes or until a golden-brown color is achieved.

315. PUMPKIN SEEDS

Prep & Cook Time: 55 minutes | Servings: 1 ½ cups

INGREDIENTS

1 ½ cups of pumpkin seeds from a large
    whole pumpkin

Olive oil
1 ½ tsp. of salt

1 tsp. of smoked paprika

INSTRUCTIONS

1   Boil two quarts of well-salted water in a pot. Cook the pumpkin seeds in the boiling water for 10 minutes.
2   Dump the content of the pot into a sieve & dry the seeds on paper towels for at least 20 minutes.
3   Pre-heat the Air Fryer to 350°F.

4   Cover the seeds with olive oil, salt & smoked paprika, before placing them in the Air Fryer basket.
5   Air fry for 35 minutes. Give the basket a good shake several times throughout the cooking process to ensure the pumpkin seeds are crispy & lightly browned.
6   Let the seeds cool before serving. Alternatively, you can keep them in an air-tight container or bag for snacking or for use as a yogurt topping.

316. COCKTAIL FLANKS

Prep & Cook Time: 45 minutes | Servings: 4

INGREDIENTS

1x 12-oz. of packet cocktail franks
1x 8-oz. of can crescent rolls

INSTRUCTIONS

1   Drain the cocktail franks & dry with paper towels.
2   Unroll the crescent rolls & slice the dough into rectangular strips, roughly 1" by 1.5".
3   Wrap the franks in the strips with the ends poking out. Leave in the freezer for 5 minutes.
4   Pre-heat the Air Fryer to 330°F.
5   Take the franks out of the freezer & put them in the cooking basket. Cook for 6 – 8 minutes.
6   Reduce the heat to 390°F & cook for another 3 minutes or until a golden-brown color is achieved.

317. GARLIC MUSHROOMS

Prep & Cook Time: 30 minutes | Servings: 4

INGREDIENTS

16 small button mushrooms
For the Stuffing:
1 ½ slices of bread   1 tbsp. of flat-leafed parsley, chopped   1 ½ tbsp. of olive oil
1 garlic clove, crushed   Ground black pepper to taste

INSTRUCTIONS

1   Pre-heat the Air Fryer to 390°F.
2   Blend together the bread slices, garlic, parsley & pepper until a fine crumb is formed.
3   Mix in the olive oil.
4   Remove the mushroom stalks & spoon even amounts of the filling into the caps. Press the crumbs in well to make sure none fall out
5   Put the mushroom caps in the cooking basket & place it in the Air Fryer.
6   Cook the mushrooms for 7 – 8 minutes or until they turn golden & crispy.

318. EGGPLANT CHIPS

Prep & Cook Time: 45 minutes | Servings: 4

INGREDIENTS

2 eggplants, peeled & thinly sliced
Salt   ½ cup of water   ½ tsp. of ground black pepper, to taste
½ cup of tapioca starch   1 tsp. of garlic powder
¼ cup of canola oil   ½ tsp. of dried dill weed

INSTRUCTIONS

1   Season the eggplant slices with salt & leave for half an hour.
2   Run them under cold water to rinse off any excess salt.
3   In a bowl, coat the eggplant slices with all of the other ingredients.
4   Cook inside your Air Fryer 390°F for 13 minutes. You may need to do this in batches.
5   Serve with the dipping sauce of your choice.

319. SAGE POTATOES

Prep & Cook Time: 45 minutes | Servings: 8

INGREDIENTS

1 ½ lb. of fingerling potatoes, halved   2 sprigs of thyme, chopped   1 tbsp. of sea salt flakes
2 tbsp. of melted butter   1 tsp. of lemon zest, finely grated ½ tsp. of grated ginger
¼ cup of fresh sage leaves, chopped   ¼ tsp. of ground pepper

INSTRUCTIONS

1   Place the potatoes in a bowl of cold water & allow to absorb for about half an hour.
2   Dry them with a clean kitchen towel.
3   Transfer to the Air Fryer & roast at 400°F for 15 minutes.
4   Serve with tomato ketchup & mayonnaise if desired.

320. DIJON & QUINOA COCKTAIL MEATBALLS

Prep & Cook Time: 20 minutes | Servings: 6

INGREDIENTS

½ lb. of ground pork
½ lb. of ground beef
1 cup of quinoa, cooked
1 egg, beaten
2 scallions, finely chopped

½ tsp. of onion powder
1 ½ tbsp. of Dijon mustard
¾ cup of ketchup
1 tsp. of ancho chili powder
1 tbsp. of sesame oil

2 tbsp. of tamari sauce
¼ cup of balsamic vinegar
2 tbsp. of sugar

INSTRUCTIONS

1   In a bowl, stir together all the ingredients & combine well.
2   Use your hands to shape equal amounts of the mixture into small meatballs.
3   Place the meatballs in the Air Fryer & cook at 370°F for 10 minutes. Give the basket a good shake & allow to cook for another 5 minutes.

321. RICOTTA BALLS

Prep & Cook Time: 25 minutes | Servings: 2 – 4

INGREDIENTS

2 cups of ricotta, grated
2 eggs, separated
2 tbsp. of chives, finely chopped
2 tbsp. of fresh basil, finely chopped

4 tbsp. of flour
¼ tsp. of salt to taste
¼ tsp. of pepper powder to taste
1 tsp. orange zest, grated

For the Coating:
¼ cup of breadcrumbs
1 tbsp. of vegetable oil

INSTRUCTIONS

1.   Pre-heat your Air Fryer at 390°F.
2.   In a bowl, combine the yolks, flour, salt, pepper, chives & orange zest. Throw in the ricotta & incorporate with your hands.
3.   Mold equal amounts of the mixture into balls.
4.   Mix the oil with the breadcrumbs until a crumbly consistency is achieved.
5.   Coat the balls in the breadcrumbs & transfer each one to the Air Fryer's basket.
6.   Put the basket in the Air Fryer. Air fry for 8 minutes or until a golden-brown color is achieved.
7.   Serve with a sauce of your choosing, such as ketchup.

322. SPICED NUTS

Prep & Cook Time: 40 minutes | Servings: 3 cups

INGREDIENTS

1 egg white, lightly beaten
¼ cup of sugar
1 tsp. of salt
½ tsp. of ground cinnamon

¼ tsp. of ground cloves
¼ tsp. of ground allspice
Pinch of ground cayenne pepper
1 cup of pecan halves

1 cup of cashews
1 cup of almonds

INSTRUCTIONS

1.   In a bowl, combine the egg white with the sugar & spices.
2.   Pre-heat the Air Fryer to 300°F.
3.   Coat the inside of the Air Fryer's basket with vegetable oil.
4.   Cover the nuts with the spiced egg white. Place half of them in the Air Fryer.
5.   Air fry for 25 minutes, giving the nuts a few good stirs throughout the cooking time, until they are crunchy & toasted.
6.   Repeat with the other half of the nuts.
7.   Serve immediately or store in an airtight container for up to two weeks.

323. SHRIMP BITES

Prep & Cook Time: 45 minutes | Servings: 10

INGREDIENTS

1 ¼ lb. shrimp, peeled & deveined
1 tsp. of paprika
½ tsp. of ground black pepper

½ tsp. of red pepper flakes, crushed
1 tbsp. of salt
1 tsp. of chili powder

1 tbsp. of shallot powder
¼ tsp. of cumin powder
1 ¼ lb. of thin bacon slices

INSTRUCTIONS

1.   Coat the shrimps with all of the seasonings.
2.   Wrap a slice of bacon around each shrimp & hold it in place with a toothpick. Refrigerate for half an hour.
3.   Transfer to the Air Fryer & fry at 360°F for 7 - 8 minutes.

324. CAJUN SPICED SNACK

Prep & Cook Time: 30 minutes | Servings: 5

INGREDIENTS

2 tbsp. of Cajun or Creole seasoning
½ cup of butter, melted
2 cups of peanuts
2 cups of mini wheat thin crackers

2 cups of mini pretzels
2 tsp. of salt
1 tsp. of cayenne pepper
4 cups of plain popcorn

1 tsp. of paprika
1 tsp. of garlic
½ tsp. of thyme
½ tsp. of oregano

1 tsp. of black pepper   ½ tsp. of onion powder

INSTRUCTIONS

1. Pre-heat the Air Fryer to 370°F.
2. In a bowl, combine the Cajun spice with the melted butter.
3. In a separate bowl, stir together the peanuts, crackers, popcorn & pretzels. Coat the snacks with the butter mixture.
4. Place in the Air Fryer & fry for 8 - 10 minutes, shaking the basket frequently during the cooking time. You will have to complete this step in two batches.
5. Put the snack mix on a cookie sheet & leave to cool.
6. The snacks can be kept in an airtight container for up to one week.

325. CHEESY BROCCOLI BALLS

Prep & Cook Time: 20 minutes | Servings: 6

INGREDIENTS

2 eggs, well whisked   Seasoned salt, to taste   1 head of broccoli, chopped into florets
2 cups of Colby cheese, shredded   ¼ tsp. of ground black pepper, or more if   1 cup of crushed saltines
1 cup of flour   preferred

INSTRUCTIONS

1. Mix together the eggs, cheese, flour, salt, pepper, & broccoli until a dough-like paste is formed.
2. Refrigerate for 1 hour. Divide the mixture evenly & mold each portion into small balls. Coat the balls in the crushed saltines & spritz them all over with cooking spray.
3. Cook inside your Air Fryer at 360°F for 10 minutes. At this point, you should check how far along in the cooking process they are & allow to cook for a further 8 - 10 minutes as needed.
4. Serve with the dipping sauce of your choice.

326. GOULASH

Prep & Cook Time: 20 minutes | Servings: 2

INGREDIENTS

2 chopped bell peppers   1 lb. of ground chicken   Salt & pepper
2 diced tomatoes   ½ cup of chicken broth

INSTRUCTIONS

1. Pre-heat your Air Fryer at 365°F & spray with cooking spray.
2. Cook the bell pepper for five minutes.
3. Add in the diced tomatoes & ground chicken. Combine well, then allow to cook for a further six minutes.
4. Pour in chicken broth, & season to taste with salt & pepper. Cook for another six minutes before serving.

327. GARLICKY MEATBALLS

Prep & Cook Time: 20 minutes | Servings: 2

INGREDIENTS

½ lb. of boneless chicken thighs   1 ¼ cup of roasted pecans   1 tsp. of extra virgin olive oil
1 tsp. of minced garlic   ½ cup of mushrooms

INSTRUCTIONS

1. Preheat your Air Fryer to 375°F.
2. Cube the chicken thighs.
3. Place them in the food processor along with the garlic, pecans, & other seasonings as desired. Pulse until a smooth consistency is achieved.
4. Chop the mushrooms finely. Add to the chicken mixture & combine.
5. Using your hands, shape the mixture into balls & brush them with olive oil.
6. Put the balls into the Air Fryer & cook for eighteen minutes. Serve hot.

328. CILANTRO DRUMSTICKS

Prep & Cook Time: 30 minutes | Servings: 4

INGREDIENTS:

8 chicken drumsticks   ½ cup of chimichurri sauce   ¼ cup of lemon juice

INSTRUCTIONS

1. Coat the chicken drumsticks with chimichurri sauce & refrigerate in an airtight container for no less than an hour, ideally overnight.
2. When it's time to cook, pre-heat your Air Fryer to 400°F.
3. Remove the chicken from refrigerator & allow return to room temperature for roughly twenty minutes.
4. Cook for eighteen minutes in the Air Fryer. Drizzle with lemon juice to taste & enjoy.

329. POPPIN' POP CORN CHICKEN

Prep & Cook Time: 20 minutes | Servings: 1

INGREDIENTS

1 lb. of skinless, boneless chicken breast
1 tsp. of chili flakes
1 tsp. of garlic powder
½ cup of flour
1 tbsp. of olive oil cooking spray

INSTRUCTIONS

1. Pre-heat your Air Fryer at 365°F. Spray with olive oil.
2. Cut the chicken breasts into cubes & place in a bowl. Toss with the chili flakes, garlic powder, & additional seasonings to taste & make sure to coat entirely.
3. Add the coconut flour & toss once more.
4. Cook the chicken in the Air Fryer for ten minutes. Turnover & cook for a further five minutes before serving.

330. CRISPY CHICKEN

Prep & Cook Time: 10 minutes | Servings: 2

INGREDIENTS

1 lb. of chicken skin
1 tsp. of butter
½ tsp. of chili flakes
1 tsp. of dill

INSTRUCTIONS

1. Pre-heat the Air Fryer at 360°F.
2. Cut the chicken skin into slices.
3. Heat the butter until melted & pour it over the chicken skin. Toss with chili flakes, dill, & any additional seasonings to taste, making sure to coat well.
4. Cook the skins in the Air Fryer for three minutes. Turn them over & cook on the other side for another three minutes.
5. Serve immediately or save them for later – they can be eaten hot or at room temperature.

331. SOUTHERN FRIED CHICKEN

Prep & Cook Time: 30 minutes | Servings: 2

INGREDIENTS

2 x 6-oz. of boneless skinless chicken breasts
2 tbsp. of hot sauce
½ tsp. of onion powder
1 tbsp. of chili powder
½ oz. of flour

INSTRUCTIONS

1. Cut the chicken breasts in half lengthwise & rub in the hot sauce. Combine the onion powder with the chili powder, then rub into the chicken. Leave to marinate for at least a half hour.
2. Use the flour to coat the chicken breasts, covering them thoroughly. Place the chicken in your Air Fryer.
3. Set the Air Fryer at 350°F & cook the chicken for 13 minutes. Flip the chicken & cook the other side for another 13 minutes or until golden.
4. Test the chicken with a meat thermometer. When fully cooked, it should reach 165°F. Serve hot, with the sides of your choice.

332. JALAPENO CHICKEN BREASTS

Prep & Cook Time: 25 minutes | Servings: 2

INGREDIENTS

2 oz. of full-fat cream cheese, softened
4 slices of sugar-free bacon, cooked & crumbled
¼ cup of pickled jalapenos, sliced
½ cup of sharp cheddar cheese, shredded & divided
2 x 6-oz. of boneless skinless chicken breasts

INSTRUCTIONS

1. In a bowl, mix the cream cheese, bacon, jalapeno slices, & half of the cheddar cheese until well-combined.
2. Cut parallel slits in the chicken breasts of about ¾ the length – make sure not to cut all the way down. You should be able to make between six & eight slices, depending on the size of the chicken breast.
3. Insert evenly sized dollops of the cheese mixture into the slits of the chicken breasts. Top the chicken with sprinkles of the rest of the cheddar cheese. Place the chicken in the basket of your Air Fryer.
4. Set the Air Fryer to 350°F & cook the chicken breasts for twenty minutes.
5. Test with a meat thermometer. The chicken should be at 165°F when fully cooked. Serve hot & enjoy!

333. FAJITA STYLE CHICKEN BREAST

Prep & Cook Time: 35 minutes | Servings: 2

INGREDIENTS

2 x 6-oz. of boneless skinless chicken breasts
1 green bell pepper, sliced
¼ medium white onion, sliced
1 tbsp. of coconut oil, melted
3 tsp. of taco seasoning mix

INSTRUCTIONS

1. Cut each chicken breast in half & place each one between two sheets of cooking parchment. Using a mallet, pound the chicken to flatten to a quarter-inch thick.
2. Place the chicken on a flat surface, with the short end facing you. Place four slices of pepper & three slices of onion at the end of each piece of chicken. Roll up the chicken tightly, making sure not to let any veggies fall out. Secure with some toothpicks or with butcher's string.
3. Coat the chicken with coconut oil & then with taco seasoning. Place into your Air Fryer.
4. Turn the Air Fryer to 350°F & cook the chicken for twenty-five minutes.
5. Serve the rolls immediately with your favorite dips & sides.

334. LEMON PEPPER CHICKEN LEGS

Prep & Cook Time: 30 minutes | Servings: 4

INGREDIENTS

½ tsp. of garlic powder
2 tsp. of baking powder

8 chicken legs
4 tbsp. of salted butter, melted

1 tbsp. of lemon pepper seasoning

INSTRUCTIONS

1. In a small bowl combine the garlic powder & baking powder, then use this mixture to coat the chicken legs. Lay the chicken in the basket of your Air Fryer.
2. Cook the chicken legs at 375°F for twenty-five minutes. Halfway through, turn them over & allow to cook on the other side.
3. When the chicken has turned golden brown, test with a thermometer to ensure it has reached an ideal temperature of 165°F. Remove from the Air Fryer.
4. Mix together the melted butter & lemon pepper seasoning & toss with the chicken legs until the chicken is coated all over. Serve hot.

335. GREEK CHICKEN MEATBALLS

Prep & Cook Time: 15 minutes | Servings: 1

INGREDIENTS

½ oz. of flour
1 lb. of ground chicken

1 tsp. of Greek seasoning
⅓ cup feta, crumbled

⅓ cup of frozen spinachthawed

INSTRUCTIONS

1. Place all the ingredients in a large bowl & combine using your hands. Take equal-sized portions of this mixture & roll each into a 2-inch ball. Place the balls in your Air Fryer.
2. Cook the meatballs at 350°F for twelve minutes, in several batches if necessary.
3. Once they are golden, ensure they have reached an ideal temperature of 165°F & remove from the Air Fryer. Keep each batch warm while you move on to the next one. Serve with Tzatziki if desired.

336. CRUSTED CHICKEN

Ingredients: Prep & Cook Time: 30 minutes | Servings: 2

INGREDIENTS

¼ cup of slivered almonds
2x 6-oz. of boneless skinless chicken

breasts
2 tbsp. of full-fat mayonnaise

1 tbsp. of Dijon mustard

INSTRUCTIONS

1. Pulse the almonds in a food processor until they are finely chopped. Spread the almonds on a plate & set aside.
2. Cut each chicken breast in half lengthwise.
3. Mix the mayonnaise & mustard together & then spread evenly on top of the chicken slices.
4. Place the chicken into the plate of chopped almonds to coat completely, laying each coated slice into the basket of your Air Fryer.
5. Cook for 25 minutes at 350°F until golden. Test the temperature, making sure the chicken has reached 165°F. Serve hot.

337. BUFFALO CHICKEN TENDERS

Ingredients: Prep & Cook Time: 20 minutes | Servings: 4

INGREDIENTS

1 egg
1 cup of mozzarella cheese, shredded

¼ cup of buffalo sauce
1 cup of cooked chicken, shredded

¼ cup of feta cheese

INSTRUCTIONS

1. Combine all ingredients (except for the feta). Line the basket of your Air Fryer with a suitably sized piece of parchment paper. Lay the mixture into the Air Fryer & press it into a circle about half an inch thick. Crumble the feta cheese over it.
2. Cook for eight minutes at 400°F. Turn the Air Fryer off & allow the chicken to rest inside before removing with care.
3. Cut the mixture into slices & serve hot.

338. BUFFALO CHICKEN STRIPS

Ingredients: Prep & Cook Time: 30 minutes | Servings: 1

INGREDIENTS

¼ cup of hot sauce
1 lb. of boneless skinless chicken tenders

1 tsp. of garlic powder
½ oz. of flour

1 tsp. of chili powder

INSTRUCTIONS

1. Toss the hot sauce & chicken tenders together in a bowl, ensuring the chicken is completely coated.
2. In another bowl, combine the garlic powder, flour, & chili powder. Use this mixture to coat the tenders, covering them well. Place the chicken into your Air Fryer, taking care not to layer pieces on top of one another.
3. Cook the chicken at 375°F for twenty minutes until cooked all the way through & golden. Serve warm with your favorite dips & sides.

339. CHICKEN & PEPPERONI PIZZA

Ingredients: Prep & Cook Time: 20 minutes | Servings: 6

INGREDIENTS:

2 cups of cooked chicken, cubed
20 slices of pepperoni

1 cup of sugar-free pizza sauce
1 cup of mozzarella cheese, shredded

¼ cup of parmesan cheese, grated

INSTRUCTIONS

1. Place the chicken into the base of a four-cup baking dish & add the pepperoni & pizza sauce on top. Mix well so as to completely coat the meat with the sauce.
2. Add the parmesan & mozzarella on top of the chicken, then place the baking dish into your Air Fryer.
3. Cook for 15 minutes at 375°F.
4. When everything is bubbling & melted, remove from the Air Fryer. Serve hot.

340. ITALIAN CHICKEN THIGHS

Ingredients: Prep & Cook Time: 30 minutes | Servings: 4

INGREDIENTS

4 skin-on bone-in chicken thighs
2 tbsp. of butter, melted

3 tsp. of Italian herbs
½ tsp. of garlic powder

¼ tsp. of onion powder

INSTRUCTIONS

1. Using a brush, coat the chicken thighs with the melted butter. Combine the herbs with the garlic powder & onion powder, then massage into the chicken thighs. Place the thighs in the Air Fryer.
2. Cook at 380°F for 20 minutes, turning the chicken halfway through to cook on the other side.
3. When the thighs have achieved a golden color, test the temperature with a meat thermometer. Once they have reached 165°F, remove from the Air Fryer & serve.

341. TERIYAKI CHICKEN WINGS

Ingredients: Prep & Cook Time: 45 minutes | Servings: 4

INGREDIENTS:

¼ tsp. of ground ginger
2 tsp. of minced garlic

½ cup of sugar-free teriyaki sauce
2 lb. of chicken wings

2 tsp. of baking powder

INSTRUCTIONS

1. In a small bowl, combine together the ginger, garlic, & teriyaki sauce. Place the chicken wings in a separate, larger bowl & pour the mixture over them. Toss to coat until the chicken is well covered.
2. Refrigerate for at least an hour.
3. Remove the marinated wings from the refrigerator & add the baking powder, tossing again to coat. Then place the chicken in the basket of your Air Fryer.
4. Cook for 25 minutes at 400°F, giving the basket a shake intermittently throughout the cooking time.
5. When the wings are 165°F & golden in color, remove from the Air Fryer & serve immediately.

342. CHICKEN PIZZA CRUSTS

Ingredients: Prep & Cook Time: 35 minutes | Servings: 1

INGREDIENTS:

½ cup of mozzarella, shredded

¼ cup of parmesan cheese, grated

1 lb. of ground chicken

INSTRUCTIONS

1. In a large bowl, combine all the ingredients & then spread the mixture out, dividing it into four parts of equal size.
2. Cut a sheet of parchment paper into four circles, roughly six inches in diameter, & put some of the chicken mixture onto the center of each piece, flattening the mixture to fill out the circle.
3. Depending on the size of your Air Fryer, cook either one or two circles at a time at 375°F for 25 minutes. Halfway through, turn the crust over to cook on the other side. Keep each batch warm while you move onto the next one.
4. Once all the crusts are cooked, top with cheese & the toppings of your choice. If desired, cook the topped crusts for an additional five minutes.
5. Serve hot or freeze & save for later!

343. CRISPY CHICKEN THIGHS

Ingredients: Prep & Cook Time: 35 minutes | Servings: 1

INGREDIENTS:

1 lb. of chicken thighs
Salt & pepper

2 cups of roasted pecans
1 cup of water

1 cup of flour

INSTRUCTIONS

1. Pre-heat your Air Fryer to 400°F.
2. Season the chicken with salt & pepper, then set aside.
3. Pulse the roasted pecans in a food processor until a flour-like consistency is achieved.
4. Fill a dish with the water, another with the flour, & a third with the pecans.

5. Coat the thighs with the flour. Mix the remaining flour with the processed pecans.
6. Dredge the thighs in the water & then press into the -pecan mix, ensuring the chicken is completely covered.
7. Cook the chicken in the Air Fryer for twenty-two minutes, with an extra five minutes added if you would like the chicken a darker-brown color. Check the temperature has reached 165°F before serving.

344. STRAWBERRY TURKEY

Ingredients: Prep & Cook Time: 50 minutes | Servings: 2

INGREDIENTS:

2 lb. of turkey breast
1 tbsp. of olive oil

Salt & pepper
1 cup of fresh strawberries

INSTRUCTIONS

1. Pre-heat your Air Fryer to 375°F.
2. Massage the turkey breast with olive oil, before seasoning with a generous amount of salt & pepper.
3. Cook the turkey in the Air Fryer for fifteen minutes. Flip the turkey & cook for a further fifteen minutes.
4. During these last fifteen minutes, blend the strawberries in a food processor until a smooth consistency has been achieved.
5. Heap the strawberries over the turkey, then cook for a final seven minutes & enjoy.

345. CHIMICHURRI TURKEY

Ingredients: Prep & Cook Time: 70 minutes | Servings: 1

INGREDIENTS:

1 lb. of turkey breast
½ cup of chimichurri sauce

½ cup of butter
¼ cup of parmesan cheese, grated

¼ tsp. of garlic powder

INSTRUCTIONS

1. Massage the chimichurri sauce into the turkey breast, then refrigerate in an airtight container for at least a half hour.
2. In the meantime, prepare the herbed butter. Mix together the butter, parmesan, & garlic powder, using a hand mixer if desired (this will make it extra creamy)
3. Preheat your Air Fryer at 350°F & place a rack inside. Remove the turkey from the refrigerator & allow to return to room temperature for roughly twenty minutes while the Air Fryer warms.
4. Place the turkey in the Air Fryer & allow to cook for twenty minutes. Flip & cook on the other side for a further twenty minutes.
5. Take care when removing the turkey from the Air Fryer. Place it on a serving dish & enjoy with the herbed butter.

346. BETTY'S BAKED CHICKEN

Ingredients: Prep & Cook Time: 70 minutes | Servings: 1

INGREDIENTS:

½ cup of butter
1 tsp. of pepper

3 tbsp. of garlic, minced
1 whole chicken

INSTRUCTIONS

1. Pre-heat your Air Fryer at 350°F.
2. Allow the butter to soften at room temperature, then mix well in a small bowl with the pepper & garlic.
3. Massage the butter into the chicken. Any remaining butter can go inside the chicken.
4. Cook the chicken in the Air Fryer for half an hour. Flip, then cook on the other side for another thirty minutes.
5. Test the temperature of the chicken by sticking a meat thermometer into the fat of the thigh to make sure it has reached 165°F. Take care when removing the chicken from the Air Fryer. Let sit for ten minutes before you carve it & serve.

347. CHICKEN BREASTS & SPICED TOMATOES

Ingredients: Prep & Cook Time: 40 minutes | Servings: 1

INGREDIENTS

1 lb. of boneless chicken breast
Salt & pepper

1 cup of butter
1 cup of tomatoes, diced

1 ½ tsp. of paprika
1 tsp. of pumpkin pie spices

INSTRUCTIONS

1. Preheat your Air Fryer at 375°F.
2. Cut the chicken into relatively thick slices & put them in the Air Fryer. Sprinkle with salt & pepper to taste. Cook for fifteen minutes.
3. In the meantime, melt the butter in a saucepan over medium heat, before adding the tomatoes, paprika, & pumpkin pie spices. Leave simmering while the chicken finishes cooking.
4. When the chicken is cooked through, place it on a dish & pour the tomato mixture over. Serve hot.

348. FENNEL CHICKEN

Ingredients: Prep & Cook Time: 40 minutes | Servings: 4

INGREDIENTS

1 ½ cup of coconut milk
2 tbsp. of garam masala

1 ½ lb. of chicken thighs
¾ tbsp. of coconut oil, melted

INSTRUCTIONS

1. Combine the coconut oil & garam masala together in a bowl. Pour the mixture over the chicken thighs & leave to marinate for a half hour.
2. Pre-heat your Air Fryer at 375°F.
3. Cook the chicken into the Air Fryer for fifteen minutes.
4. Add in the coconut milk, giving it a good stir, then cook for an additional ten minutes.
5. Remove the chicken & place on a serving dish. Make sure to pour all of the coconut "gravy" over it & serve immediately.

349. ROASTED CHICKEN

Ingredients: Prep & Cook Time: 90 minutes | Servings: 6

INGREDIENTS

6 lb. of whole chicken
1 tsp. of olive oil

1 tbsp. of minced garlic
1 white onion, peeled & halved

3 tbsp. of butter

INSTRUCTIONS

1. Pre-heat the Air Fryer at 360°F.
2. Massage the chicken with the olive oil & the minced garlic.
3. Place the peeled & halved onion, as well as the butter, inside of the chicken.
4. Cook the chicken in the Air Fryer for seventy-five minutes.
5. Take care when removing the chicken from the Air Fryer, then carve & serve.

350. CHICKEN & HONEY SAUCE

Prep & Cook Time: 20 minutes | Servings: 4

INGREDIENTS

4 chicken sausages
2 tbsp. of honey

¼ cup of mayonnaise
2 tbsp. of Dijon mustard

1 tbsp. of balsamic vinegar
½ tsp. of dried rosemary

INSTRUCTIONS

1. Pre-heat your Air Fryer at 350°F.
2. Place the sausages on the grill pan of your Air Fryer & grill for about 13 minutes, flipping them halfway through the cooking time.
3. In the meantime, make the sauce by whisking together the rest of the ingredients.
4. Pour the sauce over the warm sausages before serving.

351. PENNE CHICKEN SAUSAGE MEATBALLS

Prep & Cook Time: 20 minutes | Servings: 4

INGREDIENTS

1 cup of chicken meat, ground
1 sweet red pepper, minced
¼ cup of green onions, chopped
1 green garlic, minced

4 tbsp. of breadcrumbs
½ tsp. of cumin powder
1 tbsp. of fresh coriander, minced
½ tsp. of sea salt

¼ tsp. of mixed peppercorns, ground
1 packet of penne pasta, cooked

INSTRUCTIONS

1. Pre-heat the Air Fryer at 350°F.
2. Put the chicken, red pepper, green onions, & garlic into a mixing bowl & stir together to combine.
3. Throw in the seasoned breadcrumbs & all of the seasonings. Combine again.
4. Use your hands to mold equal amounts of the mixture into small balls, each one roughly the size of a golf ball.
5. Put them in the Air Fryer & cook for 15 minutes. Shake once or twice throughout the cooking time for even results.
6. Serve with cooked penne pasta.

352. TARRAGON CHICKEN

Prep & Cook Time: 40 minutes | Servings: 4

INGREDIENTS

2 cups of roasted vegetable broth
2 chicken breasts, cut into halves
¾ tsp. of fine sea salt
¼ tsp. of mixed peppercorns, freshly cracked

1 tsp. of cumin powder
1 ½ tsp. of sesame oil
1 ½ tbsp. of Worcester sauce
½ cup of spring onions, chopped
1 Serrano pepper, deveined & chopped

1 bell pepper, deveined & chopped
1 tbsp. of tamari sauce
½ chopped fresh tarragon

INSTRUCTIONS

1. Cook the vegetable broth & chicken breasts in a large saucepan for 10 minutes.
2. Lower the heat & simmer for another 10 minutes.
3. Let the chicken cool briefly. Then tear the chicken into shreds with a stand mixer or two forks.
4. Coat the shredded chicken with the salt, cracked peppercorns, cumin, sesame oil & the Worcester sauce.
5. Transfer to the Air Fryer & air fry at 380°F for 18 minutes, or longer as needed.
6. In the meantime, cook the remaining ingredients over medium heat in a skillet, until the vegetables are tender & fragrant.
7. Take the skillet off the heat. Stir in the shredded chicken, incorporating all the ingredients well.
8. Serve immediately.

353. PIZZA STUFFED CHICKEN

Prep & Cook Time: 20 minutes | Servings: 4

INGREDIENTS

4 small boneless, skinless chicken breasts
¼ cup of pizza sauce

½ cup of Colby cheese, shredded
16 slices of pepperoni
Salt & pepper, to taste

1 ½ tbsp. of olive oil
1 ½ tbsp. of dried oregano

INSTRUCTIONS

1. Pre-heat your Air Fryer at 370°F.
2. Flatten the chicken breasts with a rolling pin.
3. Top the chicken with equal amounts of each ingredients & roll the fillets around the stuffing. Secure with a small skewer or two toothpicks.
4. Roast in the Air Fryer on the grill pan for 13 - 15 minutes.

354. SPECIAL MAPLE-GLAZED CHICKEN

Prep & Cook Time: 20 minutes | Servings: 4

INGREDIENTS

2 ½ tbsp. of maple syrup
1 tbsp. of tamari soy sauce
1 tbsp. of oyster sauce

1 tsp. of fresh lemon juice
1 tsp. of minced fresh ginger
1 tsp. of garlic puree

Seasoned salt & freshly ground pepper, to taste
2 boneless, skinless chicken breasts

INSTRUCTIONS

1. In a bowl, combine the maple syrup, tamari sauce, oyster sauce, lemon juice, fresh ginger & garlic puree. This is your marinade.
2. Sprinkle the chicken breasts with salt & pepper.
3. Coat the chicken breasts with the marinade. Place some foil over the bowl & refrigerate for 3 hours, or overnight if possible.
4. Remove the chicken from the marinade. Place it in the Air Fryer & fry for 15 minutes at 365°F, flipping each one once or twice throughout.
5. In the meantime, add the remaining marinade to a pan over medium heat. Allow the marinade to simmer for 3 - 5 minutes until it has reduced by half.
6. Pour over the cooked chicken & serve.

355. TURKEY QUINOA SKEWERS

Prep & Cook Time: 15 minutes | Servings: 8

INGREDIENTS

1 cup of red quinoa, cooked
1 ½ cups of water
14 oz. of ground turkey
2 small eggs, beaten

1 tsp. of ground ginger
2 ½ tbsp. of vegetable oil
1 cup of chopped fresh parsley
2 tbsp. of seasoned breadcrumbs

¾ tsp. of salt
1 heaped tsp. of fresh rosemary, finely chopped
½ tsp. of ground allspice

INSTRUCTIONS

1. In a bowl, combine all of the ingredients together using your hands, kneading the mixture well.
2. Mold equal amounts of the mixture into small balls.
3. Pre-heat your Air Fryer to 380°F.
4. Place the balls in the Air Fryer basket & fry for 8 - 10 minutes.
5. Skewer them & serve with the dipping sauce of your choice.

356. POTATO CAKES & CAJUN CHICKEN WINGS

Prep & Cook Time: 40 minutes | Servings: 4

INGREDIENTS

4 large-sized chicken wings
1 tsp. of Cajun seasoning
1 tsp. of maple syrup
¾ tsp. of sea salt flakes
¼ tsp. of red pepper flakes, crushed
1 tsp. of onion powder
1 tsp. porcini powder

½ tsp. celery seeds
1 small-seized head of cabbage, shredded
1 cup of mashed potatoes
1 small-sized brown onion, coarsely grated
1 tsp. of garlic puree

1 medium whole egg, well whisked
½ tsp. of salt
½ tsp. of ground black pepper
1 ½ tbsp. of flour
¾ tsp. of baking powder
1 tbsp. of cilantro
1 tbsp. of sesame oil

INSTRUCTIONS

1. Pre-heat your Air Fryer to 390°F.
2. Pat the chicken wings dry. Place them in the Air Fryer & cook for 25 - 30 minutes, ensuring they are cooked through.
3. Make the rub by combining the Cajun seasoning, maple syrup, sea salt flakes, red pepper, onion powder, porcini powder, & celery seeds.
4. Mix together the shredded cabbage, potato, onion, garlic puree, egg, table salt, black pepper, flour, baking powder & cilantro.
5. Separate the cabbage mixture into 4 portions & use your hands to mold each one into a cabbage-potato cake.
6. Douse each cake with the sesame oil.
7. Bake the cabbage-potato cakes in the Air Fryer for 10 minutes, turning them once through the cooking time. You will need to do this in multiple batches.
8. Serve the cakes & the chicken wings together.

357. PROVENÇAL CHICKEN

Prep & Cook Time: 25 minutes | Servings: 4

INGREDIENTS

4 medium-sized skin-on chicken drumsticks
1 ½ tsp. of herbs de Provence
Salt & pepper

1 tbsp. of rice vinegar
2 tbsp. of olive oil
2 garlic cloves, crushed
12 oz. of crushed canned tomatoes

1 small-size leek, thinly sliced
2 slices smoked bacon, chopped

INSTRUCTIONS

1. Season the chicken drumsticks with herbs de Provence, salt & pepper. Pour over a light drizzling of the rice vinegar & olive oil.
2. Cook in the baking pan at 360°F for 8 - 10 minutes.
3. Pause the Air Fryer. Add in the rest of the ingredients, give them a stir, & resume cooking for 15 more minutes, checking them occasionally to ensure they don't overcook.
4. Serve with rice & lemon wedges.

358. GOURMET CHICKEN OMELET

Prep & Cook Time: 15 minutes | Servings: 2

INGREDIENTS

4 eggs, whisked
4 oz. of ground chicken
½ cup of scallions, finely chopped

2 cloves garlic, finely minced
½ tsp. of salt
½ tsp. of ground black pepper

½ tsp. of paprika
1 tsp. of dried thyme
Dash of hot sauce

INSTRUCTIONS

1. Mix together all the ingredients in a bowl, ensuring to incorporate everything well.
2. Lightly grease two oven-safe ramekins with vegetable oil. Divide the mixture between them.
3. Transfer them to the Air Fryer, & air fry at 350°F for 13 minutes.
4. Ensure they are cooked through & serve immediately.

359. PEPPERY TURKEY SANDWICHES

Prep & Cook Time: 25 minutes | Servings: 4

INGREDIENTS

1 cup of leftover turkey, cut into chunks
2 bell peppers, deveined & chopped
1 Serrano pepper, deveined & chopped
1 leek, sliced

½ cup of sour cream
1 tsp. of hot paprika
¾ tsp. of salt
½ tsp. of ground black pepper

1 tbsp. of fresh cilantro, chopped
Dash of Tabasco sauce
4 hamburger buns

INSTRUCTIONS

1. Combine all of the ingredients except for the hamburger buns, ensuring to coat the turkey well.
2. Place in an Air Fryer baking pan & roast for 20 minutes at 385°F.
3. Top the hamburger buns with the turkey & serve with mustard or sour cream as desired.

360. CHICKEN WINGS & PIRI PIRI SAUCE

Prep & Cook Time: 1 hr. 30 minutes | Servings: 6

INGREDIENTS

12 chicken wings
1 ½ oz. of butter, melted
1 tsp. of onion powder
½ tsp. of cumin powder
1 tsp. of garlic paste

For the Sauce:
2 oz. of piri piri peppers, chopped
1 tbsp. of pimiento, deveined & minced
1 garlic clove, chopped
2 tbsp. of fresh lemon juice

⅓ tsp. of sea salt
½ tsp. of tarragon
¾ tsp. of sugar

INSTRUCTIONS

1. Place the chicken wings in a steamer basket over a saucepan of boiling water. Lower the temperature & steam the chicken for 10 minutes over a medium heat.
2. Coat the wings with the butter, onion powder, cumin powder, & garlic paste.
3. Allow the chicken wings to cool slightly. Place them in the refrigerator for 45 - 50 minutes.
4. Pre-heat your Air Fryer at 330°F.
5. Roast the chicken wings in the Air Fryer for 25 - 30 minutes, turning them once halfway through the cooking time.
6. In the meantime, make the Piri Piri sauce. Blend together all of the sauce ingredients in a food processor.
7. Coat the chicken wings in the sauce before serving.

361. MARROD'S MEATBALLS

Prep & Cook Time: 15 minutes | Servings: 6

INGREDIENTS

1 lb. of ground turkey
1 tbsp. of fresh mint leaves, chopped
1 tsp. of onion powder

1 ½ tsp.of garlic paste
1 tsp. of crushed red pepper flakes
¼ cup of melted butter

¾ tsp. of fine sea salt
¼ cup of grated Pecorino Romano

INSTRUCTIONS
1. In a bowl, combine all of the ingredients well. Using an ice cream scoop, mold the meat into balls.
2. Air fry the meatballs at 380°F for about 7 minutes, in batches if necessary. Shake the basket frequently throughout the cooking time for even results.
3. Serve with basil leaves & tomato sauce if desired.

362. TURMERIC & MUSTARD CHICKEN THIGHS

Prep & Cook Time: 20 minutes | Servings: 6

INGREDIENTS
1 large egg, well whisked
2 tbsp. of whole-grain Dijon mustard
¼ cup of mayonnaise
¼ cup of chili sauce

½ tsp. of sugar
1 tsp. of fine sea salt
½ tsp. of ground black pepper, or more to taste

½ tsp. of turmeric powder
10 chicken thighs
2 cups of crushed saltines

INSTRUCTIONS
1. In a large bowl, combine the egg, mustard, mayonnaise, chili sauce, sugar, salt, pepper, & turmeric, incorporating everything well.
2. Coat the chicken thighs with the mixture. Place a layer of aluminum foil over the bowl, transfer it to the refrigerator & allow the chicken to marinate for at least 5 hours or overnight.
3. Pre-heat the Air Fryer to 360°F.
4. Separate the chicken from the marinade.
5. Put the crushed saltines into a shallow dish & use them to coat the chicken.
6. Place the chicken in the Air Fryer & cook for 15 minutes, ensuring the thighs are cooked through.
7. Serve with the rest of the marinade as a sauce.

363. ROASTED TURKEY THIGHS

Prep & Cook Time: 1 hr. 15 minute | Servings: 4

INGREDIENTS
1 red onion, cut into wedges
1 carrot, trimmed & sliced
1 celery stalk, trimmed & sliced
1 cup of Brussels sprouts, halved
1 cup of roasted vegetable broth

1 tbsp. of apple cider vinegar
1 tsp. of maple syrup
2 turkey thighs
½ tsp. of mixed peppercorns
1 tsp. of fine sea salt

1 tsp. of cayenne pepper
1 tsp. of onion powder
½ tsp. of garlic powder
⅓ tsp. of mustard seeds

INSTRUCTIONS
1. Put the vegetables into a baking dish small enough to fit inside your Air Fryer & add in the roasted vegetable broth.
2. In a large bowl, pour in the rest of the ingredients, & set aside for 30 minutes.
3. Place them on the top of the vegetables.
4. Roast at 330°F for 40 - 45 minutes.

364. VEGETABLES & ITALIAN TURKEY SAUSAGE

Prep & Cook Time: 40 minutes | Servings: 4

INGREDIENTS
1 onion, cut into wedges
2 carrots, trimmed & sliced
1 parsnip, trimmed & sliced
2 potatoes, peeled & diced

1 tsp. of dried thyme
½ tsp. of dried marjoram
1 tsp. of dried basil
½ tsp. of celery seeds

Sea salt & ground black pepper to taste
1 tbsp. of melted butter
¾ lb. of sweet Italian turkey sausage

INSTRUCTIONS
1. Cover the vegetables with all of the seasonings & the melted butter.
2. Place the vegetables in the Air Fryer basket.
3. Add the sausage on top.
4. Roast at 360°F for 33 - 37 minutes, ensuring the sausages are no longer pink, giving the basket a good shake halfway through the cooking time. You may need to cook everything in batches.

365. RICOTTA WRAPS & SPRING CHICKEN

Prep & Cook Time: 20 minutes | Servings: 12

INGREDIENTS
2 large-sized chicken breasts, cooked & shredded
⅓ tsp. of sea salt
¼ tsp. of ground black pepper, or more to taste

2 spring onions, chopped
¼ cup of soy sauce
1 tbsp. of molasses
1 tbsp. of rice vinegar
10 oz. of Ricotta cheese

1 tsp. of grated fresh ginger
50 wonton wrappers

INSTRUCTIONS

1. In a bowl, combine all of the ingredients, minus the wonton wrappers.
2. Unroll the wrappers & spritz with cooking spray.
3. Fill each of the wonton wrappers with equal amounts of the mixture.
4. Dampen the edges with a little water as an adhesive & roll up the wrappers, fully enclosing the filling.
5. Cook the rolls in the Air Fryer for 5 minutes at 375°F. You will need to do this step in batches.
6. Serve with your preferred sauce.

366. CAJUN-MUSTARD TURKEY FINGERS

Prep & Cook Time: 20 minutes | Servings: 4

INGREDIENTS

½ cup of cornmeal mix
½ cup of flour
1 ½ tbsp. of Cajun seasoning
1 ½ tbsp. of whole-grain mustard

1 ½ cups of buttermilk
1 tsp. of soy sauce
¾ lb. of turkey tenderloins, cut into finger-sized strips

Salt & ground black pepper to taste

INSTRUCTIONS

1. In a bowl, combine the cornmeal, flour, & Cajun seasoning.
2. In a separate bowl, combine the whole-grain mustard, buttermilk & soy sauce.
3. Sprinkle some salt & pepper on the turkey fingers.
4. Dredge each finger in the buttermilk mixture, before coating them completely with the cornmeal mixture.
5. Place the prepared turkey fingers in the Air Fryer baking pan & cook for 15 minutes at 360°F.
6. Serve immediately, with ketchup if desired.

367. HONEY GLAZED TURKEY BREAST

Prep & Cook Time: 55 minutes | Servings: 6

INGREDIENTS

2 tsp. of butter, softened
1 tsp. of dried sage
2 sprigs rosemary, chopped
1 tsp. of salt

¼ tsp. of freshly ground black pepper, or more if desired
1 whole turkey breast
2 tbsp. of turkey broth

¼ cup of honey
2 tbsp. of whole-grain mustard
1 tbsp. of butter

INSTRUCTIONS

1. Pre-heat your Air Fryer to 360°F.
2. Mix together the 2 tbsp. of butter, sage, rosemary, salt, & pepper.
3. Rub the turkey breast with this mixture.
4. Place the turkey in your Air Fryer's cooking basket & roast for 20 minutes. Turn the turkey breast over & allow to cook for another 15 - 16 minutes.
5. Finally turn it once more & roast for another 12 minutes.
6. In the meantime, mix together the remaining ingredients in a saucepan using a whisk.
7. Coat the turkey breast with the glaze.
8. Place the turkey back in the Air Fryer & cook for an additional 5 minutes. Remove it from the Air Fryer, let it rest, & carve before serving.

368. CHICKEN CURRY

Prep & Cook Time: 60 minutes | Servings: 2

INGREDIENTS

2 chicken thighs
1 small zucchini
2 cloves garlic
6 dried apricots
1 tsp. of curry powder

3 ½ oz. of long turnip
6 basil leaves
1 tbsp. of whole pistachios
1 tbsp. of raisin soup

1 tbsp. of olive oil
Salt
Pepper

INSTRUCTIONS

1. Pre-heat Air Fryer at 320°F.
2. Cut the chicken into 2 thin slices & chop up the vegetables into bite-sized pieces.
3. In a dish, combine all of the ingredients, incorporating everything well.
4. Place in the Air Fryer & cook for a minimum of 30 minutes.
5. Serve with rice if desired.

369. MARJORAM CHICKEN

Prep & Cook Time: 1 hr. | Servings: 2

INGREDIENTS

2 skinless, small chicken breasts
2 tbsp. of butter

1 tsp. of sea salt
½ tsp. of red pepper flakes, crushed

2 tsp. of marjoram
¼ tsp. of lemon pepper

INSTRUCTIONS

1. In a bowl, coat the chicken breasts with all of the other ingredients. Set aside to marinate for 30 – 60 minutes.
2. Pre-heat your Air Fryer to 390°F.
3. Cook for 20 minutes, turning halfway through cooking time.
4. Check for doneness using an instant-read thermometer. Serve over jasmine rice.

370. HOISIN GLAZED TURKEY DRUMSTICKS

Prep & Cook Time: 40 minutes + marinating time | Servings: 4

INGREDIENTS

2 turkey drumsticks
2 tbsp. of balsamic vinegar
2 tbsp. of dry white wine
1 tbsp. of extra-virgin olive oil
1 sprig of rosemary, chopped

Salt & ground black pepper, to taste
2 ½ tbsp. of butter, melted

For the Hoisin Glaze:
2 tbsp. of hoisin sauce
1 tbsp. of honey
1 tbsp. of honey mustard

INSTRUCTIONS

1. In a bowl, coat the turkey drumsticks with the vinegar, wine, olive oil, & rosemary. Allow to marinate for 3 hours.
2. Pre-heat the Air Fryer to 350°F.
3. Sprinkle the turkey drumsticks with salt & black pepper. Cover the surface of each drumstick with the butter.
4. Place the turkey in the Air Fryer & cook at 350°F for 30 - 35 minutes, flipping it occasionally through the cooking time. You may have to do this in batches.
5. In the meantime, make the Hoisin glaze by combining all the glaze ingredients.
6. Pour the glaze over the turkey, & roast for another 5 minutes.
7. Allow the drumsticks to rest for about 10 minutes before carving.

371. TURKEY SLIDERS & CHIVE MAYONNAISE

Prep & Cook Time: 20 minutes | Servings: 6

INGREDIENTS

For the Turkey Sliders:
¾ lb. of turkey mince
¼ cup of pickled jalapeno, chopped
1 tbsp. of oyster sauce
1 – 2 cloves garlic, minced

1 tbsp. of chopped fresh cilantro
2 tbsp. of chopped scallions
Sea salt & ground black pepper to taste

For the Chive Mayo:
1 cup of mayonnaise
1 tbsp. of chives
1 tsp. of salt
Zest of 1 lime

INSTRUCTIONS:

1. In a bowl, combine together all of the ingredients for the turkey sliders. Use your hands to shape 6 equal amounts of the mixture into slider patties.
2. Transfer the patties to the Air Fryer & fry them at 365°F for 15 minutes.
3. In the meantime, prepare the Chive Mayo by combining the rest of the ingredients.
4. Make sandwiches by placing each patty between two burger buns & serve with the mayo.

372. THAI TURKEY WINGS

Prep & Cook Time: 40 minutes | Servings: 4

INGREDIENTS

¾ lb. of turkey wings, cut into pieces
1 tsp. of ginger powder
1 tsp. of garlic powder
¾ tsp. of paprika
2 tbsp. of soy sauce

1 handful of minced lemongrass
Sea salt flakes & ground black pepper to taste
2 tbsp. of rice wine vinegar
¼ cup of peanut butter

1 tbsp. of sesame oil
½ cup of Thai sweet chili sauce

INSTRUCTIONS

1. Boil the turkey wings in a saucepan full of water for 20 minutes.
2. Put the turkey wings in a large bowl & cover them with the remaining ingredients, minus the Thai sweet chili sauce.
3. Transfer to the Air Fryer & fry for 20 minutes at 350°F, turning once halfway through the cooking time. Ensure they are cooked through before serving with the Thai sweet chili sauce, as well as some lemon wedges if desired.

373. STUFFED TURKEY ROULADE

Prep & Cook Time: 50 minutes | Servings: 4

INGREDIENTS

1 turkey fillet
Salt & garlic pepper to taste
⅓ tsp. of onion powder
½ tsp. of dried basil

⅓ tsp. of ground red chipotle pepper
1 ½ tbsp. of mustard seeds
½ tsp. of fennel seeds
2 tbsp. of melted butter

3 tbsp. of coriander, finely chopped
½ cup of scallions, finely chopped
2 cloves of garlic, finely minced

INSTRUCTIONS

1. Flatten out the turkey fillets with a mallet, until they are about a half-inch thick.
2. Season each one with salt, garlic pepper, & onion powder.

3. In a small bowl, mix together the basil, chipotle pepper, mustard seeds, fennel seeds & butter.
4. Use a pallet knife to spread the mixture over the fillets, leaving the edges uncovered.
5. Add the coriander, scallions & garlic on top.
6. Roll up the fillets into a log & wrap a piece of twine around them to hold them in place.
7. Place them in the Air Fryer cooking basket.
8. Roast at 350°F for about 50 minutes, flipping it at the halfway point. Cook for longer if necessary. Serve warm.

374. MAC'S CHICKEN NUGGETS

Prep & Cook Time: 40 minutes | Servings: 4

INGREDIENTS

2 slices of breadcrumbs
9 oz. of chicken breast, chopped
1 tsp. of garlic, minced

1 tsp. of tomato ketchup
2 medium egg
1 tbsp. of olive oil

1 tsp. of paprika
1 tsp. of parsley
Salt & pepper

INSTRUCTIONS

1. Combine the breadcrumbs, paprika, salt, pepper & oil into a thick batter.
2. Coat the chopped chicken with the parsley, one egg & ketchup.
3. Shape the mixture into several nuggets & dredge each one in the other egg. Roll the nuggets into the breadcrumbs.
4. Cook at 390°F for 10 minutes in the Air Fryer.
5. Serve the nuggets with a side of mayo dip if desired.

375. COLBY'S TURKEY MEATLOAF

Prep & Cook Time: 50 minutes | Servings: 6

INGREDIENTS

1 lb. of turkey mince
½ cup scallions, finely chopped
2 garlic cloves, finely minced
1 tsp. of dried thyme
½ tsp. of dried basil

¾ cup of Colby cheese, shredded
¾ cup of crushed saltines
1 tbsp. of tamari sauce
Salt & black pepper, to taste
¼ cup of red pepper sauce

1 tsp. of sugar
¾ tbsp. of olive oil
1 medium egg, well beaten

INSTRUCTIONS

1. Over a medium heat, fry up the turkey mince, scallions, garlic, thyme, & basil until soft & fragrant.
2. Pre-heat the Air Fryer to 360°F.
3. Combine the mixture with the cheese, saltines & tamari sauce, before shaping it into a loaf.
4. Stir together the remaining items & top the meatloaf with them.
5. Place in the Air Fryer baking pan & allow to cook for 45 - 47 minutes.

376. CHICKEN DRUMSTICKS

Prep & Cook Time: 35 minutes | Servings: 4

INGREDIENTS

8 chicken drumsticks
1 tsp. of cayenne pepper
2 tbsp. of mustard powder
2 tbsp. of oregano

2 tbsp. of thyme
3 tbsp. of coconut milk
1 large egg, lightly beaten
⅓ cup of cauliflower

⅓ cup of oats
Salt & pepper

INSTRUCTIONS

1. Pre-heat the Air Fryer to 350°F.
2. Sprinkle salt & pepper over the chicken drumsticks & massage the coconut milk into them.
3. Put all the ingredients except the egg into the food processor & pulse to create a bread crumb-like mixture.
4. Transfer to a bowl.
5. In a separate bowl, put the beaten egg. Coat each chicken drumstick in the bread crumb mixture before dredging it in the egg. Roll it in the breadcrumbs once more.
6. Put the coated chicken drumsticks in Air Fryer basket & cook for 20 minutes. Serve hot.

377. BACON-WRAPPED CHICKEN

Prep & Cook Time: 20 minutes | Servings: 6

INGREDIENTS

1 chicken breast, cut into 6 pieces

6 rashers of back bacon

1 tbsp. of soft cheese

INSTRUCTIONS

1. Put the bacon rashers on a flat surface & cover one side with the soft cheese.
2. Lay the chicken pieces on each bacon rasher. Wrap the bacon around the chicken & use a toothpick stick to hold each one in place. Put them in Air Fryer basket.
3. Air fry at 350°F for 15 minutes. Serve!

378. FAMILY FARM'S CHICKEN WINGS

Prep & Cook Time: 20 minutes | Servings: 6

INGREDIENTS

6 chicken wings
1 tbsp. of honey

2 cloves garlic, chopped
1 tsp. of red chili flakes

2 tbsp. of Worcestershire sauce
Salt & pepper

INSTRUCTIONS

1. Place all the ingredients, except for the chicken wings, in a bowl & combine well.
2. Coat the chicken with the mixture & refrigerate for 1 hour.
3. Put the marinated chicken wings in the Air Fryer basket & spritz with cooking spray.
4. Air fry the chicken wings at 320°F for 8 minutes. Raise the temperature to 350°F & cook for an additional 4 minutes. Serve hot.

379. CHICKEN SURPRISE

Prep & Cook Time: 30 minutes | Servings: 2

INGREDIENTS

2 chicken breasts, boneless & skinless
2 large eggs
½ cup of skimmed milk
6 tbsp. of soy sauce

1 cup of flour
1 tsp. of smoked paprika
1 tsp. of salt
¼ tsp. of black pepper

½ tsp. of garlic powder
1 tbsp. of olive oil
4 hamburger buns

INSTRUCTIONS

1. Slice the chicken breast into 2 – 3 pieces.
2. Place in a large bowl & drizzle with the soy sauce. Sprinkle on the smoked paprika, black pepper, salt, & garlic powder & mix well.
3. Allow to marinate for 30 – 40 minutes.
4. In the meantime, combine the eggs with the milk in a bowl. Put the flour in a separate bowl.
5. Dip the marinated chicken into the egg mixture before coating it with the flour. Cover each piece of chicken evenly.
6. Pre-heat the Air Fryer to 380°F.
7. Drizzle on the olive oil & put chicken pieces in the Air Fryer.
8. Cook for 10 – 12 minutes. Flip the chicken once throughout the cooking process.
9. Toast the hamburger buns & put each slice of chicken between two buns to make a sandwich. Serve with ketchup or any other sauce of your choice.

380. LEMON & GARLIC CHICKEN

Prep & Cook Time: 25 minutes | Servings: 1

INGREDIENTS

1 chicken breast
1 tsp. of garlic, minced

1 tbsp. of chicken seasoning
1 lemon juice

Handful of black peppercorns
Salt & pepper

INSTRUCTIONS

1. Pre-heat the Air Fryer to 350°F.
2. Sprinkle the chicken with pepper & salt. Massage the chicken seasoning into the chicken breast, coating it well, & lay the seasoned chicken on a sheet of aluminum foil.
3. Top the chicken with the garlic, lemon juice, & black peppercorns. Wrap the foil to seal the chicken tightly.
4. Cook the chicken in the Air Fryer basket for 15 minutes.

381. CAJUN SEASONED CHICKEN

Prep & Cook Time: 15 minutes | Servings: 2

INGREDIENTS

2 boneless chicken breasts
3 tbsp. of Cajun spice

INSTRUCTIONS

1. Coat both sides of the chicken breasts with Cajun spice. Put the seasoned chicken in Air Fryer basket.
2. Air fry at 350°F for 10 minutes, ensuring they are cooked through before slicing up & serving.

382. CHICKEN FILLETS

Prep & Cook Time: 30 minutes | Servings: 3

INGREDIENTS

8 pieces of chicken fillets
1 egg
1 oz. of salted butter, melted

1 cup of breadcrumbs
1 tsp. of garlic powder
½ cup of parmesan cheese

1 tsp. of Italian herbs

INSTRUCTIONS

1. Cover the chicken pieces in the whisked egg, melted butter, garlic powder, & Italian herbs. Allow to marinate for about 10 minutes.
2. In a bowl, mix together the Panko breadcrumbs & parmesan. Use this mixture to coat the marinated chicken.
3. Put the aluminum foil in your Air Fryer basket.
4. Set the Air Fryer to 390°F & briefly allow to warm. Line the basket with aluminum foil.
5. Place 4 pieces of the chicken in the basket. Cook for 6 minutes until golden brown. Don't turn the chicken over.

6. Repeat with the rest of the chicken pieces.
7. Serve the chicken fillets hot.

383. CHICKEN NUGGETS

Prep & Cook Time: 30 minutes | Servings: 4

INGREDIENTS

½ lb. of chicken breast, cut into pieces
1 tsp. of parsley
1 tsp. of paprika

1 tbsp. of olive oil
2 eggs, beaten
1 tsp. of tomato ketchup

1 tsp. of garlic, minced
½ cup of breadcrumbs
Salt & pepper

INSTRUCTIONS

1. In a bowl, combine the breadcrumbs, olive oil, paprika, pepper, & salt.
2. Place the chicken, ketchup, one egg, garlic, & parsley in a food processor & pulse together.
3. Put the other egg in a bowl.
4. Shape equal amounts of the pureed chicken into nuggets. Dredge each one in the egg before coating it in breadcrumbs.
5. Put the coated chicken nuggets in the Air Fryer basket & cook at 390°F for 10 minutes.
6. Serve the nuggets hot.

384. CRACKED CHICKEN TENDERS

Prep & Cook Time: 30 minutes | Servings: 4

INGREDIENTS

2 lb. of skinless chicken tenders
3 large eggs
6 tbsp. of skimmed milk

½ cup of flour
1 cup of breadcrumbs
¼ tsp. of black pepper

1 tsp. of salt
2 tbsp. of olive oil

INSTRUCTIONS

1. In a large bowl, combine the breadcrumbs & olive oil.
2. In a separate bowl, stir together the eggs & milk using a whisk. Sprinkle in the salt & black pepper.
3. Put the flour in a third bowl.
4. Slice up the chicken tenders into 1-inch strips. Coat each piece of chicken in the flour, before dipping it into the egg mixture, followed by the breadcrumbs.
5. Pre-heat the Air Fryer to 380°F.
6. Cook the coated chicken tenders for about 13 – 15 minutes, shaking the basket a few times to ensure they turn crispy. Serve hot, with mashed potatoes & a dipping sauce if desired.

385. RANDY'S ROASTED CHICKEN

Prep & Cook Time: 55 minutes | Servings: 4

INGREDIENTS

5 – 7 lb. of whole chicken with skin
1 tsp. of garlic powder
1 tsp. of onion powder

½ tsp. of dried thyme
½ tsp. of dried basil
½ tsp. of dried rosemary

½ tsp. of black pepper
2 tsp. of salt
2 tbsp. of extra virgin olive oil

INSTRUCTIONS

1. Massage the salt, pepper, herbs, & olive oil into the chicken. Allow to marinade for a minimum of 20 – 30 minutes.
2. In the meantime, pre-heat the Air Fryer to 340 F.
3. Place the chicken in the Air Fryer & cook for 18 – 20 minutes.
4. Flip the chicken over & cook for an additional 20 minutes.
5. Leave the chicken to rest for about 10 minutes before carving & serving.

386. HERBED CHICKEN

Prep & Cook Time: 40 minutes | Servings: 6

INGREDIENTS

4 lb. of chicken wings
6 tbsp. of red wine vinegar
6 tbsp. lime juice
1 tsp. of fresh ginger, minced
1 tbsp. of sugar

1 tsp. of thyme, chopped
½ tsp. of white pepper
¼ tsp. of ground cinnamon
1 habanero pepper, chopped
6 garlic cloves, chopped

2 tbsp. of soy sauce
2 ½ tbsp. of olive oil
¼ tsp. of salt

INSTRUCTIONS

1. Place all of the ingredients in a bowl & combine well, ensuring to coat the chicken entirely.
2. Put the chicken in the refrigerator to marinate for 1 hour.
3. Pre-heat the Air Fryer to 390°F.
4. Put half of the marinated chicken in the Air Fryer basket & cook for 15 minutes, shaking the basket once throughout the cooking process.
5. Repeat with the other half of the chicken.
6. Serve hot.

387. ROSEMARY CHICKEN

Prep & Cook Time: 30 minutes | Servings: 2

INGREDIENTS

¾ lb. of chicken
½ tbsp. of olive oil
1 tbsp. of soy sauce

1 tsp. of fresh ginger, minced
1 tbsp. of oyster sauce
3 tbsp. of sugar

1 tbsp. of fresh rosemary, chopped
½ fresh lemon, cut into wedges

INSTRUCTIONS

1. In a bowl, combine the chicken, oil, soy sauce, & ginger, coating the chicken well.
2. Refrigerate for 30 minutes.
3. Pre-heat the Air Fryer to 390°F for 3 minutes.
4. Place the chicken in the baking pan, transfer to the Air Fryer & cook for 6 minutes.
5. In the meantime, put the rosemary, sugar, & oyster sauce in a bowl & mix together.
6. Add the rosemary mixture in the Air Fryer over the chicken & top the chicken with the lemon wedges.
7. Resume cooking for another 13 minutes, turning the chicken halfway through.

388. CHICKEN STRIPS

Prep & Cook Time: 25 minutes | Servings: 2

INGREDIENTS

1 chicken breast, cut into strips
1 egg, beaten
¼ cup of flour

¾ cup of breadcrumbs
1 tsp. of mix spice
1 tbsp. of plain oats

1 tbsp. of desiccated coconut
Salt & pepper

INSTRUCTIONS

1. In a bowl, mix together the breadcrumbs, mix spice, oats, coconut, pepper, & salt.
2. Put the beaten egg in a separate bowl. Pour the flour into a shallow dish.
3. Roll the chicken strips in the flour. Dredge each one in the egg & coat with the bread crumb mixture. Put the coated chicken strips in the Air Fryer basket & air fry at 350°F for 8 minutes.
4. Reduce the heat to 320°F & cook for another 4 minutes. Serve hot.

389. GRANDMA'S CHICKEN

Prep & Cook Time: 20 minutes | Servings: 4

INGREDIENTS

12 oz. of chicken breast, diced
6 oz. of general Tso sauce

½ tsp. of white pepper
¼ cup of milk

1 cup of cornstarch

INSTRUCTIONS

1. Place the chicken & milk in a bowl.
2. Separate the milk from the chicken & coat the chicken with cornstarch.
3. Put the chicken in the Air Fryer basket & air fry at 350°F for 12 minutes.
4. Plate up the chicken & season with the white pepper.
5. Pour the Tso sauce over the chicken before serving.

390. WORCESTERSHIRE CHICKEN WINGS

Prep & Cook Time: 40 minutes | Servings: 6

INGREDIENTS

6 chicken wings
1 ½ tbsp. of Worcestershire sauce
1 tbsp. of sugar
Juice & zest of 1 orange

½ tsp. of thyme, dried
½ tsp. of sage
1 tsp. of mint
1 tsp. of basil

½ tsp. of oregano
1 tsp. of parsley
1 tsp. of rosemary
Salt & pepper

INSTRUCTIONS

1. Combine all of the ingredients in a bowl, coating the chicken wings well with the other ingredients.
2. Refrigerate the marinated chicken for 30 minutes.
3. Pre-heat the Air Fryer to 350°F.
4. Wrap the marinated chicken in a sheet of aluminum foil, ensuring to seal with the juices. Put the wrapped chicken in Air Fryer basket & cook at 350°F for 20 minutes.
5. Unfold the foil, remove the orange zest & air fry the chicken wings at 350°F for a further 15 minutes. Serve hot.

391. LIME & HONEY CHICKEN WINGS

Prep & Cook Time: 7 hours | Servings: 2

INGREDIENTS

16 winglets
½ tsp. of sea salt
2 tbsp. of light soya sauce

¼ tsp. of white pepper powder
½ crush of black pepper
2 tbsp. of honey

2 tbsp. of lime juice

INSTRUCTIONS

1. Place all of the ingredients in a glass dish. Coat the winglets well & allow to marinate in the refrigerator for a minimum of 6 hours.
2. Allow to return to room temperature for 30 minutes.
3. Put the wings in the Air Fryer & air fry at 355°F for 6 minutes. Turn each wing over before cooking for another 6 minutes.
4. Allow the chicken to cool before serving with a wedge of lemon.

392. CHICKEN KEBABS

Prep & Cook Time: 30 minutes | Servings: 3

INGREDIENTS

1 lb. of chicken breasts, diced
5 tbsp. of honey
½ cup of soy sauce
6 large mushrooms, cut in halves

3 medium bell peppers, cut
1 small zucchini, cut into rings
2 medium tomatoes, cut into rings
Salt & pepper

¼ cup of sesame seeds
1 tbsp. of olive oil

INSTRUCTIONS

1. Cube the chicken breasts & place them in a large bowl.
2. Season with some salt & pepper. Drizzle over one tbsp. of olive oil & mix well.
3. Pour in the honey & soy sauce & add in the sesame seeds.
4. Leave to marinate for 15 – 30 minutes.
5. Slice up the vegetables.
6. Thread the chicken & vegetables on wooden skewers, in alternating patterns.
7. Pre-heat the Air Fryer to 340°F
8. Put the chicken kebabs into the Air Fryer basket.
9. Cook for about 15 minutes, flipping once during cooking. Serve once crispy & brown.

393. CHICKEN TENDERLOINS

Prep & Cook Time: 25 minutes | Servings: 4

INGREDIENTS

8 chicken tenderloins
1 egg, beaten

2 tbsp. of olive oil
1 cup of breadcrumbs

Salt & pepper

INSTRUCTIONS

1. Pre-heat the Air Fryer to 350°F.
2. Combine the breadcrumbs, olive oil, pepper, & salt in a shallow dish.
3. Put the beaten egg in separate dish.
4. Dip the chicken tenderloins into the egg before rolling them in the breadcrumbs.
5. Transfer to the Air Fryer basket. Air fry the chicken for 12 minutes.

394. BUFFALO WINGS

Prep & Cook Time: 35 min. + [2 - 12 hours marinate] | Servings: 4

INGREDIENTS

2 lb. of chicken wings, no wing tips
¼ cup + ¼ cup hot sauce, separately

3 + 3 tbsp. of melted butter, separately
Sea salt to taste

Blue cheese, optional
Celery sticks, optional

INSTRUCTIONS

1. Prepare the chicken wings by separating the drumettes from the wingettes & put them into a bowl.
2. In a separate bowl, thoroughly combine 3 tbsp. of melted butter & ¼ cup of hot sauce.
3. Use this mixture to coat the chicken & marinate for 2 hours or overnight if possible.
4. Briefly pre-heat the Air Fryer to 400°F.
5. Divide the chicken into 2 batches. Put the first batch in the Air Fryer & cook for about 12 minutes. Give the basket a good shake at the halfway point. Repeat with the second batch.
6. Combine the cooked batches & return them to the Air Fryer, cooking for an additional 2 minutes.
7. In the meantime, make the sauce by stirring together the remaining 3 tbsp. of butter & ¼ cup of hot sauce.
8. Coat the cooked wings in the sauce before serving with a side of celery sticks & blue cheese if desired.

395. MOROCCAN CHICKEN

Prep & Cook Time: 25 minutes | Servings: 2

INGREDIENTS

½ lb. of shredded chicken
1 cup broth
1 carrot

1 broccoli, chopped
Pinch of cinnamon
Pinch of cumin

Pinch of red pepper
Pinch of sea salt

INSTRUCTIONS

1. In a bowl, cover the shredded chicken with cumin, red pepper, sea salt & cinnamon.
2. Chop up the carrots into small pieces. Put the carrot & broccoli into the bowl with the chicken.
3. Add the broth & stir everything well. Set aside for about 30 minutes.
4. Transfer to the Air Fryer. Cook for about 15 minutes at 390°F. Serve hot.

396. CHINESE CHICKEN WINGS

Prep & Cook Time: 45 minutes | Servings: 4

INGREDIENTS

8 chicken wings
2 tbsp. of five spice

2 tbsp. of soy sauce
1 tbsp. of mixed spices

Salt & pepper

INSTRUCTIONS

1. In a bowl, mix together all of the ingredients.
2. Cover the base of the Air Fryer with an aluminum foil & pre-heat the Air Fryer to 360°F.
3. Add in some oil & pour in the mixture. Cook for 15 minutes.
4. Turn up the heat to 390°F, turn the chicken wings & cook for another 5 minutes. Serve with mayo dip if desired.

397. CHICKEN & POTATOES

Prep & Cook Time: 45 minutes | Servings: 6

INGREDIENTS

1 lb. of potatoes
2 lb. of chicken

2 tbsp. of olive oil
Salt & pepper

INSTRUCTIONS

1. Pre-heat the Air Fryer to 350°F.
2. Place the chicken in Air Fryer basket along with the potatoes. Sprinkle on the pepper & salt.
3. Add a drizzling of the olive oil, making sure to cover the chicken & potatoes well.
4. Cook for 40 minutes.

398. CHICKEN TENDERS

Prep & Cook Time: 30 minutes | Servings: 4

INGREDIENTS

1 lb. of chicken tenders
1 tsp. ginger, minced
4 garlic cloves, minced

2 tbsp. of sesame oil
6 tbsp. of pineapple juice
2 tbsp. of soy sauce

½ tsp. of pepper

INSTRUCTIONS

1. Put all of the ingredients, except for the chicken, in a bowl & combine well.
2. Thread the chicken onto skewers & coat with the seasonings. Allow to marinate for 2 hours.
3. Pre-heat the Air Fryer to 350°F.
4. Put the marinated chicken in Air Fryer basket & cook for 18 minutes. Serve hot.

399. LIME DIJON CHICKEN

Prep & Cook Time: 20 minutes | Servings: 6

INGREDIENTS

8 chicken drumsticks
1 lime juice
1 lime zest

Kosher salt to taste
1 tbsp. of light mayonnaise
¾ tsp. of black pepper

1 clove garlic, crushed
3 tbsp. of Dijon mustard
1 tsp. of dried parsley

INSTRUCTIONS

1. Pre-heat the Air Fryer to 375°F.
2. Remove the chicken skin & sprinkle the chicken with the salt.
3. In a bowl, mix the Dijon mustard with the lime juice, before stirring in the lime zest, pepper, parsley & garlic.
4. Cover the chicken with the lime mixture. Allow it to marinate for roughly 10 - 15 minutes.
5. Drizzle some oil in the bottom of your Air Fryer. Transfer the chicken drumsticks inside & cook for 5 minutes.
6. Give the basket a shake & fry for an additional 5 minutes.
7. Serve immediately, with a side of mayo.

400. FRIED CHICKEN THIGHS

Prep & Cook Time: 35 minutes | Servings: 4

INGREDIENTS

4 chicken thighs
1 ½ tbsp. Cajun seasoning

1 egg, beaten
½ cup of flour

1 tsp. of seasoning salt

INSTRUCTIONS

1. Pre-heat the Air Fryer to 350°F.
2. In a bowl combine the flour, Cajun seasoning, & seasoning salt.
3. Place the beaten egg in another bowl.
4. Coat the chicken with the flour before dredging it in the egg. Roll once more in the flour.
5. Put the chicken in the Air Fryer & cook for 25 minutes. Serve hot.

401. FRIED WINGS

Prep & Cook Time: 35 minutes | Servings: 6

INGREDIENTS

4 Lb. of chicken wings
1 tbsp. of sugar
1 tbsp. of Worcestershire sauce

½ cup of butter, melted
½ cup of hot sauce
½ tsp. of salt

INSTRUCTIONS

1. In a bowl, combine the sugar, Worcestershire sauce, butter, salt, & hot sauce.
2. Place the chicken wings in the Air Fryer basket & air fry at 380°F for 25 minutes, giving the basket a good shake halfway through the cooking time.
3. Raise the temperature to 400°F & continue to cook for another 5 minutes.
4. Place the air fried chicken wings in the bowl with the sugar mixture & toss to coat. Serve right away.

402. TERIYAKI CHICKEN

Prep & Cook Time: 30 minutes | Servings: 2

INGREDIENTS

2 boneless chicken drumsticks
1 tsp. of ginger, grated

1 tbsp. of cooking wine
3 tbsp. of teriyaki sauce

INSTRUCTIONS

1. Combine all of the ingredients in a bowl. Refrigerate for half an hour.
2. Place the chicken in the Air Fryer baking pan & fry at 350°F for 8 minutes. Turn the chicken over & raise the temperature to 380°F. Allow to cook for another 6 minutes. Serve hot.

403. ASIAN STYLE CHICKEN

Prep & Cook Time: 25 minutes | Servings: 3

INGREDIENTS

1 lb. of skinless & chicken breasts
3 garlic cloves, minced
1 tbsp. of grated ginger

¼ tsp. of ground black pepper
½ cup of soy sauce
½ cup of pineapple juice

1 tbsp. of olive oil
2 tbsp. of sesame seeds

INSTRUCTIONS

1. Mix together all of the ingredients except for the chicken in a large bowl.
2. Slice up the chicken breasts & coat in the mixture. Allow to marinade for at least 30 – 40 minutes.
3. Transfer the marinated chicken to the Air Fryer & cook at 380°F for about 10 – 15 minutes.
4. Top with sesame seeds before serving.

404. WHOLE CHICKEN

Prep & Cook Time: 30 minutes | Servings: 2

INGREDIENTS

1 whole chicken
1 lemon, juiced

1 tsp. of lemon zest
1 tbsp. of soy sauce

1 ½ tbsp. of honey

INSTRUCTIONS

1. Place all of the ingredients in a bowl & combine well. Refrigerate for 1 hour.
2. Put the marinated chicken in the Air Fryer baking pan. Air fry at 320°F for 18 minutes.
3. Raise the heat to 350°F & cook for another 10 minutes or until chicken has turned light brown.

405. HONEY & GARLIC CHICKEN WINGS

Prep & Cook Time: 25 minutes | Servings: 4

INGREDIENTS

16 chicken wings
½ tsp. of salt

¾ cup of potato starch
¼ cup of butter, melted

4 cloves garlic, minced
¼ cup of honey

INSTRUCTIONS

1. Pre-heat your Air Fryer to 370°F.
2. Put the chicken wings in a bowl & cover them well with the potato starch.
3. Spritz a baking dish with cooking spray.
4. Transfer the wings to the dish, place inside the Air Fryer & cook for 5 minutes.
5. In the meantime, mix together the rest of the ingredients with a whisk.
6. Top the chicken with this mixture & allow to cook for another 10 minutes before serving.

406. BUFFALO CHICKEN WINGS

INGREDIENTS

2 lb. of chicken wings
1 tsp. of salt

¼ tsp. of black pepper
1 cup buffalo sauce

INSTRUCTIONS

1. Wash the chicken wings & pat them dry with clean kitchen towels.
2. Place the chicken wings in a large bowl & sprinkle on salt & pepper.
3. Pre-heat the Air Fryer to 380°F.
4. Place the wings in the Air Fryer & cook for 15 minutes, giving them an occasional stir throughout.
5. Place the wings in a bowl. Pour over the buffalo sauce & toss well to coat.
6. Put the chicken back in the Air Fryer & cook for a final 5 – 6 minutes.

407. CHICKEN MEATBALLS

Prep & Cook Time: 20 minutes | Servings: 10

INGREDIENTS

2 chicken breasts
1 tbsp. of mustard powder
1 tbsp. of cumin
1 tbsp. of basil

1 tbsp. of thyme
1 tsp. of chili powder
3 tbsp. of soy sauce
2 tbsp. of honey

1 onion, diced
Salt & pepper

INSTRUCTIONS

1. Blend the chicken in your food processor to make a mince. Place the rest of the ingredients in the processor & pulse to combine well.
2. Shape the mixture into several small meatballs & place each one in the basket of the Air Fryer.
3. Air fry at 350°F for 15 minutes. Serve hot.

408. CHICKEN LEGS

Prep & Cook Time: 35 minutes | Servings: 4

INGREDIENTS

3 chicken legs, bone-in, with ski
3 chicken thighs, bone-in, with skin
2 cups of flour
1 cup of buttermilk

1 tsp. of salt
1 tsp. of ground black pepper
1 tsp. of garlic powder
1 tsp. of onion powder

1 tsp. of ground cumin
2 tbsp. of extra virgin olive oil

INSTRUCTIONS

1. Wash the chicken, dry it, & place it in a large bowl.
2. Pour the buttermilk over the chicken & refrigerate for 2 hours.
3. In a separate bowl, combine the flour with all of the seasonings.
4. Dip the chicken into the flour mixture. Dredge it the buttermilk before rolling it in the flour again.
5. Pre-heat the Air Fryer to 360°F
6. Put the chicken legs & thighs in the Air Fryer basket. Drizzle on the olive oil & cook for roughly 20 minutes, flipping each piece of chicken a few times throughout the cooking time, until cooked through & crisped up.

409. BEASTLY BBQ DRUMSTICKS

Prep & Cook Time: 45 minutes | Servings: 4

INGREDIENTS

4 chicken drumsticks
½ tbsp. of mustard
1 clove garlic, crushed

1 tsp. of chili powder
2 tsp. of sugar
1 tbsp. of olive oil

Freshly ground black pepper

INSTRUCTIONS

1. Pre-heat the Air Fryer to 390°F.
2. Mix together the garlic, sugar, mustard, a pinch of salt, freshly ground pepper, chili powder & oil.
3. Massage this mixture into the drumsticks & leave to marinate for a minimum of 20 minutes.
4. Put the drumsticks in the Air Fryer basket & cook for 10 minutes.
5. Bring the temperature down to 300°F & continue to cook the drumsticks for a further10 minutes. When cooked through, serve with bread & corn salad.

410. TURKEY LOAF

Prep & Cook Time: 50 minutes | Servings: 4

INGREDIENTS

⅔ cup of finely chopped walnuts
1 egg
1 tbsp. of organic tomato paste
1 ½ lb. of turkey breast, diced
1 tbsp. of Dijon mustard

½ tsp. of dried savory or dill
1 tbsp. of onion flakes
½ tsp. of ground allspice
1 small garlic clove, minced
½ tsp. of sea salt

¼ tsp. of black pepper
1 tbsp. of soy sauce
2 tbsp. of grated parmesan cheese

INSTRUCTIONS

1. Pre-heat Air Fryer to 375°F.
2. Coat the inside of a baking dish with a little oil.
3. Mix together the egg, dill, tomato paste, soy sauce, mustard, salt, dill, garlic, pepper & allspice using a whisk. Stir in the diced turkey, followed by the walnuts, cheese & onion flakes.
4. Transfer the mixture to the greased baking dish & bake in the Air Fryer for 40 minutes.
5. Serve hot.

411. CHARCOAL CHICKEN

Prep & Cook Time: 20 minutes | Servings: 2

INGREDIENTS

2 medium skinless, boneless chicken breasts

½ tsp. of salt
3 tbsp. of Cajun spice

1 tbsp. of olive oil

INSTRUCTIONS

1. Massage the salt & Cajun spice into the chicken breasts. Drizzle with olive oil.
2. Pre-heat the Air Fryer to 370°F.
3. Place the chicken in the Air Fryer & cook for 7 minutes.
4. Flip both chicken breasts over & cook for an additional 3 – 4 minutes.
5. Slice up before serving.

412. BATTERED CHICKEN THIGHS

Prep & Cook Time: 4 hours 45 minutes | Servings: 4

INGREDIENTS

2 cups of buttermilk
3 tsp. of salt
1 tsp. of cayenne pepper

1 tbsp. of paprika
1 ½ lb. of chicken thighs
2 tsp. of black pepper

2 cups of flour
1 tbsp. of garlic powder
1 tbsp. of baking powder

INSTRUCTIONS

1. Put the chicken thighs in a large bowl.
2. In a separate bowl, combine the buttermilk, salt, cayenne, & black pepper.
3. Coat the thighs with the buttermilk mixture. Place a sheet of aluminum foil over the bowl & set in the refrigerator for 4 hours.
4. Pre-heat your Air Fryer to 400°F.
5. Combine together the flour, baking powder, & paprika in a shallow bowl. Cover a baking dish with a layer of parchment paper.
6. Coat the chicken thighs in the flour mixture & bake in the Air Fryer for 10 minutes. Turn the thighs over & air fry for another 8 minutes. You will have to do this in two batches.

413. CHICKEN BITES

Prep & Cook Time: 30 minutes | Servings: 4

INGREDIENTS

1 lb. of skinless, boneless chicken breasts
¼ cup of blue cheese salad dressing
¼ cup of blue cheese, crumbled

½ cup of sour cream
1 cup of breadcrumbs
1 tbsp. of olive oil

½ tsp. of salt
¼ tsp. of black pepper

INSTRUCTIONS

1. In a large bowl, combine the salad dressing, sour cream, & blue cheese.
2. In a separate bowl, combine the breadcrumbs, olive oil, salt & pepper.
3. Chop the chicken breast into 1 - 2-inch pieces & coat in the breadcrumbs.
4. Pre-heat the Air Fryer to 380°F.
5. Place the chicken bites in your Air Fryer's basket.
6. Cook for 12 – 15 minutes. When cooked through & crispy, serve with the sauce of your choice.

414. COCONUT CHICKEN

Prep & Cook Time: 45 minutes | Servings: 2 – 4

INGREDIENTS

3 pcs of whole chicken leg [skinless or with skin, it's up to you]
1.8 oz. pure coconut paste [alternatively,

1.8 oz. of coconut milk]
4 – 5 tsp. of ground turmeric
1.8 oz. of old ginger

1.8 oz. of galangal [a.k.a. lengkuas]
¾ tbsp. of salt

INSTRUCTIONS

1. Mix together all of the ingredients, except for the chicken.
2. Slice a few slits into the chicken leg, mainly around the thick parts. This will help the chicken absorb the marinade.
3. Coat the chicken in the mixture & set aside to absorb.
4. Pre-heat the Air Fryer at 375°F.
5. Air fry the chicken for 20 – 25 minutes, turning it once halfway through, until golden brown.

415. SIMPLE TURKEY BREASTS

Prep & Cook Time: 35 minutes | Servings: 5

INGREDIENTS

6 – 7 lb. of skinless, boneless turkey breast

2 tsp. of salt
1 tsp. of black pepper

½ tsp. of dried cumin
2 tbsp. of olive oil

INSTRUCTIONS

1. Massage all of the other ingredients into the turkey breast.
2. Pre-heat the Air Fryer to 340°F,
3. Cook the turkey breast for 15 minutes. Turn it over & cook for an additional 10 – 15 minutes, until cooked through & crispy.
4. Slice & serve the turkey with rice or fresh vegetables.

---

416. CHICKEN WRAPPED IN BACON

Prep & Cook Time: 25 minutes | Servings: 6

INGREDIENTS

6 rashers of unsmoked back bacon

1 small chicken breast

1 tbsp. of garlic soft cheese

INSTRUCTIONS

1. Cut the chicken breast into six bite-sized pieces.
2. Spread the soft cheese across one side of each slice of bacon.
3. Put the chicken on top of the cheese & wrap the bacon around it, holding it in place with a toothpick.
4. Transfer the wrapped chicken pieces to the Air Fryer & cook for 15 minutes at 350°F.

---

417. CHICKEN, RICE & VEGETABLES

Prep & Cook Time: 30 minutes | Servings: 4

INGREDIENTS

1 lb. of skinless, boneless chicken breasts
½ lb. of button mushrooms, sliced
1 medium onion, chopped

1 packet [10 oz.] of Alfredo sauce
2 cups of cooked rice
½ tsp. of dried thyme

1 tbsp. of olive oil
Salt & black pepper to taste

INSTRUCTIONS

1. Slice up the chicken breasts into 1-inch cubes.
2. In a large bowl, combine all of the ingredients. Sprinkle on salt & dried thyme & mix again.
3. Pre-heat the Air Fryer to 370°F & drizzle the basket with the olive oil.
4. Place the chicken & vegetables in the Air Fryer & cook for 10 – 12 minutes. Stir the contents now & again.
5. Pour in the Alfredo sauce & allow to cook for an additional 3 – 4 minutes.
6. Serve with rice if desired.

---

418. BREADCRUMB TURKEY BREASTS

Prep & Cook Time: 25 minutes | Servings: 6

INGREDIENTS

6 turkey breasts
1 stick butter, melted

1 tsp. of salt
2 cups of breadcrumbs

½ tsp. of cayenne pepper
½ tsp. of black pepper

INSTRUCTIONS

1. Put the breadcrumbs, half a tsp. of the salt, a quarter tsp. of the pepper, & the cayenne pepper in a large bowl. Combine well.
2. In a separate bowl, sprinkle the melted butter with the rest of the salt & pepper.
3. Coat the turkey breasts with the butter using a brush. Roll the turkey in the breadcrumbs & transfer to a lined baking dish. Place in the Air Fryer.
4. Air fry at 390°F for 15 minutes.

---

419. CHICKEN ESCALLOPS

Prep & Cook Time: 45 minutes | Servings: 4

INGREDIENTS

4 skinless chicken breasts
6 sage leaves
¼ cup of breadcrumbs

2 eggs, beaten
½ cup of flour
¼ cup of parmesan cheese

Cooking spray

INSTRUCTIONS

1. Cut the chicken breasts into thin slices.
2. In a bowl, combine the sage & parmesan. Add in the flour, beaten eggs, salt & pepper & mix well.
3. Cover the chicken in the mixture before rolling it in the breadcrumbs.
4. Grease the pan with the cooking spray.
5. Pre-heat your Air Fryer to 390°F & cook the chicken for 20 minutes, until it turns golden. Serve with rice.

---

420. TURKEY & MAPLE MUSTARD

Prep & Cook Time: 70 minutes | Servings: 6

INGREDIENTS

5 lb. of whole turkey breast
1 tbsp. of olive oil
1 tsp. of dried thyme
½ tsp. of smoked paprika

½ tsp. of dried sage
1 tsp. of sea salt
½ tsp. of black pepper
1 tbsp. of butter, melted

2 tbsp. of Dijon mustard
¼ cup of maple syrup

INSTRUCTIONS

1. Pre-heat the Air Fryer to 350°F.
2. Brush the turkey breast with the olive oil.
3. Mix together the thyme, paprika, sage, salt, & pepper. Coat the turkey breast all over with this mixture.
4. Put the turkey breast in the Air Fryer basket & allow to cook for 25 minutes.
5. Flip it over & cook on the other side for a further 12 minutes.
6. Turn it once again & cook for another 12 minutes.
7. Check the temperature with a meat thermometer & ensure it has reached 165°F before removing it from the Air Fryer.
8. In the meantime, combine the maple syrup, mustard, & melted butter in a saucepan over a medium heat. Stir continuously until a smooth consistency is achieved.
9. Pour the sauce over the cooked turkey in the Air Fryer.
10. Cook for a final 5 minutes, ensuring the turkey turns brown & crispy.
11. Allow the turkey to rest, under a layer of aluminum foil, before carving up & serving.

421. CHICKEN WINGS

Prep & Cook Time: 55 minutes | Servings: 4

INGREDIENTS

3 lb. of bone-in chicken wings
¾ cup of flour

1 tbsp. of old bay seasoning
4 tbsp. of butter

Couple fresh lemons

INSTRUCTIONS

1. In a bowl, combine the all-purpose flour & Old Bay seasoning.
2. Toss the chicken wings with the mixture to coat each one well.
3. Pre-heat the Air Fryer to 375°F.
4. Give the wings a shake to shed any excess flour & place each one in the Air Fryer. You may have to do this in multiple batches, so as to not overlap any.
5. Cook for 30 – 40 minutes, shaking the basket frequently, until the wings are cooked through & crispy.
6. In the meantime, melt the butter in a frying pan over a low heat. Squeeze one or two lemons & add the juice to the pan. Mix well.
7. Serve the wings topped with the sauce.

422. MOZ.ZARELLA TURKEY ROLLS

Prep & Cook Time: 20 minutes | Servings: 4

INGREDIENTS

4 slices of turkey breast
1 cup of sliced fresh mozzarella

1 tomato, sliced
½ cup of fresh basil

4 chive shoots

INSTRUCTIONS

1. Pre-heat your Air Fryer to 390°F.
2. Lay the slices of mozzarella, tomato & basil on top of each turkey slice.
3. Roll the turkey up, enclosing the filling well, & secure by tying a chive shoot around each one.
4. Put in the Air Fryer & cook for 10 minutes. Serve with a salad if desired.

423. SAGE & ONION TURKEY BALLS

Prep & Cook Time: 40 minutes | Servings: 2

INGREDIENTS

3.5 oz. of turkey mince
½ small onion, diced
1 medium egg

1 tsp. of sage
½ tsp. of garlic, pureed
3 tbsp. of breadcrumbs

Salt
Pepper

INSTRUCTIONS

1. Put all of the ingredients in a bowl & mix together well.
2. Take equal portions of the mixture & mold each one into a small ball. Transfer to the Air Fryer & cook for 15 minutes at 350°F.
3. Serve with tartar sauce & mashed potatoes.

424. MARINATED FLANK STEAK

Prep & Cook Time: 15 minutes | Servings: 4

INGREDIENTS

¾ lb. of flank steak
1 ½ tbsp. Of sake

1 tbsp.of brown miso paste
1 tsp. of honey

2 cloves garlic, pressed
1 tbsp. of olive oil

INSTRUCTIONS

1. Put all of the ingredients in a Ziploc bag. Shake to cover the steak well with the seasonings & refrigerate for at least 1 hour.
2. Coat all sides of the steak with cooking spray.
3. Put the steak in the Air Fryer baking pan.
4. Cook at 400°F for 12 minutes, turning the steak twice during the cooking time, then serve immediately.

425. FRIED STEAK

Prep & Cook Time: 15 minutes | Servings: 1

INGREDIENTS

3 cm-thick of beef steak
Salt & pepper

INSTRUCTIONS

1. Pre-heat the Air Fryer 400°F for 5 minutes.
2. Place the beef steak in the baking tray & sprinkle on pepper & salt.
3. Spritz the steak with cooking spray.
4. Allow to cook for 3 minutes. Turn the steak over & cook on the other side for 3 more minutes. Serve hot.

426. HOMEMADE MEATBALLS

Prep & Cook Time: 20 minutes | Servings: 4

INGREDIENTS

1 lb. of ground beef	½ lime, rind & juice	2 tsp. of lemongrass, finely chopped
1 tsp. of red Thai curry paste	1 tsp. of Chinese spice	1 tbsp. of sesame oil

INSTRUCTIONS

1. Mix all of the ingredients in a bowl, combining well.
2. Take 24 equal amounts of the mixture & shape each one into a meatball. Put them in the Air Fryer cooking basket.
3. Cook at 380°F for 10 minutes.
4. Turn them over & cook for a further 5 minutes on the other side, ensuring they are well-cooked before serving with your favorite dipping sauce.

427. CRUMBED FILET MIGNON

Prep & Cook Time: 20 minutes | Servings: 4

INGREDIENTS

½ lb. of filet mignon	1 tsp. of dried basil	1 tbsp. of sesame oil
Sea salt & ground black pepper, to taste	1 tsp. of dried rosemary	1 small-sized egg, well-whisked
½ tsp. of cayenne pepper	1 tsp. of dried thyme	½ cup of breadcrumbs

INSTRUCTIONS

1. Cover the filet mignon with the salt, black pepper, cayenne pepper, basil, rosemary, & thyme. Coat with a light brushing of sesame oil.
2. Put the egg in a shallow plate.
3. Pour the breadcrumbs in another plate.
4. Dip the filet mignon into the egg. Roll it into the crumbs.
5. Transfer the steak to the Air Fryer & cook for 10 to 13 minutes at 360°F or until it turns golden.
6. Serve with a salad.

428. GRILLED BEEF RIBS

Prep & Cook Time: 20 minutes + marinating time | Servings: 4

INGREDIENTS

1 lb. of meaty beef ribs	2 garlic cloves, finely chopped	Kosher salt & black pepper, to taste
3 tbsp. of apple cider vinegar	1 chipotle powder	½ cup of vegetable oil
1 cup of coriander, finely chopped	1 tsp. of fennel seeds	
1 heaped tbsp. of fresh basil leaves	1 tsp. of hot paprika	

INSTRUCTIONS

1. Wash & dry the ribs.
2. Coat the ribs with the rest of the ingredients & refrigerate for a minimum of 3 hours.
3. Separate the ribs from the marinade & put them on an Air Fryer grill pan.
4. Cook at 360°F for 8 minutes, or longer as needed.
5. Pour the remaining marinade over the ribs before serving immediately.

429. LONDON BROIL

Prep & Cook Time: 30 minutes + marinating time | Servings: 8

INGREDIENTS

2 lb. of London broil	3 large garlic cloves, minced	3 tbsp. of balsamic vinegar

3 tbsp. of whole-grain mustard
2 tbsp. of olive oil

Sea salt & ground black pepper, to taste
½ tsp. of dried hot red pepper flakes

INSTRUCTIONS

1. Wash & dry the London broil. Score its sides with a knife.
2. Mix together the rest of the ingredients. Rub this mixture into the broil, coating it well. Allow to marinate for a minimum of 3 hours.
3. Cook the meat at 400°F for 15 minutes.
4. Turn it over & cook for an additional 10 - 12 minutes before serving.

430. SMOKED BEEF ROAST

Prep & Cook Time: 45 minutes | Servings: 8

NGREDIENTS

2 lb. of roast beef, at room temperature
2 tbsp. of extra-virgin olive oil
1 tsp. of sea salt flakes

1 tsp. of black pepper, preferably freshly ground
1 tsp. of smoked paprika

Few dashes of liquid smoke
2 jalapeño peppers, thinly sliced

INSTRUCTIONS

1. Pre-heat the Air Fryer to 330°F.
2. With kitchen towels, pat the beef dry.
3. Massage the extra-virgin olive oil & seasonings into the meat. Cover with liquid smoke.
4. Place the beef in the Air Fryer & roast for 30 minutes. Flip the roast over & allow to cook for another 15 minutes.
5. When cooked through, serve topped with sliced jalapeños.

431. VEGETABLES & BEEF CUBES

Prep & Cook Time: 20 minutes + marinating time | Servings: 4

INGREDIENTS

1 lb. of top round steak, cut into cubes
2 tbsp. of olive oil
1 tbsp. of apple cider vinegar
1 tsp. of fine sea salt
½ tsp. of ground black pepper

1 tsp. of shallot powder
¾ tsp. of smoked cayenne pepper
½ tsp. of garlic powder
¼ tsp. of ground cumin
¼ lb. of broccoli, cut into florets

¼ lb. of mushrooms, sliced
1 tsp. of dried basil
1 tsp. of celery seeds

INSTRUCTIONS

1. Massage the olive oil, vinegar, salt, black pepper, shallot powder, cayenne pepper, garlic powder, & cumin into the cubed steak, ensuring to coat each piece evenly.
2. Allow to marinate for a minimum of 3 hours.
3. Put the beef cubes in the Air Fryer cooking basket & allow to cook at 365°F for 12 minutes.
4. When the steak is cooked through, place it in a bowl.
5. Wipe the grease from the cooking basket & pour in the vegetables. Season them with basil & celery seeds.
6. Cook at 400°F for 5 to 6 minutes. When the vegetables are hot, serve them with the steak.

432. BEEF & KALE OMELET

Prep & Cook Time: 20 minutes | Servings: 4

INGREDIENTS

Cooking spray
½ lb. of leftover beef, coarsely chopped
2 garlic cloves, pressed
1 cup of kale, torn into pieces & wilted

1 tomato, chopped
¼ tsp. of sugar
4 eggs, beaten
4 tbsp. of heavy cream

½ tsp. of turmeric powder
Salt & ground black pepper to taste
1/8 tsp. of ground allspice

INSTRUCTIONS

1. Grease four ramekins with cooking spray.
2. Place equal amounts of each of the ingredients into each ramekin & mix well.
3. Air fry at 360°F for 16 minutes, or longer if necessary. Serve immediately.

433. CHEESEBURGERS

Prep & Cook Time: 15 minutes | Servings: 4

INGREDIENTS

¾ lb. of ground chuck
1 envelope onion soup mix
Kosher salt

Black pepper, to taste
1 tsp. of paprika
4 slices of Monterey-Jack cheese

4 ciabatta rolls
Mustard & pickled salad, to serve

INSTRUCTIONS

1. In a bowl, stir together the ground chuck, onion soup mix, salt, black pepper, & paprika to combine well.
2. Pre-heat your Air Fryer at 385°F.
3. Take four equal portions of the mixture & mold each one into a patty. Transfer to the Air Fryer & air fry for 10 minutes.
4. Put the slices of cheese on the top of the burgers.

5. Cook for another minute before serving on ciabatta rolls along with mustard & the pickled salad of your choosing.

434. SIMPLE BEEF

Prep & Cook Time: 25 minutes | Servings: 1

INGREDIENTS

1 thin beef schnitzel
1 egg, beaten

½ cup of breadcrumbs
2 tbsp. of olive oil

Salt & pepper

INSTRUCTIONS

1. Pre-heat the Air Fryer to 350°F.
2. In a shallow dish, combine the breadcrumbs, oil, pepper, & salt.
3. In a second shallow dish, place the beaten egg.
4. Dredge the schnitzel in the egg before rolling it in the breadcrumbs.
5. Put the coated schnitzel in the Air Fryer basket & air fry for 12 minutes.

435. MEATLOAF

Prep & Cook Time: 30 minutes | Servings: 4

INGREDIENTS

1 lb. of ground beef
1 egg, beaten
1 mushroom, sliced

1 tbsp. of thyme
1 small onion, chopped
3 tbsp. of breadcrumbs

Pepper

INSTRUCTIONS

1. Pre-heat the Air Fryer at 400°F.
2. Place all the ingredients into a large bowl & combine entirely.
3. Transfer the meatloaf mixture into the loaf pan & move it to the Air Fryer basket.
4. Cook for 25 minutes. Slice up before serving.

436. BEEF BURGERS

Prep & Cook Time: 65 minutes | Servings: 4

INGREDIENTS

10.5 oz. of beef, minced
1 onion, diced
1 tsp. of garlic, minced or pureed
1 tsp. of tomato, pureed

1 tsp. of mustard
1 tsp. of basil
1 tsp. of mixed herbs
Salt

Pepper
1 oz. of cheddar cheese
4 buns
Salad leaves

INSTRUCTIONS

1. Drizzle the Air Fryer with one tsp. of olive oil & allow it to warm up.
2. Place the diced onion in the Air Fryer & fry until they turn golden brown.
3. Mix in all of the seasoning & cook for 25 minutes at 390°F.
4. Lay 2 – 3 onion rings & pureed tomato on two of the buns. Place one slice of cheese & the layer of beef on top. Top with salad leaves & any other condiments you desire before closing off the sandwich with the other buns.
5. Serve with ketchup, cold drink & French fries.

437. BRUSSELS SPROUTS & TENDER BEEF CHUCK

Prep & Cook Time: 25 minutes + marinating time | Servings: 4

INGREDIENTS

1 lb. of beef chuck shoulder steak
2 tbsp. of vegetable oil
1 tbsp. of red wine vinegar
1 tsp. of fine sea salt

½ tsp. of ground black pepper
1 tsp. of smoked paprika
1 tsp. of onion powder
½ tsp. of garlic powder

½ lb. of Brussels sprouts, halved
½ tsp. of fennel seeds
1 tsp. of dried basil
1 tsp. of dried sage

INSTRUCTIONS

1. Massage the beef with the vegetable oil, wine vinegar, salt, black pepper, paprika, onion powder, & garlic powder, coating it well.
2. Allow to marinate for a minimum of 3 hours.
3. Air fry at 390°F for 10 minutes.
4. Put the prepared Brussels sprouts in the Air Fryer along with the fennel seeds, basil, & sage.
5. Lower the heat to 380°F & cook everything for another 5 minutes.
6. Pause the machine & give the contents a good stir. Cook for an additional 10 minutes.
7. Take out the beef & allow the vegetables too cook for a few more minutes if necessary or desired.
8. Serve everything together with the sauce of your choice.

438. SWEDISH MEATBALLS

Prep & Cook Time: 25 minutes | Servings: 8

INGREDIENTS

1 lb. ground beef
2 bread slices, crumbled
1 small onion, minced

½ tsp. of garlic salt
1 cup of tomato sauce
2 cups of pasta sauce

1 egg, beaten
2 carrots, shredded
Salt & pepper

INSTRUCTIONS
1. Pre-heat Air Fryer to 400°F.
2. In a bowl, combine the ground beef, egg, carrots, crumbled bread, onion, garlic salt, pepper & salt.
3. Divide the mixture into equal amounts & shape each one into a small meatball.
4. Put them in the Air Fryer basket & cook for 7 minutes.
5. Transfer the meatballs to an oven-safe dish & top with the tomato sauce.
6. Set the dish into the Air Fryer basket & allow to cook at 320°F for 5 more minutes. Serve hot.

439. GERMAN SCHNITZEL

Prep & Cook Time: 15 minutes | Servings: 4

INGREDIENTS

4 thin beef schnitzel
1 tbsp. of sesame seeds
2 tbsp. of paprika

3 tbsp. of olive oil
4 tbsp. of flour
2 eggs, beaten

1 cup of breadcrumbs
Salt & pepper

INSTRUCTIONS
1. Pre-heat the Air Fryer at 350°F.
2. Sprinkle the pepper & salt on the schnitzel.
3. In a shallow dish, combine the paprika, flour, & salt
4. In a second shallow dish, mix the breadcrumbs with the sesame seeds.
5. Place the beaten eggs in a bowl.
6. Coat the schnitzel in the flour mixture. Dip it into the egg before rolling it in the breadcrumbs.
7. Put the coated schnitzel in the Air Fryer basket & allow to cook for 12 minutes before serving hot.

440. STEAK TOTAL

Prep & Cook Time: 30 minutes | Servings: 4

INGREDIENTS

2 lb. of rib eye steak

1 tbsp. of olive oil

1 tbsp. of steak rub

INSTRUCTIONS
1. Set the Air Fryer to 400°F & allow to warm for 4 minutes.
2. Massage the olive oil & steak rub into both sides of the steak.
3. Put the steak in the Air Fryer's basket & cook for 14 minutes. Turn the steak over & cook on the other side for another 7 minutes.
4. Serve hot.

441. BETTY'S BEEF ROAST

Prep & Cook Time: 65 minutes | Servings: 6

INGREDIENTS

2 lb. of beef
1 tbsp. of olive oil
1 tsp. of dried rosemary

1 tsp. of dried thyme
½ tsp. of black pepper
½ tsp. of oregano

½ tsp. of garlic powder
1 tsp. of salt
1 tsp. of onion powder

INSTRUCTIONS
1. Preheat the Air Fryer to 330°F.
2. In a small bowl, mix together all of the spices.
3. Coat the beef with a brushing of olive oil.
4. Massage the spice mixture into the beef.
5. Transfer the meat to the Air Fryer & cook for 30 minutes. Turn it over & cook on the other side for another 25 minutes.

442. BEEF MEATLOAF

Prep & Cook Time: 30 minutes | Servings: 4

INGREDIENTS

¾ lb. of ground chuck
¼ lb. of ground pork sausage
1 cup of shallots, finely chopped
2 eggs, well beaten
3 tbsp. of plain milk

1 tbsp. of oyster sauce
1 tsp. of porcini mushrooms
½ tsp. of cumin powder
1 tsp. of garlic paste
1 tbsp. of fresh parsley

Seasoned salt & crushed red pepper
flakes to taste
1 cup of crushed saltines

INSTRUCTIONS
1. Mix together all of the ingredients in a large bowl, combining everything well.
2. Transfer to the Air Fryer baking dish & cook at 360°F for 25 minutes.
3. Serve hot.

443. STUFFED BELL PEPPER

Prep & Cook Time: 25 minutes | Servings: 4

INGREDIENTS

4 bell peppers, cut top of bell pepper
16 oz. of ground beef
⅔ cup of cheese, shredded
½ cup of rice, cooked

1 tsp. of basil, dried
½ tsp. of chili powder
1 tsp. of black pepper
1 tsp. of garlic salt

2 tsp. of Worcestershire sauce
8 oz. of tomato sauce
2 garlic cloves, minced
1 small onion, chopped

INSTRUCTIONS

1. Grease a frying pan with cooking spray & fry the onion & garlic over a medium heat.
2. Stir in the beef, basil, chili powder, black pepper, & garlic salt, combining everything well. Allow to cook until the beef is nicely browned, before taking the pan off the heat.
3. Add in half of the cheese, the rice, Worcestershire sauce, & tomato sauce & stir to combine.
4. Spoon equal amounts of the beef mixture into the four bell peppers, filling them entirely.
5. Pre-heat the Air Fryer at 400°F.
6. Spritz the Air Fryer basket with cooking spray.
7. Put the stuffed bell peppers in the basket & allow to cook for 11 minutes.
8. Add the remaining cheese on top of each bell pepper with remaining cheese & cook for a further 2 minutes. When the cheese is melted & the bell peppers are piping hot, serve immediately.

444. ASIAN BEEF BURGERS

Prep & Cook Time: 20 minutes | Servings: 4

INGREDIENTS

¾ lb. of lean ground beef
1 tbsp. of soy sauce
1 tsp. of Dijon mustard
Few dashes of liquid smoke

1 tsp. of shallot powder
1 clove of garlic, minced
½ tsp. of cumin powder
¼ cup of scallions, minced

⅓ tsp. of sea salt flakes
⅓ tsp. of peppercorns
1 tsp. of celery seeds
1 tsp. of parsley flakes

INSTRUCTIONS

1. Mix together all of the ingredients in a bowl using your hands, combining everything well.
2. Take four equal amounts of the mixture & mold each one into a patty.
3. Use the back of a spoon to create a shallow dip in the center of each patty. This will prevent them from puffing up during the cooking process.
4. Lightly coat all sides of the patties with cooking spray.
5. Place each one in the Air Fryer & cook for roughly 12 minutes at 360°F.
6. Test with a meat thermometer – the patties are ready once they have reached 160°F. Serve them on top of butter rolls with any sauces & toppings you desire.

445. BURGER PATTIES

Prep & Cook Time: 15 minutes | Servings: 6

INGREDIENTS

1 lb. of ground beef

6 cheddar cheese slices

Salt & pepper

INSTRUCTIONS

1. Pre-heat the Air Fryer to 350°F.
2. Sprinkle the salt & pepper on the ground beef.
3. Shape six equal portions of the ground beef into patties & put each one in the Air Fryer basket.
4. Air fry the patties for 10 minutes.
5. Top the patties with the cheese slices & air fry for one more minute.
6. Serve the patties on top of dinner rolls.

446. BEEF ROLLS

Prep & Cook Time: 30 minutes | Servings: 2

INGREDIENTS

2 lb. of beef flank steak
3 tsp. of pesto
1 tsp. of black pepper

6 slices of provolone cheese
3 oz. of roasted red bell peppers
¾ cup of baby spinach

1 tsp. of sea salt

INSTRUCTIONS

1. Spoon equal amounts of the pesto onto each flank steak & spread it across evenly.
2. Place the cheese, roasted red peppers & spinach on top of the meat, about three-quarters of the way down.
3. Roll the steak up, holding it in place with toothpicks. Sprinkle on the sea salt & pepper.
4. Place inside the Air Fryer & cook for 14 minutes at 400°F, turning halfway through the cooking time.
5. Allow the beef to rest for 10 minutes before slicing up & serving.

447. SPRING ROLLS

Prep & Cook Time: 35 minutes | Servings: 20

INGREDIENTS

⅓ cup of noodles
1 cup beef minced
2 tbsp. of cold water

1 packet spring roll sheets
1 tsp. of soy sauce
1 cup of fresh mix vegetables

3 garlic cloves, minced
1 small onion, diced
1 tbsp. of sesame oil

INSTRUCTIONS

1. Cook the noodle in hot water to soften them up, drain them & snip them to make them shorter.
2. In a frying pan over medium heat, cook the minced beef, soy sauce, mixed vegetables, garlic, & onion in a little oil until the beef minced is cooked through. Take the pan off the heat & throw in the noodles. Mix well to incorporate everything.
3. Unroll a spring roll sheet & lay it flat. Scatter the filling diagonally across it & roll it up, brushing the edges lightly with water to act as an adhesive. Repeat until you have used up all of the sheets & the filling.
4. Pre-heat the Air Fryer to 350°F.
5. Coat each spring roll with a light brushing of oil & transfer to the Air Fryer.
6. Cook for 8 minutes & serve hot.

448. CHEESY SCHNITZEL

Prep & Cook Time: 30 minutes | Servings: 1

INGREDIENTS

1 thin beef schnitzel
1 egg, beaten
½ cup of breadcrumbs

2 tbsp. of olive oil
3 tbsp. pasta sauce
¼ cup of parmesan cheese, grated

Salt & pepper

INSTRUCTIONS

1. Pre-heat the Air Fryer to 350°F.
2. In a shallow dish, combine the breadcrumbs, olive oil, pepper, & salt. In another shallow dish, put the beaten egg.
3. Cover the schnitzel in the egg before press it into the breadcrumb mixture & placing it in the Air Fryer basket. Cook for 15 minutes.
4. Pour the pasta sauce over the schnitzel & top with the grated cheese. Cook for an additional 5 minutes until the cheese melts. Serve hot.

449. BEEF SCHNITZEL

Prep & Cook Time: 30 minutes | Servings: 1

INGREDIENTS

1 egg
1 thin beef schnitzel

3 tbsp. of breadcrumbs
2 tbsp. of olive oil

1 parsley, roughly chopped
½ lemon, cut in wedges

INSTRUCTIONS:

1. Pre-heat your Air Fryer to the 360°F.
2. In a bowl combine the breadcrumbs & olive oil to form a loose, crumbly mixture.
3. Beat the egg with a whisk.
4. Coat the schnitzel first in the egg & then in the breadcrumbs, ensuring to cover it fully.
5. Place the schnitzel in the Air Fryer & cook for 12 – 14 minutes. Garnish the schnitzel with the lemon wedges & parsley before serving.

450. MIGHTY MEATBALLS

Prep & Cook Time: 20 minutes | Servings: 4

INGREDIENTS

1 egg
½ lb. of beef minced
½ cup of breadcrumbs

1 tbsp. of parsley, chopped
2 tbsp. of raisins
1 cup of onion, chopped & fried

½ tbsp. of pepper
½ tsp. of salt

INSTRUCTIONS

1. Place all of the ingredients in a bowl & combine well.
2. Use your hands to shape equal amounts of the mixture into small balls. Place each one in the Air Fryer basket.
3. Air fry the meatballs at 350°F for 15 minutes. Serve with the sauce of your choice.

451. BJORN'S BEEF STEAK

Prep & Cook Time: 15 minutes | Servings: 1

INGREDIENTS

1 steak, 1-inch thick
1 tbsp. of olive oil

Black pepper to taste
Sea salt to taste

INSTRUCTIONS

1. Place the baking tray inside the Air Fryer & pre-heat for about 5 minutes at 390°F.
2. Brush or spray both sides of the steak with the oil.
3. Season both sides with salt & pepper.
4. Take care when placing the steak in the baking tray & allow to cook for 3 minutes. Flip the meat over & cook for an additional 3 minutes.
5. Take it out of the Air Fryer & allow to sit for roughly 3 minutes before serving.

452. BEEF & BROCCOLI

Prep & Cook Time: 25 minutes | Servings: 4

INGREDIENTS

1 lb. of broccoli, cut into florets
¾ lb. of round steak, cut into strips
1 garlic clove, minced
1 tsp. of ginger, minced

1 tbsp. of olive oil
1 tsp. of cornstarch
1 tsp. of sugar
1 tsp. of soy sauce

⅓ cup of sherry wine
2 tsp. of sesame oil
⅓ cup oyster sauce

INSTRUCTIONS

1. In a bowl, combine the sugar, soy sauce, sherry wine, cornstarch, sesame oil, & oyster sauce.
2. Place the steak strips in the bowl, coat each one with the mixture & allow to marinate for 45 minutes.
3. Put the broccoli in the Air Fryer & lay the steak on top.
4. Top with the olive oil, garlic & ginger.
5. Cook at 350°F for 12 minutes. Serve hot with rice if desired.

453. BEEF & MUSHROOMS

Prep & Cook Time: 3 hours 15 minutes | Servings: 1

INGREDIENTS

6 oz. of beef
¼ onion, diced

½ cup of mushroom slices
2 tbsp. of favorite marinade

INSTRUCTIONS

1. Slice or cube the beef & put it in a bowl.
2. Cover the meat with the marinade, place a layer of aluminum foil or saran wrap over the bowl, & place the bowl in the refrigerator for 3 hours.
3. Put the meat in a baking dish along with the onion & mushrooms
4. Air Fry at 350°F for 10 minutes. Serve hot.

454. MAX'S MEATLOAF

Prep & Cook Time: 35 minutes | Servings: 4

INGREDIENTS

1 large onion, peeled & diced
2 kg. of minced beef
1 tsp. of Worcester sauce

3 tbsp. of tomato ketchup
1 tbsp. of basil
1 tbsp. of oregano

1 tbsp. of mixed herbs
1 tbsp. of breadcrumbs
Salt & pepper

INSTRUCTIONS

1. In a large bowl, combine the mince with the herbs, Worcester sauce, onion & tomato ketchup, incorporating every component well.
2. Pour in the breadcrumbs & give it another stir.
3. Transfer the mixture to a small dish & cook for 25 minutes in the Air Fryer at 350°F.

455. PARMESAN ARTICHOKES

Prep & Cook Time: 35 minutes | Servings: 4

INGREDIENTS

2 medium artichokes, trimmed & quartered, with the centers removed

2 tbsp. of coconut oil, melted
1 egg, beaten

½ cup of parmesan cheese, grated
¼ cup blanched, finely ground flour

INSTRUCTIONS

1. Place the artichokes in a bowl with the coconut oil & toss to coat, then dip the artichokes into a bowl of beaten egg.
2. In a separate bowl, mix together the parmesan cheese & the flour. Combine with the pieces of artichoke, making sure to coat each piece well. Transfer the artichoke to the Air Fryer.
3. Cook at 400°F for ten minutes, shaking occasionally throughout the cooking time. Serve hot.

456. CHEESE PIZZA WITH BROCCOLI CRUST

Prep & Cook Time: 30 minutes | Servings: 1

INGREDIENTS

3 cups of broccoli rice, steamed
½ cup of parmesan cheese, grated

1 egg
3 tbsp. of Alfredo sauce

½ cup of parmesan cheese, grated

INSTRUCTIONS

1. Drain the broccoli rice & combine with the parmesan cheese & egg in a bowl, mixing well.
2. Cut a piece of parchment paper roughly the size of the base of the Air Fryer's basket. Spoon four equal-sized amounts of the broccoli mixture onto the paper & press each portion into the shape of a pizza crust. You may have to complete this part in two batches. Transfer the parchment to the Air Fryer.
3. Cook at 370°F for five minutes. When the crust is firm, flip it over & cook for an additional two minutes.
4. Add the Alfredo sauce & mozzarella cheese on top of the crusts & cook for an additional seven minutes. The crusts are ready when the sauce & cheese have melted. Serve hot.

457. STUFFED EGGPLANT

Prep & Cook Time: 35 minutes | Servings: 2

INGREDIENTS

large eggplant
¼ medium yellow onion, diced

2 tbsp. of red bell pepper, diced
1 cup of spinach

¼ cup of artichoke hearts, chopped

INSTRUCTIONS

1. Cut the eggplant lengthwise into slices & spoon out the flesh, leaving a shell about a half-inch thick. Chop it up & set aside.
2. Set a skillet over a medium heat & spritz with cooking spray. Cook the onions for about three to five minutes to soften. Then add the pepper, spinach, artichokes, & the flesh of eggplant. Fry for a further five minutes, then remove from the heat.
3. Scoop this mixture in equal parts into the eggplant shells & place each one in the Air Fryer.
4. Cook for twenty minutes at 320°F until the eggplant shells are soft. Serve warm.

458. BROCCOLI SALAD

Prep & Cook Time: 15 minutes | Servings: 2

INGREDIENTS

3 cups fresh broccoli florets
2 tbsp. of coconut oil, melted

¼ cup of sliced spinach
½ medium lemon, juiced

INSTRUCTIONS

1. Take a six-inch baking dish & fill with the broccoli florets. Pour the melted coconut oil over the broccoli & add in the sliced spinach. Toss together. Put the dish in the Air Fryer.
2. Cook at 380°F for seven minutes, stirring at the halfway point.
3. Place the broccoli in a bowl & drizzle the lemon juice over it.

459. ROASTED CAULIFLOWER

Prep & Cook Time: 20 minutes | Servings: 2

INGREDIENTS

1 medium head of cauliflower
2 tbsp. of salted butter, melted

1 medium lemon
1 tsp. of dried parsley

½ tsp. of garlic powder

INSTRUCTIONS

1. Having removed the leaves from the cauliflower head, brush it with the melted butter. Grate the rind of the lemon over it & then drizzle some juice. Finally add the parsley & garlic powder on top.
2. Transfer the cauliflower to the basket of the Air Fryer.
3. Cook for fifteen minutes at 350°F, checking regularly to ensure it doesn't overcook. The cauliflower is ready when it is hot & fork tender.
4. Take care when removing it from the Air Fryer, cut up & serve.

460. MUSHROOM LOAF

Prep & Cook Time: 20 minutes | Servings: 2

INGREDIENTS

2 cups of mushrooms, chopped
½ cups of cheddar cheese, shredded

¾ cup of flour
2 tbsp. of butter, melted

2 eggs

INSTRUCTIONS

1. In a food processor, pulse together the mushrooms, cheese, flour, melted butter, & eggs, along with some salt & pepper if desired, until a uniform consistency is achieved.
2. Transfer into a silicone loaf pan, spreading & levelling with a palette knife.
3. Pre-heat the Air Fryer at 375°F & put the rack inside.
4. Set the loaf pan on the rack & cook for fifteen minutes.
5. Take care when removing the pan from the Air Fryer & leave it to cool. Then slice & serve.

461. GREEN BEAN CASSEROLE

Prep & Cook Time: 10 minutes | Servings: 2

INGREDIENTS

1 tbsp. of butter, melted
1 cup of green beans

6 oz. of cheddar cheese, shredded
7 oz. of parmesan cheese, shredded

¼ cup of heavy cream

INSTRUCTIONS

1. Pre-heat your Air Fryer at 400°F.
2. Take a baking dish small enough to fit inside the Air Fryer & cover the bottom with melted butter. Throw in the green beans, cheddar cheese, & any seasoning as desired, then give it a stir. Add the parmesan on top & finally the heavy cream.
3. Cook in the Air Fryer for six minutes. Allow to cool before serving.

462. CABBAGE STEAKS

INGREDIENTS

Small head of cabbage
1 tsp. of butter, butter

1 tsp. of paprika
1 tsp. of olive oil

INSTRUCTIONS

1. Halve the cabbage.
2. In a bowl, mix together the melted butter, paprika, & olive oil. Massage into the cabbage slices, making sure to coat it well. Season as desired with salt & pepper or any other seasonings of your choosing.
3. Pre-heat the Air Fryer at 400°F & set the rack inside.
4. Put the cabbage in the Air Fryer & cook for three minutes. Flip it & cook on the other side for another two minutes. Enjoy!

463. ZUCCHINI GRATIN

Prep & Cook Time: 15 minutes | Servings: 2

INGREDIENTS

5 oz. of parmesan cheese, shredded
1 tbsp. of coconut flour

1 tbsp. of dried parsley
2 zucchinis

1 tsp. of butter, melted

INSTRUCTIONS

1. Mix the parmesan & coconut flour together in a bowl, seasoning with parsley to taste.
2. Cut the zucchini in half lengthwise & chop the halves into four slices.
3. Pre-heat the Air Fryer at 400°F.
4. Pour the melted butter over the zucchini & then dip the zucchini into the parmesan-flour mixture, coating it all over. Cook the zucchini in the Air Fryer for thirteen minutes.

464. CHEESY KALE

Prep & Cook Time: 15 minutes | Servings: 2

INGREDIENTS

1 lb. of kale
8 oz. of parmesan cheese, shredded

1 onion, diced
1 tsp. of butter

1 cup of heavy cream

INSTRUCTIONS

1. Dice up the kale, discarding any hard stems. In a baking dish small enough to fit inside the Air Fryer, combine the kale with the parmesan, onion, butter & cream.
2. Pre-heat the Air Fryer at 250°F.
3. Set the baking dish in the Air Fryer & cook for twelve minutes. Make sure to give it a good stir before serving.

465. SPAGHETTI SQUASH

Prep & Cook Time: 45 minutes | Servings: 2

INGREDIENTS

spaghetti squash
1 tsp. of olive oil

Salt & pepper
4 tbsp. of heavy cream

1 tsp. of butter

INSTRUCTIONS

1. Pre-heat your Air Fryer at 360°F.
2. Cut & de-seed the spaghetti squash. Brush with the olive oil & season with salt & pepper to taste.
3. Put the squash inside the Air Fryer, placing it cut-side-down. Cook for thirty minutes. Halfway through cooking, fluff the spaghetti inside the squash with a fork.
4. When the squash is ready, fluff the spaghetti some more, then pour some heavy cream & butter over it & give it a good stir. Serve with the tomato sauce of your choice.

466. CHIPOTLE JICAMA HASH

Prep & Cook Time: 15 minutes | Servings: 2

INGREDIENTS

4 slices of bacon, chopped
12 oz. of jicama, peeled & diced

4 oz. of purple onion, chopped
1 oz. of green bell pepper (or poblano),

seeded & chopped
4 tbsp. of Chipotle mayonnaise

INSTRUCTIONS

1. Inside your Air Fryer, fry the bacon at 400°F for 10 minutes.
2. Remove & place on a towel to drain the grease.
3. Use the remaining grease to fry the onions & jicama until brown.
4. When ready, add the bell pepper & cook the hash until tender.
5. Transfer the hash onto two plates & serve each plate with 4 tbsp. of Chipotle mayonnaise.

467. FRIED QUESO BLANCO

Prep & Cook Time: 170 minutes | Servings: 4

INGREDIENTS

5 oz. of queso blanco

1 ½ tbsp. of olive oil

3 oz. of cheese

2 oz. of olives

1 pinch of red pepper flakes

INSTRUCTIONS

1. Cube some cheese & freeze it for 1-2 hours.
2. Pour the oil inside a dish and place the dish inside your Air Fryer.
3. Add the cheese cubes. Close the lid.
4. Cook at 400°F for 20 minutes, flipping regularly.
5. While flipping, fold the cheese into itself to form crispy layers.
6. Use a spatula to roll it into a block.
7. Remove the dish from the Air Fryer, allow it to cool, cut it into small cubes, & serve.

468. SPINACH WITH BACON & SHALLOTS

Prep & Cook Time: 30 minutes | Servings: 4

INGREDIENTS

16 oz. of raw spinach

½ cup of chopped white onion

½ cup of chopped shallot

½ lb. of raw bacon slices

2 tbsp. of butter

INSTRUCTIONS

1. Slice the bacon strips into small narrow pieces.
2. Inside your Air Fryer, heat the butter & add the chopped onion, shallots & bacon.
3. Cook at 350°F for 15-20 minutes or until the onions start to caramelize & the bacon is cooked.
4. Add the spinach & sauté on a medium heat. Stir frequently to ensure the leaves touch the skillet while cooking.
5. Serve!

469. BACON-WRAPPED SAUSAGE SKEWERS

Prep & Cook Time: 8 minutes | Servings: 2

INGREDIENTS

5 Italian chicken sausages

10 slices of bacon

INSTRUCTIONS

1. Preheat your Air Fryer to 370°F/190°C.
2. Cut the sausage into four pieces.
3. Slice the bacon in half.
4. Wrap the bacon over the sausage.
5. Skewer the sausage.
6. Fry for 4-5 minutes until browned.

470. ROASTED BRUSSELS SPROUTS & BACON

Prep & Cook Time: 45 minutes | Servings: 2

INGREDIENTS

24 oz. of brussels sprouts

¼ cup of fish sauce

¼ cup of bacon grease

6 strips of bacon

Pepper

INSTRUCTIONS

1. De-stem & quarter the brussels sprouts.
2. Mix them with the bacon grease & fish sauce.
3. Slice the bacon into small strips & cook.
4. Add the bacon & pepper to the sprouts.
5. Spread onto a greased pan & cook inside your Air Fryer at 450°F/230°C for 35 minutes.
6. Stir every 5 minute or so.
7. Broil for a few more minutes & serve.

471. HOT HAM & CHEESE ROLLS

Prep & Cook Time: 5 minutes | Servings: 4

INGREDIENTS

16 slices of ham

1 packet of chive & onion cream cheese (8 oz.)

16 slices thin Swiss cheese

INSTRUCTIONS

1. Place the ham slices inside your Air Fryer. Flash fry at 400°F for 3 minutes.
2. Remove and dry the slices with a paper towel.
3. Thinly spread 2 teaspoons of Swiss cheese over each slice of ham.
4. On the clean section of ham, add a half inch slice of cheese.
5. On the cheese side, fold the ham over the cheese & roll it up. Serve!

472. HILLBILLY CHEESE SURPRISE

Prep & Cook Time: 40 minutes | Servings: 6

INGREDIENTS

4 cups of broccoli florets
¼ cup of ranch dressing

½ cup of sharp cheddar cheese, shredded

¼ cup of heavy whipping cream
Kosher salt & pepper to taste

INSTRUCTIONS

1. Preheat your Air Fryer to 375°F/190°C.
2. In a bowl, combine all of the ingredients until the broccoli is well-covered.
3. In a casserole dish, spread out the broccoli mixture.
4. Bake for 30 minutes.
5. Take out of your Air Fryer & mix.
6. If the florets are not tender, bake for another 5 minutes until tender.
7. Serve.

473. PARMESAN & GARLIC CAULIFLOWER

Prep & Cook Time: 40 minutes | Servings: 4

INGREDIENTS

¾ cup of cauliflower florets
2 tbsp. of butter

1 clove garlic, sliced thinly
2 tbsp. of shredded parmesan

Salt

INSTRUCTIONS

1. Preheat your Air Fryer to 350°F/175°C.
2. On a low heat, melt the butter with the garlic for 5-10 minutes.
3. Strain the garlic in a sieve.
4. Add the cauliflower, parmesan & salt.
5. Bake for 20 minutes or until golden.

474. JALAPEÑO GUACAMOLE

Prep & Cook Time: 30 minutes | Servings: 4

INGREDIENTS

2 avocados, ripe
¼ red onion

1 jalapeño
1 tbsp. of fresh lime juice

Sea salt

INSTRUCTIONS

1. Spoon the avocado innings into your Air Fryer. Cook at 350°F/175°C for 5 minutes.
2. Dice the jalapeño & onion.
3. Mash the avocado to the desired consistency.
4. Add in the onion, jalapeño & lime juice.
5. Sprinkle with salt

475. GREEN BEANS & SPINACH

Prep & Cook Time: 15 minutes | Servings: 4

INGREDIENTS

1 lb. of fresh green beans, trimmed
2 tbsp. of butter

¼ cup of sliced spinach
2 tsp. of lemon pepper

INSTRUCTIONS

1. Cook the green beans in your Air Fryer at 350°F/175°C for 8 minutes, until tender, then drain.
2. On a medium heat, melt the butter in a skillet.
3. Sauté the spinach until browned.
4. Sprinkle with salt & pepper.
5. Mix in the green beans.

476. SUGAR SNAP BACON

Prep & Cook Time: 25 minutes | Servings: 4

INGREDIENTS

3 cups of sugar snap peas
½ tbsp. of lemon juice

2 tbsp. of bacon fat
2 tsp. of garlic

½ tsp. of red pepper flakes

INSTRUCTIONS

1. Inside your Air Fryer, cook the bacon fat at 400°F for 15 minutes, until it begins to smoke.
2. Add the garlic & cook for 2 minutes.
3. Add the sugar peas & lemon juice.
4. Cook for 2-3 minutes.
5. Remove & sprinkle with red pepper flakes & lemon zest. Serve!

6. Serve!

477. FLAX CHEESE CHIPS

Prep & Cook Time: 20 minutes | Servings: 2

INGREDIENTS

1 ½ cup of cheddar cheese

4 tbsp. of ground flaxseed meal

Seasonings of your choice

INSTRUCTIONS

1. Preheat your Air Fryer to 425°F/220°C.
2. Spoon 2 tbsp. of cheddar cheese into a mound, onto a non-stick pad.
3. Spread out a pinch of flax seed on each chip.
4. Season & bake for 10-15 minutes.

478. COUNTRY STYLE CHARD

Prep & Cook Time: 30 minutes | Servings: 2

INGREDIENTS

4 slices of bacon, chopped
2 tbsp. of butter

2 tbsp. of fresh lemon juice
½ tsp. of garlic paste

1 bunch of Swiss chard, stems removed, leaves cut into 1-inch pieces

INSTRUCTIONS

1. Cook the bacon inside your Air Fryer at 400°F for 20 minutes, until the fat begins to brown.
2. Melt the butter in the skillet & add the lemon juice & garlic paste.
3. Add the chard leaves & cook until they begin to wilt.
4. Cover & turn up the heat to high.
5. Cook for 3 minutes.
6. Plate the bacon and add the chard. Sprinkle with salt & serve.

479. BAKED TORTILLAS

Prep & Cook Time: 30 minutes | Servings: 4

INGREDIENTS

1 large head of cauliflower divided into florets.
4 large eggs

2 garlic cloves (minced)
1 ½ tsp. of herbs (whatever your favorite is - basil, oregano, thyme)

½ tsp. of salt

INSTRUCTIONS

1. Preheat your Air Fryer to 375°F/190°C.
2. Put parchment paper on two baking sheets.
3. In a food processor, break down the cauliflower into rice.
4. Add ¼ cup of water & the riced cauliflower to a saucepan.
5. Cook on a medium high heat until tender for 10 minutes. Drain.
6. Dry with a clean kitchen towel.
7. Mix the cauliflower, eggs, garlic, herbs & salt.
8. Make 4 thin circles on the parchment paper.
9. Bake for 20 minutes, until dry.

480. HOMEMADE MAYONNAISE

Prep & Cook Time: 30 minutes | Servings: 4

INGREDIENTS

1 large egg
Juice from 1 lemon.

1 tsp. of dry mustard
½ tsp. of black pepper

1 cup avocado oil

INSTRUCTIONS

1. Combine the egg & lemon juice inside a dish and let sit for 10 minutes.
2. Add the dry mustard, pepper, & avocado oil.
3. Place the dish inside your Air Fryer and flash fry at 400°F for 2 minutes.
4. Remove and whisk the warm sauce for 30 seconds.
5. Transfer to a sealed container & store in your refrigerator overnight. Serve!

481. HOLLANDAISE SAUCE

Prep & Cook Time: 3 minutes | Servings: 8

INGREDIENTS

8 large egg yolks
½ tsp. of salt

2 tbsp. of fresh lemon juice
1 cup of butter

INSTRUCTIONS

1. Combine the egg yolks, salt, & lemon juice inside a dish until smooth.

2. Place the dish inside your Air Fryer and cook at 400°F for 2 minutes.
3. Serve!

482. GRANNY'S GREEN BEANS

Prep & Cook Time: 10 minutes | Servings: 4

INGREDIENTS

1 lb. of green beans, trimmed
1 cup of butter

2 cloves garlic, minced
1 cup of toasted pine nuts

INSTRUCTIONS

1. Add the green beans to a dish and place it inside your Air Fryer & bake until tender at 350°F for 5 minutes.
2. Heat the butter in a large skillet over a high heat. Add the garlic & pine nuts & sauté for 2 minutes or until the pine nuts are lightly browned.
3. Transfer the green beans to the skillet & turn until coated.
4. Serve!

483. MINI PEPPER POPPERS

Prep & Cook Time: 10 minutes | Servings: 4

INGREDIENTS

8 mini sweet peppers
¼ cup of pepper jack cheese, shredded

4 slices of sugar-free bacon, cooked &
crumbled

4 oz. of full-fat cream cheese, softened

INSTRUCTIONS

1. Prepare the peppers by cutting off the tops & halving them lengthwise. Then take out the membrane & the seeds.
2. In a small bowl, combine the pepper jack cheese, bacon, & cream cheese, making sure to incorporate everything well
3. Spoon equal-sized portions of the cheese-bacon mixture into each of the pepper halves.
4. Place the peppers inside your Air Fryer & cook for eight minutes at 400°F. Take care when removing them from the Air Fryer & enjoy warm.

484. BACON-WRAPPED JALAPENO POPPER

Prep & Cook Time: 20 minutes | Servings: 4

INGREDIENTS

6 jalapenos
⅓ cup medium cheddar cheese

¼ tsp. of garlic powder
3 oz. of full-fat cream cheese

12 slices of sugar-free bacon

INSTRUCTIONS

1. Prepare the jalapenos by slicing off the tops & halving each one lengthwise. Take care when removing the seeds & membranes, wearing gloves if necessary.
2. In a microwavable bowl, combine the cheddar cheese, garlic powder, & cream cheese. Microwave for half a minute & mix again, before spooning equal parts of this mixture into each of the jalapeno halves.
3. Take a slice of bacon & wrap it around one of the jalapeno halves, covering it entirely. Place it in the basket of your Air Fryer. Repeat with the rest of the bacon & jalapenos.
4. Cook at 400°F for twelve minutes, flipping the peppers halfway through in order to ensure the bacon gets crispy. Make sure not to let any of the contents spill out of the jalapeno halves when turning them.
5. Eat the peppers hot or at room temperature.

485. CHEESY BACON BREAD

Prep & Cook Time: 25 minutes | Servings: 2

INGREDIENTS

4 slices of sugar-free bacon, cooked &
chopped

2 eggs
¼ cup of pickled jalapenos, chopped

¼ cup of parmesan cheese, grated
2 cups of mozzarella cheese, shredded

INSTRUCTIONS

1. Add all of the ingredients together in a bowl & mix together.
2. Cut out a piece of parchment paper that will fit the base of your Air Fryer's basket. Place it inside the Air Fryer
3. With slightly wet hands, roll the mixture into a circle. You may have to form two circles to cook in separate batches, depending on the size of your Air Fryer.
4. Place the circle on top of the parchment paper inside your Air Fryer. Cook at 320°F for ten minutes.
5. Turn the bread over & cook for another five minutes.
6. The bread is ready when it is golden & cooked all the way through. Slice & serve warm.

486. MOZZARELLA STICKS

Prep & Cook Time: 60 minutes | Servings: 4

INGREDIENTS

6 x 1-oz. of mozzarella string cheese
sticks

1 tsp. of dried parsley
½ oz. of flour

½ cup of parmesan cheese, grated
2 eggs

INSTRUCTIONS

1. Halve the mozzarella sticks & freeze for forty-five minutes. Optionally you can leave them longer & place in a Ziploc bag to prevent them from becoming freezer burned.
2. In a small bowl, combine the dried parsley, flour & parmesan cheese.
3. In a separate bowl, beat the eggs with a fork.
4. Take a frozen mozzarella stick & dip it into the eggs, then into the flour mixture, making sure to coat it all over. Proceed with the rest of the cheese sticks, placing each coated stick in the basket of your Air Fryer.
5. Cook at 400°F for ten minutes, until they are golden brown.
6. Serve hot, with some homemade marinara sauce if desired.

487. BEEF JERKY

Prep & Cook Time: 250 minutes | Servings: 4

INGREDIENTS

¼ tsp. of garlic powder
¼ tsp. of onion powder

¼ cup of soy sauce
2 tsp. of Worcestershire sauce

1 lb. of flat iron steak, thinly sliced

INSTRUCTIONS

1. In a bowl, combine the garlic powder, onion powder, soy sauce, & Worcestershire sauce. Marinade the beef slices with the mixture in an airtight bag, shaking it well to ensure the beef is well-coated. Leave to marinate for at least two hours
2. Place the meat in the basket of your Air Fryer, making sure it is evenly spaced. Cook the beef slices in more than one batch if necessary.
3. Cook for four hours at 160°F.
4. Allow to cool before serving. You can keep the jerky in an airtight container for up to a week, if you can resist it that long.

488. BACON-WRAPPED BRIE

Prep & Cook Time: 15 minutes | Servings: 1

INGREDIENTS

4 slices of sugar-free bacon

8 oz. of brie cheese

INSTRUCTIONS

1. On a cutting board, lay out the slices of bacon across each other in a star shape (two Xs overlaid). Then place the entire round of brie in the center of this star.
2. Lift each slice of bacon to wrap it over the brie & use toothpicks to hold everything in place. Cut up a piece of parchment paper to fit in your Air Fryer's basket & place it inside, followed by the wrapped brie, setting it in the center of the sheet of parchment.
3. Cook at 400°F for seven minutes. Turn the brie over & cook for a further three minutes.
4. It is ready once the bacon is crisp, & cheese is melted on the inside.
5. Slice up the brie & enjoy hot.

489. CRUST-LESS MEATY PIZZA

Prep & Cook Time: 15 minutes | Servings: 1

INGREDIENTS

½ cup of mozzarella cheese, shredded
2 slices of sugar-free bacon, cooked & crumbled

¼ cup ground sausage, cooked
7 slices of pepperoni
1 tbsp. of parmesan cheese, grated

INSTRUCTIONS

1. Spread the mozzarella across the bottom of a six-inch cake pan. Throw on the bacon, sausage, & pepperoni, then add a sprinkle of the parmesan cheese on top. Place the pan inside your Air Fryer.
2. Cook at 400°F for five minutes. The cheese is ready once brown in color & bubbly. Take care when removing the pan from the Air Fryer & serve.

490. RADISH CHIPS

Prep & Cook Time: 15 minutes | Servings: 1

INGREDIENTS

2 cups of water
1 lb. of radishes

½ tsp. of garlic powder
¼ tsp. of onion powder

2 tbsp. of coconut oil, melted

INSTRUCTIONS

1. Boil the water over the stove.
2. In the meantime, prepare the radish chips. Slice off the tops & bottoms &, using a mandolin, shave into thin slices of equal size. Alternatively, this step can be completed using your food processor if it has a slicing blade.
3. Put the radish chips in the pot of boiling water & allow to cook for five minutes, ensuring they become translucent. Take care when removing from the water & place them on a paper towel to dry.
4. Add the radish chips, garlic powder, onion powder, & melted coconut oil into a bowl & toss to coat. Transfer the chips to your Air Fryer.
5. Cook at 320°F for five minutes, occasionally giving the basket a good shake to ensure even cooking. The chips are done when cooked through & crispy. Serve immediately.

491. PARMESAN ZUCCHINI CHIPS

Prep & Cook Time: 10 minutes | Servings: 1

INGREDIENTS

2 medium zucchinis	½ cup of parmesan cheese, grated
1 oz. of flour	1 egg

INSTRUCTIONS

1. Cut the zucchini into slices about a quarter-inch thick. Lay on a paper towel to dry.
2. In a bowl, combine the flour & the grated parmesan.
3. In a separate bowl, beat the egg with a fork.
4. Take a zucchini slice & dip it into the egg, then into the parmesan mixture, making sure to coat it evenly. Repeat with the rest of the slices. Lay them in the basket of your Air Fryer, taking care not to overlap. This step may need to be completed in more than one batch.
5. Cook at 320°F for five minutes. Turn the chips over & allow to cook for another five minutes.
6. Allow to cool to achieve a crispier texture or serve warm. Enjoy!

492. BUFFALO CAULIFLOWER

Prep & Cook Time: 10 minutes | Servings: 1

INGREDIENTS

½ packet of dry ranch seasoning	Cauliflower florets
2 tbsp. of salted butter, melted	¼ cup of buffalo sauce

INSTRUCTIONS

1. In a bowl, combine the dry ranch seasoning & butter. Toss with the cauliflower florets to coat & transfer them to the Air Fryer.
2. Cook at 400°F for five minutes, shaking the basket occasionally to ensure the florets cook evenly.
3. Remove the cauliflower from the Air Fryer, pour the buffalo sauce over it, & enjoy.

493. ZESTY CILANTRO ROASTED CAULIFLOWER

Prep & Cook Time: 10 minutes | Servings: 2

INGREDIENTS

2 cups of cauliflower florets, chopped	2 ½ tsp. of taco seasoning mix	2 tbsp. of cilantro, chopped
2 tbsp. of coconut oil, melted	1 medium lime	

INSTRUCTIONS

1. Mix the cauliflower with the melted coconut oil & the taco seasoning, ensuring to coat the florets all over.
2. Air bake at 350°F for seven minutes, shaking the basket a few times through the cooking time. Then transfer the cauliflower to a bowl.
3. Squeeze the lime juice over the cauliflower & season with the cilantro. Toss once more to coat & enjoy.

494. FRIED GREEN TOMATOES

Prep & Cook Time: 10 minutes | Servings: 2

INGREDIENTS

2 medium green tomatoes	¼ cup of blanched finely ground flour
1 egg	⅓ cup of parmesan cheese, grated

INSTRUCTIONS

1. Slice the tomatoes about a half-inch thick.
2. Crack the egg into a bowl & beat it with a whisk. In a separate bowl, mix together the flour & parmesan cheese.
3. Dredge the tomato slices in egg, then dip them into the flour-cheese mixture to coat. Place each slice into the Air Fryer basket. They may need to be cooked in multiple batches.
4. Cook at 400°F for seven minutes, turning them halfway through the cooking time, & then serve warm.

495. AVOCADO STICKS

Prep & Cook Time: 10 minutes | Servings: 2

INGREDIENTS

2 avocados	1 ½ tbsp. of water	1 cup of flour
4 egg yolks	Salt & pepper	1 cup herbed butter

INSTRUCTIONS

1. Halve the avocados, twist to open, & take out the pits. Cut each half into three equal slices.
2. In a bowl, combine the egg yolks & water. Season with salt & pepper to taste & whisk together.
3. Pour the flour into a shallow bowl.
4. Coat each slice of avocado in the flour, then in the egg, before dipping it in the flour again. Ensure the flour coats the avocado well & firmly.
5. Pre-heat the Air Fryer at 400°F. When it is warm, put the avocados inside & cook for eight minutes.
6. Take care when removing the avocados from the Air Fryer & enjoy with a side of the herbed butter.

496. CHEESY CAULIFLOWER BITES

Prep & Cook Time: 20 minutes | Servings: 3

INGREDIENTS

2 cup of cauliflower florets
¾ cup of cheddar cheese, shredded

½ cup of onion, chopped
1 tsp. of seasoning salt

2 tbsp. of butter, melted
2 cloves garlic, minced

INSTRUCTIONS
1. Pulse the cauliflower florets in the food processor until they become crumbly. Use a cheesecloth to remove all the moisture from the cauliflower.
2. In a bowl, combine the cauliflower with the cheese, onion, seasoning salt, & melted butter. With your hands, roll the mixture into balls.
3. Pre-heat the Air Fryer at 400°F.
4. Fry the balls for fourteen minutes, leaving them in the Air Fryer for an additional two minutes if you like them browner. Serve hot.

497. BRUSSELS SPROUTS WITH CHEESE SAUCE

Prep & Cook Time: 10 minutes | Servings: 2

INGREDIENTS

¾ cups of Brussels sprouts
1 tbsp. of extra virgin olive oil

¼ tsp. of salt
¼ cup of mozzarella cheese, shredded

INSTRUCTIONS
1. Halve the Brussels sprouts & drizzle with the olive oil. Season with salt & toss to coat.
2. Pre-heat your Air Fryer at 375°F. When warm, transfer the Brussels sprouts inside & add the shredded mozzarella on top.
3. Cook for five minutes, serving when the cheese is melted.

498. VEGETABLE MIX

Prep & Cook Time: 45 minutes | Servings: 4

INGREDIENTS

3.5 oz. of radish
½ tsp. of parsley
3.5 oz. of celeriac
1 yellow carrot

1 orange carrot
1 red onion
3.5 oz. of pumpkin
3.5 oz. of parsnips

Salt
Epaulette pepper to taste
1 tbsp. of olive oil
4 cloves garlic, unpeeled

INSTRUCTIONS
1. Peel & slice up all the vegetables into 2- to 3-cm pieces.
2. Pre-heat your Air Fryer to 390°F.
3. Pour in the oil & allow it to warm before placing the vegetables in the Air Fryer, followed by the garlic, salt & pepper.
4. Roast for 18 – 20 minutes.
5. Top with parsley & serve hot with rice if desired.

499. POTATO CHIPS

Prep & Cook Time: 45 minutes | Servings: 4

INGREDIENTS

2 large potatoes, peel & sliced
1 tbsp. of rosemary

3.5 oz. of sour cream
¼ tsp. of salt

INSTRUCTIONS
1. Place the potato slices in water & allow to absorb for 30 minutes.
2. Drain the potato slices & transfer to a large bowl. Toss with the rosemary, sour cream, & salt.
3. Pre-heat the Air Fryer to 320°F
4. Put the coated potato slices in the Air Fryer's basket & cook for 35 minutes. Serve hot.

500. BRUSSELS SPROUTS

Prep & Cook Time: 15 minutes | Servings: 2

INGREDIENTS

2 cups of Brussels sprouts, sliced in half
1 tbsp. of balsamic vinegar

1 tbsp. of olive oil
¼ tsp. of salt

INSTRUCTIONS
1. Toss all of the ingredients together in a bowl, coating the Brussels sprouts well.
2. Place the sprouts in the Air Fryer basket & air fry at 400°F for 10 minutes, shaking the basket at the halfway point.

501. GARLIC POTATOES

Prep & Cook Time: 40 minutes | Servings: 4

INGREDIENTS

1 lb. of russet baking potatoes
1 tbsp. of garlic powder

1 tbsp. of freshly chopped parsley
½ tsp. of salt

¼ tsp. of black pepper
1 – 2 tbsp. of olive oil

INSTRUCTIONS
1. Wash the potatoes & pat them dry with clean paper towels.
2. Pierce each potato several times with a fork.
3. Place the potatoes in a large bowl & season with the garlic powder, salt & pepper.

4. Pour over the olive oil & mix well.
5. Pre-heat the Air Fryer to 360°F.
6. Place the potatoes in the Air Fryer & cook for about 30 minutes, shaking the basket a few times throughout the cooking time.
7. Garnish the potatoes with the chopped parsley & serve with butter, sour cream or another dipping sauce if desired.

502. ZUCCHINI ROLLS

Prep & Cook Time: 15 minutes | Servings: 2 – 4

INGREDIENTS

3 zucchinis, sliced thinly lengthwise with a mandolin or very sharp knife

1 tbsp. of olive oil
1 cup goat cheese

¼ tsp. of black pepper

INSTRUCTIONS

1. Preheat your Air Fryer to 390°F.
2. Coat each zucchini strip with a light brushing of olive oil.
3. Combine the sea salt, black pepper & goat cheese.
4. Scoop a small, equal amount of the goat cheese onto the center of each strip of zucchini. Roll up the strips & secure with a toothpick.
5. Transfer to the Air Fryer & cook for 5 minutes until the cheese is warm & the zucchini slightly crispy. If desired, add some tomato sauce on top.

503. ASPARAGUS

Prep & Cook Time: 15 minutes | Servings: 4

INGREDIENTS

10 asparagus spears, woody end cut off
1 clove garlic, minced

4 tbsp. of olive oil
Pepper

Salt

INSTRUCTIONS

1. Set the Air Fryer to 400°F & allow to heat for 5 minutes.
2. In a bowl, combine the garlic & oil.
3. Cover the asparagus with this mixture & put it in the Air Fryer basket. Sprinkle over some pepper & salt.
4. Cook for 10 minutes & serve hot.

504. ZUCCHINI CHIPS

Prep & Cook Time: 30 minutes | Servings: 2

INGREDIENTS

3 medium zucchinis, sliced
1 tsp. of parsley, chopped

3 tbsp. of parmesan cheese, grated
Pepper

Salt

INSTRUCTIONS

1. Pre-heat the Air Fryer to 425°F.
2. Put the sliced zucchini on a sheet of baking paper & spritz with cooking spray.
3. Combine the cheese, pepper, parsley, & salt. Use this mixture to sprinkle over the zucchini.
4. Transfer to the Air Fryer & cook for 25 minutes, ensuring the zucchini slices have crisped up nicely before serving.

505. SWEET POTATO WEDGES

Prep & Cook Time: 25 minutes | Servings: 2

INGREDIENTS

2 large, sweet potatoes, cut into wedges
1 tbsp. of olive oil
1 tsp. of chili powder

1 tsp. of mustard powder
1 tsp. of cumin
1 tbsp. Mexican seasoning

Pepper
Salt

INSTRUCTIONS

1. Pre-heat the Air Fryer at 350°F.
2. Place all of the ingredients into a bowl & combine well to coat the sweet potatoes entirely.
3. Place the wedges in the Air Fryer basket & air fry for 20 minutes, shaking the basket at 5-minute intervals.

506. POTATO WEDGES

Prep & Cook Time: 30 minutes | Servings: 4

INGREDIENTS

4 medium potatoes, cut into wedges
1 tbsp. of Cajun spice

1 tbsp. of olive oil
Pepper

Salt

INSTRUCTIONS

1. Place the potato wedges in the Air Fryer basket & pour in the olive oil.
2. Cook wedges at 370°F for 25 minutes, shaking the basket twice throughout the cooking time.
3. Put the cooked wedges in a bowl & coat them with the Cajun spice, pepper, & salt. Serve warm.

507. BANANA CHIPS

Prep & Cook Time: 20 minutes | Servings: 3

INGREDIENTS

2 large raw bananas, peel & sliced
½ tsp. of red chili powder

1 tsp. of olive oil
¼ tsp. of turmeric powder

1 tsp. of salt

INSTRUCTIONS

1. Put some water in a bowl along with the turmeric powder & salt.
2. Place the sliced bananas in the bowl & allow to soak for 10 minutes.
3. Dump the contents into a sieve to strain the banana slices before drying them with a paper towel.
4. Pre-heat the Air Fryer to 350°F.
5. Put the banana slices in a bowl & coat them with the olive oil, chili powder & salt.
6. Transfer the chips to the Air Fryer basket & air fry for 15 minutes.

---

508. HONEY CARROTS

Prep & Cook Time: 20 minutes | Servings: 4

INGREDIENTS

1 tbsp. of honey
3 cups baby carrots or carrots, sliced

1 tbsp. of olive oil
Sea salt to taste

Ground black pepper to taste

INSTRUCTIONS

1. In a bowl, combine the carrots, honey, & olive oil, coating the carrots completely. Sprinkle on some salt & ground black pepper.
2. Transfer the carrots to the Air Fryer & cook at 390°F for 12 minutes. Serve immediately.

---

509. POTATO TOTES

Prep & Cook Time: 20 minutes | Servings: 2

INGREDIENTS

1 large potato, diced
1 tsp. of onion, minced

1 tsp. of olive oil
Pepper

Salt

INSTRUCTIONS

1. Boil the potatoes in a saucepan of water over a medium-high heat.
2. Strain the potatoes, transfer them to bowl, & mash them thoroughly.
3. Combine with the olive oil, onion, pepper & salt in mashed potato.
4. Shape equal amounts of the mixture into small tots & place each one in the Air Fryer basket. Cook at 380°F for 8 minutes.
5. Give the basket a good shake & cook for an additional 5 minutes before serving.

---

510. ZUCCHINI

Prep & Cook Time: 30 minutes | Servings: 6

INGREDIENTS

6 medium zucchinis, cut into sticks
4 tbsp. of parmesan cheese, grated
4 egg whites, beaten

½ tsp. of garlic powder
1 cup of breadcrumbs
Pepper

Salt

INSTRUCTIONS

1. Pre-heat the Air Fryer to 400°F.
2. In a bowl, mix the beaten egg whites with some salt & pepper.
3. In a separate bowl, combine the breadcrumbs, garlic powder, & parmesan cheese.
4. Dredge each zucchini stick in the egg whites before rolling in the breadcrumbs.
5. Place the coated zucchini in the Air Fryer basket & allow to cook for 20 minutes.

---

511. CARROTS & CUMIN

Prep & Cook Time: 25 minutes | Servings: 4

INGREDIENTS

2 cups carrots, peeled & chopped
1 tsp. of cumin seeds

1 tbsp. of olive oil
¼ cup of coriander

INSTRUCTIONS

1. Cover the carrots with the cumin & oil.
2. Transfer to the Air Fryer & cook at 390°F for 12 minutes.
3. Season with the coriander before serving.

---

512. CHEESE STICKS

Prep & Cook Time: 15 minutes | Servings: 4

INGREDIENTS

1 lb. of mozzarella cheese
2 eggs, beaten
1 tsp. of cayenne pepper

1 cup of breadcrumbs
1 tsp. of onion powder
1 tsp. of garlic powder

1 cup of flour
½ tsp. of salt

INSTRUCTIONS

1. Slice the mozzarella cheese into 3- x ½-inch sticks.
2. Put the beaten eggs in a bowl.
3. Pour the flour into a shallow dish.
4. In a second bowl combine the breadcrumbs, cayenne pepper, onion powder, garlic powder, & salt.
5. Dredge the mozzarella strips in the beaten egg before coating it in the flour. Dip it in the egg again. Lastly, press it into the breadcrumbs.
6. Refrigerate for 20 minutes.
7. Pre-heat the Air Fryer to 400°F.
8. Spritz the Air Fryer basket with cooking spray.
9. Put the coated cheese sticks in the Air Fryer basket & cook for 5 minutes. Serve immediately.

513. ONION RINGS

Prep & Cook Time: 25 minutes | Servings: 2

INGREDIENTS

1 large onion, cut into slices
1 egg, beaten
¾ cup of breadcrumbs

1 cup of milk
1 tsp. of baking powder
1 ¼ cup of flour

1 tsp. of salt

INSTRUCTIONS

1. Pre-heat the Air Fryer for 5 minutes.
2. In a small bowl, combine the baking powder, flour, & salt
3. In a second bowl, stir together the milk & egg using a whisk.
4. Put the breadcrumbs in a shallow dish.
5. Coat each slice of onion with the flour, then dredge it in the egg mixture. Lastly, press it into the breadcrumbs.
6. Transfer the coated onion rings to the Air Fryer basket & cook at
7. 350°F for 10 minutes.

514. VEGAN VEGGIE DISH

Prep & Cook Time: 30 minutes | Servings: 4

INGREDIENTS

1 large zucchini, sliced
3 – 4 cherry tomatoes on the vine
1 medium carrot, peeled & cubed
1 large parsnip, peeled & cubed

1 green pepper, sliced
1 tsp. of mustard
1 tsp. of mixed herbs
2 cloves garlic, crushed

2 tbsp. of honey
3+3 tbsp. of olive oil, separately
Sea salt to taste
Black pepper to taste

INSTRUCTIONS

1. Place the slices of zucchini, green pepper, parsnip, carrot & cherry tomatoes inside the Air Fryer.
2. Pour 3 tbsp. of oil over the vegetables & cook at 360°F for 15 minutes.
3. In the meantime, make the marinade by mixing together all of the other ingredients in the Air Fryer baking dish.
4. Transfer the cooked vegetables to the baking dish & coat it completely with the marinade. Season with pepper & salt as desired.
5. Return to the Air Fryer & cook at 390°F for 5 minutes. Serve hot.

515. TOFU

Prep & Cook Time: 20 minutes | Servings: 4

INGREDIENTS

15 oz. extra firm tofu, drained & cut into cubes
1 tsp. chili flakes

¾ cup cornstarch
¼ cup cornmeal
Pepper

Salt

INSTRUCTIONS

1. In a bowl, combine the cornmeal, cornstarch, chili flakes, pepper, & salt.
2. Coat the tofu cubes completely with the mixture.
3. Pre-heat your Air Fryer at 350°F.
4. Spritz the basket with cooking spray.
5. Transfer the coated tofu to the basket & air fry for 8 minutes, shaking the basket at the 4-minute mark.

516. FRIDAY'S FRIES

Prep & Cook Time: 25 minutes | Servings: 2

INGREDIENTS

1 large eggplant, cut into 3-inch slices
¼ cup of water

1 tbsp. of olive oil
¼ cup of cornstarch

¼ tsp. of salt

INSTRUCTIONS
1. Pre-heat the Air Fryer to 400°F.
2. In a bowl, combine the water, olive oil, cornstarch, & salt.
3. Coat the sliced eggplant with the mixture.
4. Put the coated eggplant slices in the Air Fryer basket & cook for 20 minutes.

517. SWEET POTATO BITES
Prep & Cook Time: 30 minutes | Servings: 2

INGREDIENTS

2 sweet potatoes, diced into 1-inch cubes
1 tsp. of red chili flakes

2 tsp. of cinnamon
2 tbsp. of olive oil

2 tbsp. of honey
½ cup of fresh parsley, chopped

INSTRUCTIONS
1. Pre-heat the Air Fryer at 350°F.
2. Place all of the ingredients in a bowl & stir well to coat the sweet potato cubes entirely.
3. Put the sweet potato mixture into the Air Fryer basket & cook for 15 minutes.

518. KALE CHIPS
Prep & Cook Time: 15 minutes | Servings: 2

INGREDIENTS

1 head of kale

1 tbsp. of olive oil

1 tsp. of soy sauce

INSTRUCTIONS
1. De-stem the head of kale & shred each leaf into a 1 ½" piece. Wash & dry well.
2. Toss the kale with the olive oil & soy sauce to coat it completely.
3. Transfer to the Air Fryer & cook at 390°F for 2 to 3 minutes, giving the leaves a good toss at the halfway mark.

519. STUFFED TOMATOES
Prep & Cook Time: 30 minutes | Servings: 4

INGREDIENTS

4 large tomatoes, without tops
1 clove garlic, crushed
1 onion, cubed
1 cup frozen peas

2 cups of cooked rice, cold
1 tbsp. of soy sauce
1 carrot, cubed
1 tbsp. of olive oil

Parsley to taste, roughly chopped
Cooking spray

INSTRUCTIONS
1. Fry up the rice in a pan with the olive oil over a low heat.
2. Add in the cubed onion, carrots, crushed garlic, & frozen peas & allow to cook for 2 minutes, stirring occasionally.
3. Pour in the soy sauce & toss to coat. Remove the pan from the heat.
4. Pre-heat the Air Fryer to 360°F.
5. Stuff each tomato with the rice & vegetables
6. Put the tomatoes in the Air Fryer & cook for 20 minutes.
7. Garnish the cooked tomatoes with the chopped parsley & serve.

520. MIXED NUTS
Prep & Cook Time: 15 minutes | Servings: 8

INGREDIENTS

2 cups of mixed nuts
1 tsp. of chipotle chili powder

1 tsp. of ground cumin
1 tbsp. of butter, melted

1 tsp. of pepper
1 tsp. of salt

INSTRUCTIONS
1. In a bowl, combine all of the ingredients, coating the nuts well.
2. Set your Air Fryer to 350°F & allow to heat for 5 minutes.
3. Place the mixed nuts in the Air Fryer basket & roast for 4 minutes, shaking the basket halfway through the cooking time.

521. CHEESY POTATOES
Prep & Cook Time: 20 minutes | Servings: 4

INGREDIENTS

11 oz. of potatoes, diced & boiled
1 egg yolk
2 tbsp. of flour

3 tbsp. of parmesan cheese
3 tbsp. of breadcrumbs
Pepper

Nutmeg to taste
Salt

INSTRUCTIONS
1. Pre-heat Air Fryer at 390°F.
2. Mash up the potatoes & combine with all of the ingredients, minus the breadcrumbs.
3. Shape equal amounts of the mixture into medium-sized balls & roll each one in the breadcrumbs.

4. Place the potato balls in the Air Fryer & cook for 4 minutes.

522. BAKED POTATOES

Prep & Cook Time: 45 minutes | Servings: 3

INGREDIENTS

3 Idaho or russet baking potatoes, washed
2 cloves garlic, crushed

1 tbsp. of olive oil
1 tbsp. of sea salt
Parsley, roughly chopped

Sour cream to taste

INSTRUCTIONS

1. Pierce each potato several times with a fork.
2. Sprinkle the potatoes with salt & coat with the garlic puree & olive oil.
3. Place the potatoes in the Air Fryer basket & cook at 390°F for 35 - 40 minutes until soft. Serve with parsley & sour cream, or whatever toppings you desire.

523. BABY CORN

Prep & Cook Time: 20 minutes | Servings: 4

INGREDIENTS

8 oz. of baby corns, boiled
1 cup of flour
1 tsp. of garlic powder

½ tsp. of carom seeds
¼ tsp. of chili powder
Pinch of baking soda

Salt

INSTRUCTIONS

1. In a bowl, combine the flour, chili powder, garlic powder, cooking soda, salt & carom seed. Add in a little water to create a batter-like consistency.
2. Coat each baby corn in the batter.
3. Pre-heat the Air Fryer at 350°F.
4. Cover the Air Fryer basket with aluminum foil before laying the coated baby corns on top of the foil.
5. Cook for 10 minutes.

524. FRENCH FRIES

Prep & Cook Time: 25 minutes | Servings: 4

INGREDIENTS

1 lb. of russet potatoes
1 tsp. of salt

½ tsp. of black pepper
1 tbsp. of olive oil

INSTRUCTIONS

1. In a pot filled with water, blanch the potatoes until softened.
2. Remove from the heat & allow to cool. Slice the potatoes into matchstick shapes.
3. Place them in a large bowl & coat with the olive oil, salt & pepper.
4. Pre-heat the Air Fryer to 390°F.
5. Cook the French fries for about 15 minutes, giving the basket a shake now & again throughout the cooking time. Serve with freshly chopped herbs if desired.

525. ROASTED CORN

Prep & Cook Time: 15 minutes | Servings: 8

INGREDIENTS

4 fresh ears of corn

2 to 3 tsp. of vegetable oil

Salt & pepper

INSTRUCTIONS

1. Remove the husks from the corn, before washing & drying the corn. Slice up the corn to fit your Air Fryer basket if necessary.
2. Pour a drizzling of vegetable oil over the corn, coating it well. Sprinkle on salt & pepper.
3. Place in the Air Fryer & cook at 400°F for about 10 minutes.

526. ROASTED CARROTS

Prep & Cook Time: 20 minutes | Servings: 2

INGREDIENTS

1 tbsp. of olive oil
3 cups of baby carrots or carrots

1 tbsp. of honey
Salt & pepper

INSTRUCTIONS

1. In a bowl, coat the carrots with the honey & olive oil before sprinkling on some salt & pepper.
2. Place into the Air Fryer & cook at 390°F for 12 minutes. Serve hot.

527. FRIED KALE CHIPS

Prep & Cook Time: 10 minutes | Servings: 2

INGREDIENTS

1 head of kale, torn into 1 ½-inch pieces   1 tbsp. of olive oil   1 tsp. of soy sauce

INSTRUCTIONS

1. Wash & dry the kale pieces.
2. Transfer the kale to a bowl & coat with the soy sauce & oil.
3. Place it in the Air Fryer & cook at 400°F for 3 minutes, tossing it halfway through the cooking process.

---

528. ORANGE CAULIFLOWER

Prep & Cook Time: 30 minutes | Servings: 2

INGREDIENTS

½ lemon, juiced   ½ tbsp. of olive oil   Sea salt to taste
1 head of cauliflower   1 tsp. of curry powder   Ground black pepper to taste

INSTRUCTIONS

1. Wash the cauliflower. Cut out the leaves & core.
2. Chop the cauliflower into equally sized florets.
3. Coat the inside of the Air Fryer with the oil & allow it to warm up for about 2 minutes at 390°F.
4. In a bowl, mix together the fresh lemon juice & curry powder. Add in the cauliflower florets. Sprinkle in the pepper & salt & mix again, coating the florets well.
5. Transfer to the Air Fryer, cook for 20 minutes, & serve warm.

---

529. LEMON GREEN BEANS

Prep & Cook Time: 20 minutes | Servings: 4

INGREDIENTS

1 lemon, juiced   ¼ tsp. of extra virgin olive oil   Black pepper to taste
1 lb. of green beans, washed   Sea salt to taste

INSTRUCTIONS

1. Pre-heat the Air Fryer to 400°F.
2. Put the green beans in your Air Fryer basket & drizzle the lemon juice over them.
3. Sprinkle on the pepper & salt. Pour in the oil & toss to coat the green beans well.
4. Cook for 10 – 12 minutes & serve warm.

---

530. BROCCOLI FLORETS

Prep & Cook Time: 20 minutes | Servings: 4

INGREDIENTS

1 lb. of broccoli, cut into florets   1 tbsp. of olive oil   3 garlic cloves, minced
1 tbsp. of lemon juice   1 tbsp. of sesame seeds

INSTRUCTIONS

1. In a bowl, combine all of the ingredients, coating the broccoli well.
2. Transfer to the Air Fryer basket & air fry at 400°F for 13 minutes.

---

531. AVOCADO FRIES

Prep & Cook Time: 20 minutes | Servings: 4

INGREDIENTS

½ cup of panko   1 whole avocado
½ tsp. of salt   1 oz. of aquafaba

INSTRUCTIONS

1. In a shallow bowl, stir together the panko & salt.
2. In a separate shallow bowl, add the aquafaba.
3. Dip the avocado slices into the aquafaba, before coating each one in the panko.
4. Place the slices in your Air Fryer basket, taking care not to overlap any. Air fry for 10 minutes at 390°F.

---

532. ORIENTAL SPINACH SAMOSA

Prep & Cook Time: 45 minutes | Servings: 2

INGREDIENTS

¾ cup of boiled & blended spinach puree   taste   ¼ cup of boiled & cut potatoes
¼ cup of green peas   2 tsp. of olive oil   ½ 1 cup of flour
½ tsp. of sesame seeds   1 tsp. of chopped fresh coriander leaves   ½ tsp. of cooking soda
Ajwain, salt, chaat masala, chili powder to   1 tsp. of garam masala

INSTRUCTIONS

1. In a bowl, combine the Ajwain, flour, cooking soda & salt to form a dough-like consistency. Pour in one tsp. of the oil & the spinach puree. Continue to mix the dough, ensuring it is smooth.
2. Refrigerate for 20 minutes. Add another tsp. of oil to a saucepan & sauté the potatoes & peas for 5 minutes.
3. Stir in the sesame seeds, coriander, & any other spices you desire.
4. Use your hands to shape equal sized amounts of the dough into small balls. Mold these balls into cone-shapes.
5. Fill each cone with the potatoes & peas mixture & seal.
6. Pre-heat your Air Fryer to 390°F.
7. Put the samosas in the basket & cook for 10 minutes.
8. Serve the samosas with the sauce of your choice.

533. TOMATOES & HERBS

Prep & Cook Time: 30 minutes | Servings: 2

INGREDIENTS

2 large tomatoes, washed & cut into halves
Herbs, such as oregano, basil, thyme,
rosemary, sage to taste
Cooking spray
Pepper
Parmesan, grated [optional]
Parsley, minced [optional]

INSTRUCTIONS

1. Spritz both sides of each tomato half with a small amount of cooking spray.
2. Coat the tomatoes with a light sprinkling of pepper & the herbs of your choice.
3. Place the tomatoes in your Air Fryer basket, cut-side-up. Cook at 320°F for 20 minutes, or longer if necessary.
4. Serve hot, at room temperature, or chilled as a refreshing summer snack. Optionally, you can garnish them with grated Parmesan & minced parsley before serving.

534. VEGETABLE FRITTERS

Prep & Cook Time: 15 minutes | Servings: 4

INGREDIENTS

1 cup of bell peppers, deveined & chopped
1 tsp. of sea salt flakes
1 tsp. Of cumin
¼ tsp. of paprika
½ cup of shallots, chopped
2 cloves of garlic, minced
1 ½ tbsp. of fresh chopped cilantro
1 egg, whisked
¾ cup of cheddar cheese, grated
¼ cup of cooked quinoa
¼ cup of flour

INSTRUCTIONS

1. In a bowl, combine all of the ingredients well.
2. Divide the mixture into equal portions & shape each one into a ball. Use your palm to flatten each ball very slightly to form patties.
3. Lightly coat the patties with a cooking spray.
4. Put the patties in your Air Fryer cooking basket, taking care not to overlap them.
5. Cook at 340°F for 10 minutes, turning them over halfway through.

535. CHEESECAKE CUPS

Prep & Cook Time: 25 minutes | Servings: 4

INGREDIENTS

8 oz. of cream cheese, softened
2 oz. of heavy cream
1 tsp. of sugar
1 tsp. of vanilla flavoring

INSTRUCTIONS

1. Combine all the ingredients.
2. Whip until a pudding consistency is achieved.
3. Divide in cups.
4. Cook inside your Air Fryer at 325°F/160°C for 20 minutes until warm.
5. Refrigerate and serve!

536. STRAWBERRY SHAKE

Prep & Cook Time: 5 minutes | Servings: 1

INGREDIENTS

¾ cup of coconut milk (from the carton)
¼ cup of heavy cream
7 ice cubes
2 tbsp. of sugar-free strawberry Torani syrup
¼ tsp. Xanthan Gum

INSTRUCTIONS

1. Combine all the ingredients into blender.
2. Blend for 1-2 minutes.
3. Cook inside your Air Fryer at 325°F/160°C for 2 minutes until warm.
4. Serve!

537. RASPBERRY PUDDING SURPRISE

Prep & Cook Time: 40 minutes | Servings: 1

INGREDIENTS

3 tbsp. of chia seeds

½ cup of milk

1 scoop of chocolate protein powder

¼ cup of raspberries, fresh or frozen

1 tsp. of honey

INSTRUCTIONS

1. Combine the milk, protein powder & chia seeds together.
2. Let rest for 5 minutes before stirring.
3. Cook inside your Air Fryer at 325°F/160°C for 25 minutes until warm.
4. Top with raspberries.
5. Serve!

538. VANILLA BEAN DREAM

Prep & Cook Time: 35 minutes | Servings: 1

INGREDIENTS

½ cup of extra virgin coconut oil, softened

½ cup of coconut butter, softened

Juice of 1 lemon

Seeds from ½ a vanilla bean

INSTRUCTIONS

1. Whisk the ingredients in an easy-to-pour cup.
2. Pour into a lined cupcake or loaf pan.
3. Cook inside your Air Fryer at 325°F/160°C for 30 minutes until warm.
4. Serve!

539. WHITE CHOCOLATE BERRY CHEESECAKE

Prep & Cook Time: 5-10 minutes | Servings: 4

INGREDIENTS

8 oz. of cream cheese, softened

2 oz. of heavy cream

½ tsp. of sugar

1 tsp. of raspberries

1 tbsp. of white chocolate syrup

INSTRUCTIONS

1. Whip together the ingredients to a thick consistency inside a greased pan. Place the pan inside your Air Fryer at 325°F/160°C for 5 minutes.
2. Divide in cups.
3. Refrigerate.
4. Serve!

540. COCONUT PILLOW

Prep & Cook Time: 1-2 days | Servings: 4

INGREDIENTS

1 can of coconut milk

Berries of choice

Dark chocolate

INSTRUCTIONS

1. Refrigerate the coconut milk for 24 hours.
2. Remove it from your refrigerator & whip for 2-3 minutes.
3. Fold in the berries.
4. Cook inside your Air Fryer at 325°F/160°C for 5 minutes until warm.
5. Season with the chocolate shavings.
6. Serve!

541. COFFEE SURPRISE

Prep & Cook Time: 8 minutes | Servings: 1

INGREDIENTS

2 heaped tbsp. of flaxseed, ground

100ml of cooking cream 35% fat

½ tsp. of cocoa powder, dark

1 tbsp. of goji berries

Freshly brewed coffee

INSTRUCTIONS

1. Mix together the flaxseeds, cream & cocoa & coffee.
2. Season with goji berries.
3. Cook inside your Air Fryer at 325°F/160°C for 5 minutes until warm.
4. Serve!

542. CHOCOLATE CHEESECAKE

Prep & Cook Time: 60 minutes | Servings: 4

INGREDIENTS

4 oz. of cream cheese

½ oz. of heavy cream

1 tsp. of sugar glycerite

1 tsp. of sugar

1 oz. of chocolate chips

INSTRUCTIONS

1. Combine all the ingredients except the chocolate to a thick consistency.
2. Fold in the chocolate chips.
3. Cook inside your Air Fryer at 325°F/160°C for 30 minutes.
4. Serve!

543. CRUSTY

Prep & Cook Time: 40 minutes | Servings: 3

INGREDIENTS

2 cups of flour
4 tsp. of melted butter

2 large eggs
½ tsp. of salt

INSTRUCTIONS

1. Mix together the flour & butter.
2. Add in the eggs & salt & combine well to form a dough ball.
3. Place the dough between two pieces of parchment paper. Roll out to 10" by 16" & ¼ inch thick.
4. Place inside your Air Fryer and cook at 375°F/190°C for 30 minutes.
5. Serve.

544. CHOCOLATE PEANUT BUTTER CUPS

Prep & Cook Time: 40 minutes | Servings: 2

INGREDIENTS

1 stick of butter
1 oz. / 1 cube of chocolate

5 tbsp. of sugar
1 tbsp. of heavy cream

4 tbsp. of peanut butter

INSTRUCTIONS

1. In a microwave, melt the butter & chocolate.
2. Add the sugar.
3. Stir in the cream & peanut butter.
4. Line the muffin tins. Fill the muffin cups.
5. Cook inside your Air Fryer and cook at 375°F/190°C for 30 minutes.
6. Serve!

545. MACAROON BITES

Prep & Cook Time: 30 minutes | Servings: 2

INGREDIENTS

4 egg whites
½ tsp. of vanilla

½ tsp. of sugar
4½ tsp. of water

1 cup of coconut

INSTRUCTIONS

1. Preheat your Air Fryer to 375°F/190°C.
2. Combine the egg whites, liquids & coconut.
3. Put into the Air Fryer & reduce the heat to 325°F/160°C.
4. Bake for 15 minutes.
5. Serve!

546. CHOCO-BERRY FUDGE SAUCE

Prep & Cook Time: 15 minutes | Servings: 2

INGREDIENTS

4 oz. of cream cheese, softened
1-3.5 oz. 90% of chocolate Lindt bar

¼ cup of sugar
¼ cup of heavy cream

1 tbsp. of raspberry syrup

INSTRUCTIONS

1. Inside your Air Fryer, melt together the cream cheese & chocolate at 325°F/160°C for 5 minutes.
2. Open halfway and stir in the sugar.
3. Finish cooking and once cool, mix in the cream & syrup.
4. Serve!

547. CHOCO-COCONUT PUDDIN

Prep & Cook Time: 45 minutes | Servings: 1

INGREDIENTS

1 cup of coconut milk
2 tbsp. of cacao powder or organic cocoa

½ tsp. of sugar
½ tbsp. of quality gelatin

1 tbsp. of water

INSTRUCTIONS

1. Inside your Air Fryer, combine the coconut milk, cocoa & sugar at 325°F/160°C for 30 minutes.

2. In a separate bowl, mix in the gelatin & water.
3. Add to the Air Fryer & stir until fully dissolved.
4. Pour into small dishes & refrigerate for 1 hour.
5. Serve!

548. STRAWBERRY DESSERT

Prep & Cook Time: 45 minutes | Servings: 1

INGREDIENTS

½ cup of strawberry preserves
½ cup of sugar

2 cups of Greek Yogurt
Ice cream maker

INSTRUCTIONS

1. In a food processor, purée the strawberries. Add the strawberry preserves.
2. Add the Greek yogurt & fully mix.
3. Cook inside your Air Fryer at 325°F/160°C for 30 minutes until baked.
4. Serve!

549. BERRY LAYER CAKE

Prep & Cook Time: 8 minutes | Servings: 1

INGREDIENTS

¼ lemon of pound cake
¼ cup of whipping cream

½ tsp. of sugar
Eighth tsp. of orange flavor

1 cup of mixed berries

INSTRUCTIONS

1. Using a sharp knife, divide the lemon cake into small cubes.
2. Dice the strawberries.
3. Combine the whipping cream, sugar, & orange flavor.
4. Cook inside your Air Fryer at 325°F/160°C for 2 minutes until warm.
5. Layer the fruit, cake & cream in a glass.
6. Serve!

550. CHOCOLATE PUDDING

Prep & Cook Time: 50 minutes | Servings: 1

INGREDIENTS

3 tbsp. of chia seeds
1 cup of milk

1 scoop of cocoa powder
¼ cup of fresh raspberries

½ tsp. of honey

INSTRUCTIONS

1. Mix together all of the ingredients in a large bowl.
2. Let it rest for 15 minutes but stir halfway through.
3. Stir it again & refrigerate for 30 minutes. Garnish with raspberries.
4. Place inside your Air Fryer at 325°F/160°C for 2 minutes until warm.
5. Serve!

551. CRANBERRY CREAM SURPRISE

Prep & Cook Time: 30 minutes | Servings: 1

INGREDIENTS

1 cup mashed cranberries
½ cup of sugar

2 tsp. of natural cherry flavoring
2 tsp. of natural rum flavoring

1 cup of organic heavy cream

INSTRUCTIONS

1. Combine the mashed cranberries, sugar, cherry & rum flavorings.
2. Cover & refrigerate for 20 minutes.
3. Whip the heavy cream until soft peaks form.
4. Layer the whipped cream & cranberry mixture.
5. Top with fresh cranberries, mint leaves or grated dark chocolate.
6. Place inside your Air Fryer at 325°F/160°C for 2 minutes until warm.
7. Serve!

552. BANANA CHOCOLATE CAKE

Prep & Cook Time: 30 minutes | Servings: 10

INGREDIENTS

1 stick of softened butter
½ cup of sugar
1 egg

1 banana, mashed
2 tbsp. of maple syrup
2 cups of flour

¼ tsp. of anise star, ground
¼ tsp. of ground mace
¼ tsp. of ground cinnamon

¼ tsp. of crystallized ginger
½ tsp. of vanilla paste

Pinch of kosher salt
½ cup of cocoa powder

INSTRUCTIONS
1. Beat together the softened butter & sugar to combine well.
2. Mix together the egg, mashed banana & maple syrup using a whisk.
3. Combine the two mixtures, stirring well until pale & creamy.
4. Add in the flour, anise star, mace, cinnamon, crystallized ginger, vanilla paste, salt, & cocoa powder. Mix well to form the batter.
5. Grease two cake pans with cooking spray.
6. Transfer the batter into the cake pans & place them in the Air Fryer.
7. Cook at 330°F for 30 minutes. Frost with chocolate glaze if desired

553. LEMON BUTTER POUND CAKE

Prep & Cook Time: 2 hours 20 minutes | Servings: 8

INGREDIENTS

1 stick of softened butter
1 cup of sugar
1 medium egg
1 ¼ cups of flour

1 tsp. of butter flavoring
1 tsp. of vanilla essence
Salt
¾ cup of milk

Grated zest of 1 medium-sized lemon
For the Glaze:
2 tbsp. of freshly squeezed lemon juice

INSTRUCTIONS:
1. In a large bowl, use a creamer to mix together the butter & sugar. Fold in the egg & continue to stir.
2. Add in the flour, butter flavoring, vanilla essence, & salt, combining everything well.
3. Pour in the milk, followed by the lemon zest, & continue to mix.
4. Lightly brush the inside of a cake pan with the melted butter.
5. Pour the cake batter into the cake pan.
6. Place the pan in the Air Fryer & bake at 350°F for 15 minutes.
7. After removing it from the Air Fryer, run a knife around the edges of the cake to loosen it from the pan & transfer it to a serving plate.
8. Leave it to cool completely.
9. In the meantime, make the glaze by combining with the lemon juice.
10. Pour the glaze over the cake & let it sit for a further 2 hours before serving

554. FRIED PINEAPPLE RINGS

Prep & Cook Time: 10 minutes | Servings: 6

INGREDIENTS

⅔ cup of flour
½ tsp. of baking powder
½ tsp. of baking soda
Pinch of kosher salt

½ cup of water
1 cup of rice milk
½ tsp. of ground cinnamon
¼ tsp. of ground anise star

½ tsp. of vanilla essence
4 tbsp. of sugar
¼ cup of flaked coconut
1 medium pineapple, peeled & sliced

INSTRUCTIONS
1. Mix together all of the ingredients, minus the pineapple.
2. Cover the pineapple slices with the batter.
3. Place the slices in the Air Fryer & cook at 380°F for 6 - 8 minutes.
4. Pour a drizzling of maple syrup over the pineapple & serve with a side of vanilla ice cream.

555. HAZELNUT BROWNIE CUPS

Prep & Cook Time: 30 minutes | Servings: 12

INGREDIENTS

6 oz. of chocolate chips
1 stick of butter, at room temperature
1 cup of sugar
2 large eggs

¼ cup of red wine
¼ tsp. of hazelnut extract
1 tsp. of pure vanilla extract
¾ cup of flour

2 tbsp. of cocoa powder
½ cup of ground hazelnuts
Pinch of kosher salt

INSTRUCTIONS
1. Melt the butter & chocolate chips in a microwave.
2. In a large bowl, combine the sugar, eggs, red wine, hazelnut & vanilla extract with a whisk. Pour in the chocolate mix.
3. Add in the flour, cocoa powder, ground hazelnuts, & a pinch of kosher salt, continuing to stir until a creamy, smooth consistency is achieved.
4. Take a muffin tin & place a cupcake liner in each cup. Spoon an equal amount of the batter into each one.
5. Air bake at 360°F for 28 - 30 minutes, cooking in batches if necessary.
6. Serve with a topping of ganache if desired

556. SWIRLED GERMAN CAKE

Prep & Cook Time: 25 minutes | Servings: 8

INGREDIENTS

1 cup of flour
1 tsp. of baking powder

1 cup of sugar
1/8 tsp. of salt

¼ tsp. of ground cinnamon
¼ tsp. of grated nutmeg

1 tsp. of orange zest
1 stick of butter, melted

2 eggs
1 tsp. of pure vanilla extract

¼ cup of milk
2 tbsp. of cocoa powder

INSTRUCTIONS:
1. Take a round pan that is small enough to fit inside your Air Fryer & lightly grease the inside with oil.
2. In a bowl, use an electric mixer to combine the flour, baking powder, sugar, salt, cinnamon, nutmeg, & orange zest.
3. Fold in the butter, eggs, vanilla, & milk, incorporating everything well.
4. Spoon a quarter-cup of the batter to the baking pan.
5. Stir the cocoa powder into the rest of the batter.
6. Use a spoon to drop small amounts of the brown batter into the white batter. Swirl them together with a knife.
7. Place the pan in the Air Fryer & cook at 360°F for about 15 minutes.
8. Remove the pan from the Air Fryer & leave to cool for roughly 10 minutes.

557. OATMEAL APPLE & PLUM CRUMBLE

Prep & Cook Time: 20 minutes | Servings: 6

INGREDIENTS

¼ lb. of plums, pitted & chopped
¼ lb. of Braeburn apples, cored & chopped
1 tbsp. of fresh lemon juice
2 ½ oz. of sugar

1 tbsp. of honey
½ tsp. of ground mace
½ tsp. of vanilla paste
1 cup fresh cranberries
⅓ cup of oats

⅔ cup of flour
½ stick of butter, chilled
1 tbsp. cold water

INSTRUCTIONS
1. Coat the plums & apples with the lemon juice, sugar, honey, & ground mace.
2. Lightly coat the inside of a cake pan with cooking spray.
3. Pour the fruit mixture into the pan.
4. In a bowl, mix together all of the other ingredients, combining everything well.
5. Use a palette knife to spread this mixture evenly over the fruit.
6. Place the pan in the Air Fryer & air bake at 390°F for 20 minutes. Ensure the crumble is cooked through before serving.

558. CHOCOLATE CHIP COOKIES

Prep & Cook Time: 25 minutes | Servings: 9

INGREDIENTS

1 ¼ cup of flour
⅔ cup chocolate chips, or any kind of baker's chocolate

⅓ cup of sugar
½ cup of butter
4 tbsp. of honey

1 tbsp. of milk
High quality cooking spray

INSTRUCTIONS
1. Set your Air Fryer to 320°F & allow to warm up for about 10 minutes.
2. In the meantime, in a large bowl, cream the butter to soften it.
3. Add in the sugar & combine to form a light & fluffy consistency.
4. Stir in the honey.
5. Gradually fold in the flour, incorporating it well.
6. If you are using baker's chocolate, use a rolling pin or a mallet to break it up & create chocolate chips.
7. Throw the chocolate into the bowl & mix well to ensure the chips are evenly distributed throughout the dough.
8. Finally, add in the milk & combine well.
9. Lightly spritz your Air Fryer basket with the cooking spray.
10. Transfer the cookie dough into the Air Fryer & cook for 20 minutes.
11. Slice into 9 cookies. Serve immediately. Alternatively, the cookies can be stored in an airtight container for up to 3 days.

559. HOMEMADE COCONUT BANANA TREAT

Prep & Cook Time: 20 minutes | Servings: 6

INGREDIENTS

2 tbsp. of coconut oil
¾ cup of breadcrumbs
2 tbsp. of sugar

½ tsp. of cinnamon powder
¼ tsp. of ground cloves
6 ripe bananas, peeled & halved

⅓ cup of flour
1 large egg, beaten

INSTRUCTIONS
1. Heat a skillet over a medium heat. Add in the coconut oil & the breadcrumbs & mix together for approximately 4 minutes.
2. Take the skillet off of the heat.
3. Add in the sugar, cinnamon, & cloves.
4. Cover all sides of the banana halves with the rice flour.
5. Dip each one in the beaten egg before coating them in the bread crumb mix.
6. Place the banana halves in the Air Fryer basket, taking care not to overlap them. Cook at 290°F for 10 minutes. You may need to complete this step in multiple batches.
7. Serve hot or at room temperature, topped with a sprinkling of flaked coconut if desired.

560. MINI STRAWBERRY PIES

Prep & Cook Time: 15 minutes | Servings: 8

INGREDIENTS

1 cup of sugar
¼ tsp. of ground cloves
1/8 tsp. of cinnamon powder

1 tsp. of vanilla extract
1 [12-oz.] can of biscuit dough
12 oz. of strawberry pie filling

¼ cup of butter, melted

INSTRUCTIONS

1. In a bowl, mix together the sugar, cloves, cinnamon, & vanilla.
2. With a rolling pin, roll each piece of the biscuit dough into a flat, round circle.
3. Spoon an equal amount of the strawberry pie filling onto the center of each biscuit.
4. Roll up the dough. Dip the biscuits into the melted butter & coat them with the sugar mixture.
5. Coat with a light brushing of non-stick cooking spray on all sides.
6. Transfer the cookies to the Air Fryer & bake them at 340°F for roughly 10 minutes, or until a golden-brown color is achieved.
7. Allow to cool for 5 minutes before serving.

---

561. COCONUT BROWNIES

Prep & Cook Time: 15 minutes | Servings: 8

INGREDIENTS

½ cup of coconut oil
2 oz. of dark chocolate
1 cup of sugar
2 ½ tbsp. of water
4 whisked eggs

¼ tsp. of ground cinnamon
½ tsp. of ground anise star
¼ tsp. of coconut extract
½ tsp. of vanilla extract
1 tbsp. of honey

½ cup of flour
½ cup of desiccated coconut
sugar, to dust

INSTRUCTIONS

1. Melt the coconut oil & dark chocolate in the microwave.
2. Combine with the sugar, water, eggs, cinnamon, anise, coconut extract, vanilla, & honey in a large bowl.
3. Stir in the flour & desiccated coconut. Incorporate everything well.
4. Lightly grease a baking dish with butter. Transfer the mixture to the dish.
5. Place the dish in the Air Fryer & bake at 355°F for 15 minutes.
6. Remove from the Air Fryer & allow to cool slightly.
7. Take care when taking it out of the baking dish. Slice it into squares.
8. Dust with sugar before serving.

---

562. BANANA & VANILLA PASTRY PUFFS

Prep & Cook Time: 15 minutes | Servings: 8

INGREDIENTS

1 packet [8-oz.] of dinner rolls
1 cup of milk

4 oz. of instant vanilla pudding
4 oz. of cream cheese, softened

2 bananas, peeled & sliced
1 egg, lightly beaten

INSTRUCTIONS

1. Roll out the crescent dinner rolls & slice each one into 8 squares.
2. Mix together the milk, pudding, & cream cheese using a whisk.
3. Scoop equal amounts of the mixture into the pastry squares. Add the banana slices on top.
4. Fold the squares around the filling, pressing down on the edges to seal them.
5. Apply a light brushing of the egg to each pastry puff before placing them in the Air Fryer.
6. Air bake at 355°F for 10 minutes.

---

563. DOUBLE CHOCOLATE CAKE

Prep & Cook Time: 45 minutes | Servings: 8

INGREDIENTS

½ cup of sugar
1 ¼ cups of flour
1 tsp. of baking powder
1/3 cup of cocoa powder
¼ tsp. of ground cloves

1/8 tsp. of freshly grated nutmeg
Pinch of table salt
1 egg
¼ cup of soda of your choice
¼ cup of milk

½ stick of butter, melted
2 oz. of bittersweet chocolate, melted
½ cup of hot water

INSTRUCTIONS

1. In a bowl, thoroughly combine the dry ingredients.
2. In another bowl, mix together the egg, soda, milk, butter, & chocolate.
3. Combine the two mixtures. Add in the water & stir well.
4. Take a cake pan that is small enough to fit inside your Air Fryer & transfer the mixture to the pan.
5. Place a sheet of foil on top & bake at 320°F for 35 minutes.
6. Take off the foil & bake for further 10 minutes.
7. Frost the cake with buttercream if desired before serving.

---

564. BANANA OATMEAL COOKIES

Prep & Cook Time: 20 minutes | Servings: 6

INGREDIENTS

2 cups of quick oats
¼ cup of milk

4 ripe bananas, mashed
¼ cup of coconut, shredded

INSTRUCTIONS

1. Pre-heat the Air Fryer to 350°F.
2. Combine all of the ingredients in a bowl.
3. Scoop equal amounts of the cookie dough onto a baking sheet & put it in the Air Fryer basket.
4. Bake the cookies for 15 minutes.

---

565. SUGAR BUTTER FRITTERS

Prep & Cook Time: 30 minutes | Servings: 16

INGREDIENTS

For the dough:
4 cups of flour
1 tsp. of salt
1 tsp. of sugar
3 tbsp. of butter, at room temperature

1 packet of instant yeast
1 ¼ cups of lukewarm water

For the Cakes:
1 cup of sugar
Pinch of cardamom
1 tsp. of cinnamon powder
1 stick of butter, melted

INSTRUCTIONS

1. Place all of the ingredients in a large bowl & combine well.
2. Add in the lukewarm water & mix until a soft, elastic dough forms.
3. Place the dough on a lightly floured surface & lay a greased sheet of aluminum foil on top of the dough. Refrigerate for 5 to 10 minutes.
4. Remove it from the refrigerator & divide it in two. Mold each half into a log & slice it into 20 pieces.
5. In a shallow bowl, combine the sugar, cardamom & cinnamon.
6. Coat the slices with a light brushing of melted butter & the sugar.
7. Spritz Air Fryer basket with cooking spray.
8. Transfer the slices to the Air Fryer & air fry at 360°F for roughly 10 minutes. Turn each slice once during the baking time.
9. Dust each slice with the sugar before serving.

---

566. PEAR & APPLE CRISP WITH WALNUTS

Prep & Cook Time: 25 minutes | Servings: 6

INGREDIENTS

½ lb. of apples, cored & chopped
½ lb. of pears, cored & chopped
1 cup of flour
1 cup of sugar

1 tbsp. of butter
1 tsp. of ground cinnamon
¼ tsp. of ground cloves
1 tsp. of vanilla extract

¼ cup of chopped walnuts
Whipped cream, to serve

INSTRUCTIONS

1. Lightly grease a baking pan & place the apples & pears inside and place the pan inside your Air Fryer.
2. Combine the rest of the ingredients, minus the walnuts & the whipped cream, until a course, crumbly texture is achieved.
3. Pour the mixture over the fruits & spread it evenly. Top with the chopped walnuts.
4. Air bake at 340°F for 20 minutes or until the top turns golden brown.
5. When cooked through, serve at room temperature with whipped cream.

---

567. SWEET & CRISP BANANAS

Prep & Cook Time: 20 minutes | Servings: 4

INGREDIENTS

4 ripe bananas, peeled & halved
1 tbsp. of oatmeal
1 tbsp. of cashew, crushed

1 egg, beaten
1 ½ tbsp. of coconut oil
¼ cup of flour

1 ½ tbsp. of sugar
½ cup of breadcrumbs

INSTRUCTIONS

1. Put the coconut oil in a saucepan & heat over a medium heat. Stir in the breadcrumbs & cook, stirring continuously, for 4 minutes.
2. Transfer the breadcrumbs to a bowl.
3. Add in the oatmeal & crushed cashew. Mix well.
4. Coat each of the banana halves in the corn flour, before dipping it in the beaten egg & lastly coating it with the breadcrumbs.
5. Put the coated banana halves in the Air Fryer basket. Season with the sugar.
6. Air fry at 350°F for 10 minutes.

---

568. SHORTBREAD FINGERS

Prep & Cook Time: 20 minutes | Servings: 10

INGREDIENTS

1 ½ cups of butter
1 cup of flour

¾ cup of sugar
Cooking spray

INSTRUCTIONS
1. Pre-heat your Air Fryer to 350°F.
2. In a bowl. combine the flour & sugar.
3. Cut each stick of butter into small chunks. Add the chunks into the flour & the sugar.
4. Blend the butter into the mixture to combine everything well.
5. Use your hands to knead the mixture, forming a smooth consistency.
6. Shape the mixture into 10 equal-sized finger shapes, marking them with the tines of a fork for decoration if desired.
7. Lightly spritz the Air Fryer basket with the cooking spray. Place the cookies inside, spacing them out well.
8. Bake the cookies for 12 minutes.
9. Let cool slightly before serving. Alternatively, you can store the cookies in an airtight container for up to 3 days.

569. COCONUT & BANANA CAKE

Prep & Cook Time: 1 hour 15 minutes | Servings: 5

INGREDIENTS

⅔ cup of sugar, shaved
⅔ cup of butter
3 eggs
1 ¼ cup of flour

1 ripe banana, mashed
½ tsp. of vanilla extract
1/8 tsp. of baking soda
Sea salt to taste

Topping Ingredients:
sugar to taste, shaved
Walnuts to taste, roughly chopped
Bananas to taste, sliced

INSTRUCTIONS
1. Pre-heat the Air Fryer to 360°F.
2. Mix together the flour, baking soda, & a pinch of sea salt.
3. In a separate bowl, combine the butter, vanilla extract & sugar using an electrical mixer or a blender, to achieve a fluffy consistency. Beat in the eggs one at a time.
4. Throw in half of the flour mixture & stir thoroughly. Add in the mashed banana & continue to mix. Lastly, throw in the remaining half of the flour mixture & combine until a smooth batter is formed.
5. Transfer the batter to a baking tray & top with the banana slices.
6. Scatter the chopped walnuts on top before dusting with the sugar
7. Place a sheet of foil over the tray & pierce several holes in it.
8. Put the covered tray in the Air Fryer. Cook for 48 minutes.
9. Decrease the temperature to 320°F, take off the foil, & allow to cook for an additional 10 minutes until golden brown.
10. Insert a skewer or toothpick in the center of the cake. If it comes out clean, the cake is ready.

570. ROASTED PUMPKIN SEEDS & CINNAMON

Prep & Cook Time: 35 minutes | Servings: 2

INGREDIENTS

1 cup pumpkin raw seeds
1 tbsp. of ground cinnamon

2 tbsp. of sugar
1 cup of water

1 tbsp. of olive oil

INSTRUCTIONS
1. In a frying pan, combine the pumpkin seeds, cinnamon & water.
2. Boil the mixture over a high heat for 2 - 3 minutes.
3. Pour out the water & place the seeds on a clean kitchen towel, allowing them to dry for 20 - 30 minutes.
4. In a bowl, mix together the sugar, dried seeds, a pinch of cinnamon & one tbsp. of olive oil.
5. Pre-heat the Air Fryer to 340°F.
6. Place the seed mixture in the Air Fryer basket & allow to cook for 15 minutes, shaking the basket periodically throughout.

571. PINEAPPLE STICKS

Prep & Cook Time: 20 minutes | Servings: 4

INGREDIENTS

½ fresh pineapple, cut into sticks
¼ cup desiccated coconut

INSTRUCTIONS
1. Pre-heat the Air Fryer to 400°F.
2. Coat the pineapple sticks in the desiccated coconut & put each one in the Air Fryer basket.
3. Air fry for 10 minutes.

572. SPONGE CAKE

Prep & Cook Time: 50 minutes | Servings: 8

INGREDIENTS

For the Cake:
9 oz. of sugar
9 oz. butter

3 eggs
9 oz. of flour
1 tsp. of vanilla extract

Zest of 1 lemon
1 tsp. of baking powder

For the Frosting:
Juice of 1 lemon
Zest of 1 lemon

1 tsp. yellow food coloring
7 oz. of sugar
4 egg whites

INSTRUCTIONS
1. Pre-heat your Air Fryer to 320°F.
2. Use an electric mixer to combine all of the cake ingredients.
3. Grease the insides of two round cake pans.
4. Pour an equal amount of the batter into each pan.
5. Place one pan in the Air Fryer & cook for 15 minutes, before repeating with the second pan.
6. In the meantime, mix together all of the frosting ingredients.
7. Allow the cakes to cool. Spread the frosting on top of one cake & stack the other cake on top.

573. APPLE WEDGES

Prep & Cook Time: 25 minutes | Servings: 4

INGREDIENTS
4 large apples
2 tbsp. of olive oil

½ cup of dried apricots, chopped
1 – 2 tbsp. of sugar

½ tsp. of ground cinnamon

INSTRUCTIONS
1. Peel the apples & slice them into eight wedges. Throw away the cores.
2. Coat the apple wedges with the oil.
3. Place each wedge in the Air Fryer & cook for 12 - 15 minutes at 350°F.
4. Add in the apricots & allow to cook for a further 3 minutes.
5. Stir together the sugar & cinnamon. Sprinkle this mixture over the cooked apples before serving.

574. CHOCOLATE LAVA CAKE

Prep & Cook Time: 20 minutes | Servings: 4

INGREDIENTS
1 cup of dark cocoa candy melts
1 stick butter
2 eggs
4 tbsp. of sugar

1 tbsp. of honey
4 tbsp. of flour
Pinch of kosher salt
Pinch of ground cloves

¼ tsp. of grated nutmeg
¼ tsp. of cinnamon powder

INSTRUCTIONS
1. Spritz the insides of four custard cups with cooking spray.
2. Melt the cocoa candy melts & butter in the microwave for 30 seconds to 1 minute.
3. In a large bowl, combine the eggs, sugar & honey with a whisk until frothy. Pour in the melted chocolate mix.
4. Throw in the rest of the ingredients & combine well with an electric mixer or a manual whisk.
5. Transfer equal portions of the mixture into the prepared custard cups.
6. Place in the Air Fryer & air bake at 350°F for 12 minutes.
7. Remove from the Air Fryer & allow to cool for 5 to 6 minutes.
8. Place each cup upside-down on a dessert plate & let the cake slide out. Serve with fruits & chocolate syrup if desired.

575. ENGLISH LEMON TARTS

Prep & Cook Time: 30 minutes | Servings: 4

INGREDIENTS
½ cup of butter
½ lb. of flour

2 tbsp. of sugar
1 large lemon, juiced & zested

2 tbsp. of lemon curd
Pinch of nutmeg

INSTRUCTIONS
1. In a large bowl, combine the butter, flour & sugar until a crumbly consistency is achieved.
2. Add in the lemon zest & juice, followed by a pinch of nutmeg. Continue to combine. If necessary, add a couple tbsp. of water to soften the dough.
3. Sprinkle the insides of a few small pastry tins with flour. Pour equal portions of the dough into each one & add sugar or lemon zest on top.
4. Pre-heat the Air Fryer to 360°F.
5. Place the lemon tarts inside the Air Fryer & allow to cook for 15 minutes.

576. BLUEBERRY PANCAKES

Prep & Cook Time: 20 minutes | Servings: 4

INGREDIENTS
½ tsp. of vanilla extract
2 tbsp. of honey
½ cup of blueberries

½ cup of sugar
2 cups + 2 tbsp. of flour
3 eggs, beaten

1 cup of milk
1 tsp. of baking powder
Salt

INSTRUCTIONS
1. Pre-heat the Air Fryer to 390°F.

2. In a bowl, mix together all of the dry ingredients.
3. Pour in the wet ingredients & combine with a whisk, ensuring the mixture becomes smooth.
4. Roll each blueberry in some flour to lightly coat it before folding it into the mixture. This is to ensure they do not change the color of the batter.
5. Coat the inside of a baking dish with a little oil or butter.
6. Spoon several equal amounts of the batter onto the baking dish, spreading them into pancake-shapes & ensuring to space them out well. This may have to be completed in two batches.
7. Place the dish in the Air Fryer & bake for about 10 minutes.

577. NEW ENGLAND PUMPKIN CAKE

Prep & Cook Time: 50 minutes | Servings: 4

INGREDIENTS

1 large egg
½ cup of skimmed milk
7 oz. of flour

2 tbsp. of sugar
5 oz. of pumpkin puree
Salt

Pinch of cinnamon [if desired]
Cooking spray

INSTRUCTIONS

1. Stir together the pumpkin puree & sugar in a bowl. Crack in the egg & combine using a whisk until smooth.
2. Add in the flour & salt, stirring constantly. Pour in the milk, ensuring to combine everything well.
3. Spritz a baking tin with cooking spray.
4. Transfer the batter to the baking tin.
5. Pre-heat the Air Fryer to 350°F.
6. Put the tin in the Air Fryer basket & bake for 15 minutes.

578. MIXED BERRY PUFFED PASTRY

Prep & Cook Time: 20 minutes | Servings: 3

INGREDIENTS

3 pastry dough sheets
½ cup of mixed berries, mashed

1 tbsp. of honey
2 tbsp. of cream cheese

3 tbsp. of chopped walnuts
¼ tsp. of vanilla extract

INSTRUCTIONS

1. Pre-heat your Air Fryer to 375°F.
2. Roll out the pastry sheets & spread the cream cheese over each one.
3. In a bowl, combine the berries, vanilla extract & honey.
4. Cover a baking sheet with parchment paper.
5. Spoon equal amounts of the berry mixture into the center of each sheet of pastry. Scatter the chopped walnuts on top.
6. Fold up the pastry around the filling & press down the edges with the back of a fork to seal them.
7. Transfer the baking sheet to the Air Fryer & cook for approximately 15 minutes.

579. CHERRY PIE

Prep & Cook Time: 35 minutes | Servings: 8

INGREDIENTS

1 tbsp. of milk
2 ready-made pie crusts

21 oz. of cherry pie filling
1 egg yolk

INSTRUCTIONS

1. Pre-heat the Air Fryer to 310°F.
2. Coat the inside of a pie pan with a little oil or butter & lay one of the pie crusts inside. Use a fork to pierce a few holes in the pastry.
3. Spread the pie filling evenly over the crust.
4. Slice the other crust into strips & place them on top of the pie filling to make the pie look more homemade.
5. Place in the Air Fryer & cook for 15 minutes.

580. APPLE PIE

Prep & Cook Time: 25 minutes | Servings: 7

INGREDIENTS

2 large apples
½ cup of flour

2 tbsp. of butter
1 tbsp. of sugar

½ tsp. of cinnamon

INSTRUCTIONS

1. Pre-heat the Air Fryer to 360°F
2. In a large bowl, combine the flour & butter. Pour in the sugar, continuing to mix.
3. Add in a few tbsp. of water & combine everything to create a smooth dough.
4. Grease the insides of a few small pastry tins with butter. Divide the dough between each tin & lay each portion flat inside.
5. Peel, core & dice up the apples. Put the diced apples on top of the pastry & top with a sprinkling of sugar & cinnamon.
6. Place the pastry tins in your Air Fryer & cook for 15 - 17 minutes.
7. Serve with whipped cream or ice cream if desired.

581. CHOCOLATE MOLTEN LAVA CAKE

Prep & Cook Time: 25 minutes | Servings: 4

INGREDIENTS

3 ½ oz. of butter, melted
3 ½ tbsp. of sugar

3 ½ oz. of chocolate, melted
1 ½ tbsp. of flour

2 eggs

INSTRUCTIONS

1. Pre-heat the Air Fryer to 375°F.
2. Grease four ramekins with a little butter.
3. Rigorously combine the eggs & butter before stirring in the melted chocolate.
4. Slowly fold in the flour.
5. Spoon an equal amount of the mixture into each ramekin.
6. Put them in the Air Fryer & cook for 10 minutes
7. Place the ramekins upside-down on plates & let the cakes fall out. Serve hot.

582. PINEAPPLE CAKE

Prep & Cook Time: 40 minutes | Servings: 4

INGREDIENTS

2 cups of flour
¼ lb. of butter
¼ cup of sugar

½ lb. of pineapple, chopped
½ cup of pineapple juice
1 oz. of dark chocolate, grated

1 large egg
2 tbsp. of skimmed milk

INSTRUCTIONS

1. Pre-heat the Air Fryer to 370°F.
2. Grease a cake tin with a little oil or butter.
3. In a bowl, combine the butter & flour to create a crumbly consistency.
4. Add in the sugar, diced pineapple, juice, & crushed dark chocolate & mix well.
5. In a separate bowl, combine the egg & milk. Add this mixture to the flour & stir well until a soft dough forms.
6. Pour the mixture into the cake tin & transfer to the Air Fryer.
7. Cook for 35 - 40 minutes.

583. GLAZED DONUTS

Prep & Cook Time: 25 minutes | Servings: 2 – 4

INGREDIENTS

1 can [8 oz.] of refrigerated croissant
dough

Cooking spray
1 can [16 oz.] of vanilla frosting

INSTRUCTIONS

1. Cut the croissant dough into 1-inch-round slices. Make a hole in the center of each one to create a donut.
2. Put the donuts in the Air Fryer basket, taking care not to overlap any, & spritz with cooking spray. You may need to cook everything in multiple batches.
3. Cook at 400°F for 2 minutes. Turn the donuts over & cook for another 3 minutes.
4. Place the rolls on a paper plate.
5. Microwave a half-cup of frosting for 30 seconds & pour a drizzling of the frosting over the donuts before serving.

584. APPLE DUMPLINGS

Prep & Cook Time: 40 minutes | Servings: 2

INGREDIENTS

2 tbsp. of sultanas
2 sheets of puff pastry

2 tbsp. of butter, melted
2 small apples

1 tbsp. of sugar

INSTRUCTIONS

1. Pre-heat your Air Fryer to 350°F
2. Peel the apples & remove the cores.
3. In a bowl, stir together the sugar & the sultanas.
4. Lay one apple on top of each pastry sheet & stuff the sugar & sultanas into the holes where the cores used to be.
5. Wrap the pastry around the apples, covering them completely.
6. Put them on a sheet of aluminum foil & coat each dumpling with a light brushing of melted butter
7. Transfer to the Air Fryer & bake for 25 minutes until a golden-brown color is achieved & the apples have softened inside.

585. BANANAS & ICE CREAM

Prep & Cook Time: 25 minutes | Servings: 2

INGREDIENTS

2 large bananas
1 tbsp. of butter

1 tbsp. of sugar
2 tbsp. of breadcrumbs

Vanilla ice cream for serving

INSTRUCTIONS
1. Place the butter in the Air Fryer basket & allow it to melt for 1 minute at 350°F.
2. Combine the sugar & breadcrumbs in a bowl.
3. Slice the bananas into 1-inch-round pieces. Drop them into the sugar mixture & coat them well.
4. Place the bananas in the Air Fryer & cook for 10 – 15 minutes.
5. Serve warm, with ice cream on the side if desired.

586. RASPBERRY MUFFINS

Prep & Cook Time: 35 minutes | Servings: 10

INGREDIENTS
1 egg
1 cup of flour coated raspberries
1 ½ cups of flour
½ cup of sugar

⅓ cup vegetable oil
2 tsp. of baking powder
Yogurt, as needed
1 tsp. of lemon zest

2 tbsp. of lemon juice
Pinch of sea salt

INSTRUCTIONS
1. Pre-heat the Air Fryer to 350°F
2. Place all of the dry ingredients in a bowl & combine well.
3. Beat the egg & pour it into a cup. Mix it with the oil & lemon juice. Add in the yogurt, to taste.
4. Mix together the dry & wet ingredients.
5. Add in the lemon zest & raspberries.
6. Coat the insides of 10 muffin tins with a little butter.
7. Spoon an equal amount of the mixture into each muffin tin.
8. Transfer to the Air Fryer, & cook for 10 minutes, in batches if necessary.

587. PECAN PIE

Prep & Cook Time: 1 hour 10 minutes | Servings: 4

INGREDIENTS
1x 8-inch pie dough
½ tsp. of cinnamon
¾ tsp. of vanilla extract
2 eggs

¾ cup maple syrup
1/8 tsp. of nutmeg
2 tbsp. of butter
1 tbsp. of butter, melted

2 tbsp. of sugar
½ cup of chopped pecans

INSTRUCTIONS
1. Pre-heat the Air Fryer to 370°F.
2. In a small bowl, coat the pecans in the melted butter.
3. Transfer the pecans to the Air Fryer & allow them to toast for about 10 minutes.
4. Put the pie dough in a greased pie pan & add the pecans on top.
5. In a bowl, mix together the rest of the ingredients. Pour this over the pecans.
6. Place the pan in the Air Fryer & bake for 25 minutes.

588. ORANGE CARROT CAKE

Prep & Cook Time: 30 minutes | Servings: 8

INGREDIENTS
2 large carrots, peeled & grated
1 ¾ cup of flour
¾ cup of sugar
2 eggs

10 tbsp. of olive oil
2 cups of sugar
1 tsp. of mixed spice
2 tbsp. of milk

4 tbsp. of melted butter
1 small orange, rind & juice

INSTRUCTIONS
1. Set the Air Fryer to 360°F & allow to heat up for 10 minutes.
2. Place a baking sheet inside the tin.
3. Combine the flour, sugar, grated carrots, & mixed spice.
4. Pour the milk, beaten eggs, & olive oil into the middle of the batter & mix well.
5. Pour the mixture in the tin, transfer to the Air Fryer & cook for 5 minutes.
6. Lower the heat to 320°F & allow to cook for an additional 5 minutes.
7. In the meantime, prepare the frosting by combining the melted butter, orange juice, rind, & sugar until a smooth consistency is achieved.
8. Remove the cake from the Air Fryer, allow it to cool for several minutes & add the frosting on top.

589. CHOCOLATE COOKIES

Prep & Cook Time: 30 minutes | Servings: 8

INGREDIENTS
3 oz. of sugar
4 oz. of butter

1 tbsp. of honey
6 oz. of flour

1 ½ tbsp. of milk
2 oz. of chocolate chips

INSTRUCTIONS

1. Pre-heat the Air Fryer to 350°F.
2. Mix together the sugar & butter using an electric mixer, until a fluffy texture is achieved.
3. Stir in the remaining ingredients, minus the chocolate chips.
4. Gradually fold in the chocolate chips.
5. Spoon equal portions of the mixture onto a lined baking sheet & flatten out each one with a spoon. Ensure the cookies are not touching.
6. Place in the Air Fryer & cook for 18 minutes.

590. BUTTER CAKE

Prep & Cook Time: 25 minutes | Servings: 2

INGREDIENTS

1 egg
1 ½ cup of flour
7 tbsp. of butter, at room temperature

6 tbsp. of milk
6 tbsp. of sugar
Pinch of sea salt

Cooking spray
Dusting of sugar to serve

INSTRUCTIONS

1. Pre-heat the Air Fryer to 360°F.
2. Spritz the inside of a small ring cake tin with cooking spray.
3. In a bowl, combine the butter & sugar using a whisk.
4. Stir in the egg & continue to mix everything until the mixture is smooth & fluffy.
5. Pour the flour through a sieve into the bowl.
6. Pour in the milk, before adding a pinch of salt, & combine once again to incorporate everything well.
7. Pour the batter into the tin & use the back of a spoon to make sure the surface is even.
8. Place in the Air Fryer & cook for 15 minutes.
9. Before removing it from the Air Fryer, ensure the cake is cooked through by inserting a toothpick into the center & checking that it comes out clean.
10. Allow the cake to cool & serve.

591. SWEDISH CHOCOLATE MUG CAKE

Prep & Cook Time: 15 minutes | Servings: 1

INGREDIENTS

1 tbsp. of cocoa powder
3 tbsp. of coconut oil

¼ cup of flour
3 tbsp. of whole milk

5 tbsp. of sugar

INSTRUCTIONS

1. In a bowl, stir together all of the ingredients to combine them completely.
2. Take a short, stout mug & pour the mixture into it.
3. Put the mug in your Air Fryer & cook for 10 minutes at 390°F.

592. DUNKY DOUGH DIPPERS & CHOCOLATE SAUCE

Prep & Cook Time: 45 minutes | Servings: 5

INGREDIENTS

¾ cup of sugar
1 lb. of bread dough

1 cup of heavy cream
12 oz. of chocolate chips

½ cup of butter, melted
2 tbsp. of vanilla extract

INSTRUCTIONS

1. Pre-heat the Air Fryer to 350°F.
2. Coat the inside of the basket with a little melted butter.
3. Halve & roll up the dough to create two 15-inch logs. Slice each log into 20 disks.
4. Halve each disk & twist it 3 or 4 times.
5. Lay out a cookie sheet & lay the twisted dough pieces on top. Brush the pieces with some more melted butter & sprinkle on the sugar.
6. Place the sheet in the Air Fryer & air fry for 5 minutes. Flip the dough twists over & brush the other side with more butter. Cook for an additional 3 minutes. It may be necessary to complete this step-in batches.
7. In the meantime, make the chocolate sauce. Firstly, put the heavy cream into a saucepan over the medium heat & allow it to simmer.
8. Put the chocolate chips into a large bowl & add the simmering cream on top. Whisk the chocolate chips everything together until a smooth consistency is achieved. Stir in 2 tbsp. of the vanilla extract.
9. Transfer the baked cookies in a shallow dish, pour over the rest of the melted butter & sprinkle on the sugar.
10. Drizzle on the chocolate sauce before serving.

593. PEACH CRUMBLE

Prep & Cook Time: 35 minutes | Servings: 6

INGREDIENTS

1 ½ lb. peaches, peeled & chopped
2 tbsp. of lemon juice
1 cup of flour

1 tbsp. of water
½ cup of sugar
5 tbsp. cold butter

Pinch of sea salt

INSTRUCTIONS

1. Mash the peaches a little with a fork to achieve a lumpy consistency.

2. Add in two tbsp. of sugar & the lemon juice.
3. In a bowl, combine the flour, salt, & sugar. Throw in a tbsp. of water before adding in the cold butter, mixing until crumbly.
4. Grease the inside of a baking dish & arrange the berries at the bottom. Top with the crumbs.
5. Transfer the dish to the Air Fryer & air fry for 20 minutes at 390°F.

594. BANANA WALNUT CAKE

Prep & Cook Time: 55 minutes | Servings: 6

INGREDIENTS

16 oz. bananas, mashed
8 oz. of flour
6 oz. of sugar

3.5 oz. of walnuts, chopped
2.5 oz. of butter
2 eggs

¼ tsp. of baking soda

INSTRUCTIONS

1. Coat the inside of a baking dish with a little oil.
2. Pre-heat the Air Fryer at 355°F.
3. In a bowl combine the sugar, butter, egg, flour & soda using a whisk. Throw in the bananas & walnuts.
4. Transfer the mixture to the dish. Place the dish in the Air Fryer & cook for 10 minutes.
5. Reduce the heat to 330°F & cook for another 15 minutes. Serve hot

595. CHEESY LEMON CAKE

Prep & Cook Time: 60 minutes | Servings: 6

INGREDIENTS

17.5 oz. of ricotta cheese
5.4 oz. of sugar

3 eggs
3 tbsp. of flour

1 lemon, juiced & zested
2 tsp. of vanilla extract [optional]

INSTRUCTIONS

1. Pre-heat Air Fryer to 320°F.
2. Combine all of the ingredients until a creamy consistency is achieved.
3. Place the mixture in a cake tin.
4. Transfer the tin to the Air Fryer & cook the cakes for 25 minutes.
5. Remove the cake from the Air Fryer, allow to cool, & serve.

596. CHOCOLATE BROWNIES & CARAMEL SAUCE

Prep & Cook Time: 45 minutes | Servings: 4

INGREDIENTS

½ cup of butter
1 ¾ oz. of cooking chocolate
1 cup of sugar

2 medium eggs, beaten
1 cup of flour
2 tsp. of vanilla

2 tbsp. of water
⅔ cup of milk

INSTRUCTIONS

1. In a saucepan over a medium heat, melt the butter & chocolate together.
2. Take the saucepan off the heat & stir in the sugar, eggs, flour, & vanilla, combining everything well.
3. Pre-heat your Air Fryer to 350°F.
4. Coat the inside of a baking dish with a little butter. Transfer the batter to the dish & place inside the Air Fryer.
5. Bake for 15 minutes.
6. In the meantime, prepare the caramel sauce. In a small saucepan, slowly bring the water to a boil. Cook for around 3 minutes, until the mixture turns light brown.
7. Lower the heat & allow to cook for another two minutes. Gradually add in the rest of the butter. Take the saucepan off the heat & allow the caramel to cool.
8. When the brownies are ready, slice them into squares. Pour the caramel sauce on top & add on some sliced banana if desired before serving.

597. PUMPKIN CINNAMON PUDDING

Prep & Cook Time: 25 minutes | Servings: 4

INGREDIENTS

3 cups of pumpkin puree
3 tbsp. of honey
1 tbsp. of ginger

1 tbsp. of cinnamon
1 tsp. of clove
1 tsp. of nutmeg

1 cup of full-fat cream
2 eggs
1 cup of sugar

INSTRUCTIONS

1. Pre-heat your Air Fryer to 390°F.
2. In a bowl, stir all of the ingredients together to combine.
3. Grease the inside of a small baking dish.
4. Pour the mixture into the dish & transfer to the Air Fryer. Cook for 15 minutes. Serve with whipped cream if desired

598. BANANA WALNUT BREAD

Prep & Cook Time: 40 minutes | Servings: 1 loaf

INGREDIENTS

7 oz. of flour

¼ tsp. of baking powder

2.5 oz. of butter

5.5 oz. of sugar

2 medium eggs

14 oz. bananas, peeled

2.8 oz. chopped walnuts

INSTRUCTIONS

1. Pre-heat the Air Fryer to 350°F.
2. Take a baking tin small enough to fit inside the Air Fryer & grease the inside with butter.
3. Mix together the flour & the baking powder in a bowl.
4. In a separate bowl, beat together the sugar & butter until fluffy & pale. Gradually add in the flour & egg. Stir.
5. Throw in the walnuts & combine again.
6. Mash the bananas using a fork & transfer to the bowl. Mix once more, until everything is incorporated.
7. Pour the mixture into the tin, place inside the Air Fryer & cook for 10 minutes.

599. PEACH SLICES

Prep & Cook Time: 40 minutes | Servings: 4

INGREDIENTS

4 cups of peaches, sliced

2 – 3 tbsp. of sugar

2 tbsp. of flour

⅓ cup of oats

2 tbsp. of butter

¼ tsp. of vanilla extract

1 tsp. of cinnamon

INSTRUCTIONS

1. In a large bowl, combine the peach slices, sugar, vanilla extract, & cinnamon. Pour the mixture into a baking tin & place it in the Air Fryer.
2. Cook for 20 minutes on 290°F.
3. In the meantime, combine the oats, flour, & of butter in a separate bowl.
4. Once the peach slices cooked, pour the butter mixture on top of them.
5. Cook for an additional 10 minutes at 300 - 310°F.
6. Remove from the Air Fryer & allow to crisp up for 5 – 10. Serve with ice cream if desired.

600. VANILLA SOUFFLE

Prep & Cook Time: 50 minutes | Servings: 6

INGREDIENTS

¼ cup of flour

¼ cup of butter, softened

1 cup whole milk

¼ cup of sugar

2 tsp. of vanilla extract

1 vanilla bean

5 egg whites

4 egg yolks

1 oz. of sugar

1 tsp. of cream of tartar

INSTRUCTIONS

1. Mix together the flour & butter to create a smooth paste.
2. In a saucepan, heat up the milk. Add the ¼ cup of sugar & allow it to dissolve.
3. Put the vanilla bean in the mixture & bring it to a boil.
4. Pour in the flour-butter mixture. Beat the contents of the saucepan thoroughly with a wire whisk, removing all the lumps.
5. Reduce the heat & allow the mixture to simmer & thicken for a number of minutes.
6. Take the saucepan off the heat. Remove the vanilla bean & let the mixture cool for 10 minutes in an ice bath.
7. In the meantime, grease six 3-oz. ramekins or soufflé dishes with butter & add a sprinkling of sugar to each one.
8. In a separate bowl quickly, rigorously stir the egg yolks & vanilla extract together. Combine with the milk mixture.
9. In another bowl, beat the egg whites, 1 oz. of sugar & cream of tartar to form medium stiff peaks.
10. Fold the egg whites into the soufflé base. Transfer everything to the ramekins, smoothing the surfaces with a knife or the back of a spoon.
11. Pre-heat the Air Fryer to 330°F.
12. Put the ramekins in the cooking basket & cook for 14 – 16 minutes. You may need to complete this step in multiple batches.
13. Serve the soufflés topped with powdered sugar & with a side of chocolate sauce.

601. BUTTER MARSHMALLOW FLUFF TURNOVER

Prep & Cook Time: 35 minutes | Servings: 4

INGREDIENTS

4 sheets of filo pastry, defrosted

4 tbsp. of chunky peanut butter

4 tsp. of marshmallow fluff

2 oz. of butter, melted

Pinch of sea salt

INSTRUCTIONS

1. Pre-heat the Air Fryer to 360°F.
2. Roll out the pastry sheets. Coat one with a light brushing of butter.
3. Lay a second pastry sheet on top of the first one. Brush once again with butter. Repeat until all 4 sheets have been used.
4. Slice the filo layers into four strips, measuring roughly 3 inches x 12 inches.
5. Spread one tbsp. of peanut butter & one tsp. of marshmallow fluff on the underside of each pastry strip.
6. Take the tip of each sheet & fold it backwards over the filling, forming a triangle. Repeat this action in a zigzag manner until the filling is completely enclosed.
7. Seal the ends of each turnover with a light brushing of butter.
8. Put the turnovers in the Air Fryer basket & cook for 3 – 5 minutes, until they turn golden brown & puffy.

9. Sprinkle a little sea salt over each turnover before serving.

602. CHOCOLATE-COVERED MAPLE BACON

Prep & Cook Time: 25 minutes | Servings: 4

INGREDIENTS
8 slices of sugar-free bacon
1 tbsp. of granular sugar

⅓ cup of chocolate chips
1 tsp. of coconut oil

½ tsp. of maple extract

INSTRUCTIONS
1. Place the bacon in the Air Fryer's basket & add the sugar on top. Cook for six minutes at 350°F & turn the bacon over. Leave to cook another six minutes or until the bacon is sufficiently crispy.
2. Take the bacon out of the Air Fryer & leave it to cool.
3. Microwave the chocolate chips & coconut oil together for half a minute. Remove from the microwave & mix together before stirring in the maple extract.
4. Set the bacon flat on a piece of parchment paper & pour the mixture over. Allow to harden in the refrigerator for roughly five minutes before serving.

603. SUGAR PORK RINDS

Prep & Cook Time: 10 minutes | Servings: 2

INGREDIENTS
2 oz. of pork rinds
2 tsp. of butter, melted

¼ cup of sugar
½ tsp. of ground cinnamon

INSTRUCTIONS
1. Coat the rinds with the melted butter.
2. In a separate bowl, combine the sugar & cinnamon & pour over the pork rinds, ensuring the rinds are covered completely & evenly.
3. Transfer the pork rinds into the Air Fryer & cook at 400°F for five minutes.

604. TOASTED COCONUT FLAKES

Prep & Cook Time: 5 minutes | Servings: 1

INGREDIENTS
1 cup of coconut flakes
2 tsp. of coconut oil, melted

¼ cup of sugar
Salt

INSTRUCTIONS
1. In a large bowl, combine the coconut flakes, oil, sugar, & a pinch of salt, ensuring that the flakes are coated completely.
2. Place the coconut flakes in your Air Fryer & cook at 300°F for three minutes, giving the basket a good shake a few times throughout the cooking time. Fry until golden & serve.

605. BLACKBERRY CRISP

Prep & Cook Time: 18 minutes | Servings: 1

INGREDIENTS
2 tbsp. of lemon juice
⅓ cup of sugar

2 cups of blackberries
1 cup of crunchy granola

INSTRUCTIONS
1. In a bowl, combine the lemon juice, sugar, & blackberries. Transfer to a round baking dish about six inches in diameter & seal with aluminum foil.
2. Put the dish in the Air Fryer & leave to cook for twelve minutes at 350°F.
3. Take care when removing the dish from the Air Fryer. Give the blackberries another stir & top with the granola.
4. Return the dish to the Air Fryer & cook for an additional three minutes, this time at 320°F. Serve once the granola has turned brown & enjoy.

606. CHURROS

Prep & Cook Time: 15 minutes | Servings: 1

INGREDIENTS
½ cup of water
¼ cup of butter

½ cup of flour
3 eggs

2 ½ tsp. of sugar

INSTRUCTIONS
1. In a saucepan, bring the water & butter to a boil. Once it is bubbling, add the flour & mix to create a doughy consistency.
2. Remove from the heat, allow to cool, & crack the eggs into the saucepan. Blend with a hand mixer until the dough turns fluffy.
3. Transfer the dough into a piping bag.
4. Pre-heat the Air Fryer at 380°F.
5. Pipe the dough into the Air Fryer in several three-inch-long segments. Cook for ten minutes before removing from the Air Fryer & coating in the sugar.

6. Serve with a chocolate sauce of your choice.

607. PEANUT BUTTER COOKIES

Prep & Cook Time: 15 minutes | Servings: 1

INGREDIENTS

¼ tsp. of salt
4 tbsp. of sugar

½ cup peanut butter
1 egg

INSTRUCTIONS

1. Combine the salt, sugar, & peanut butter in a bowl, incorporating everything well. Break the egg over the mixture & mix to create a dough.
2. Flatten the dough using a rolling pin & cut into shapes with a knife or cookie cutter. Make a crisscross on the top of each cookie with a fork.
3. Pre-heat your Air Fryer at 360°F.
4. Once the Air Fryer has warmed up, put the cookies inside & leave to cook for ten minutes. Take care when taking them out & allow to cook before enjoying.

608. AVOCADO PUDDING

Prep & Cook Time: 5 minutes | Servings: 1

INGREDIENTS

Avocado
3 tsp. of liquid Sugar

1 tbsp. cocoa powder
4 tsp. of milk

¼ tsp. of vanilla extract

INSTRUCTIONS

1. Pre-heat your Air Fryer at 360°F.
2. Halve the avocado, twist to open, & scoop out the pit.
3. Spoon the flesh into a bowl & mash it with a fork. Throw in the Sugar, cocoa powder, milk, & vanilla extract, & combine everything with a hand mixer.
4. Transfer this mixture to the basket of your Air Fryer & cook for three minutes.

609. CHIA PUDDING

Prep & Cook Time: 10 minutes | Servings: 1

INGREDIENTS

1 cup of chia seeds
1 cup of coconut milk

1 tsp. of liquid Sugar
1 tbsp. of coconut oil

1 tsp. of butter

INSTRUCTIONS

1. Pre-heat the Air Fryer at 360°F.
2. In a bowl, gently combine the chia seeds with the milk & Sugar, before mixing the coconut oil & butter. Spoon seven equal-sized portions into seven ramekins & set these inside the Air Fryer.
3. Cook for four minutes. Take care when removing the ramekins from the Air Fryer & allow to cool for four minutes before serving.

610. BACON COOKIES

Prep & Cook Time: 15 minutes | Servings: 2

INGREDIENTS

¼ tsp. of ginger
¼ tsp. of baking soda

⅔ cup peanut butter
2 tbsp. of swerve

3 slices of bacon, cooked & chopped

INSTRUCTIONS

1. In a bowl, mix the ginger, baking soda, peanut butter, & Swerve together, making sure to combine everything well.
2. Stir in the chopped bacon.
3. With clean hands, shape the mixture into a cylinder & cut in six. Press down each slice into a cookie with your palm.
4. Pre-heat your Air Fryer at 350°F.
5. When the Air Fryer is warm, put the cookies inside & cook for seven minutes. Take care when taking them out of the Air Fryer & allow to cool before serving.

611. LOBSTER TAILS & WHITE WINE SAUCE

Prep & Cook Time: 10 minutes | Servings: 4

INGREDIENTS

4 lobster tails, shell cut from the top
½ onion, quartered
½ cup of butter
⅓ cup of white wine

¼ cup of honey
6 garlic cloves, crushed
1 tbsp. of lemon juice
1 tsp. of salt

Pepper
Lemon slices to season
2 tbsp. fresh parsley

INSTRUCTIONS

1. Whack the lobster tails inside your Air Fryer.

2. Combine the remaining ingredients inside a mixing bowl & pour them over the lobster tails.
3. Switch your Air Fryer to 'broil' mode and cook for 15 minutes at 350°F.
4. Serve warm.

611. BROILED LOBSTER TAILS

Prep & Cook Time: 16minutes | Servings: 4

INGREDIENTS

2 lobster tails, shell cut from the top ½
1 cup of butter, melted

½ tsp. of ground paprika
Salt

White pepper, to taste
1 lemon, juiced

INSTRUCTIONS

5. Whack the lobster tails inside your Air Fryer.
6. Combine the remaining ingredients inside a mixing bowl & pour them over the lobster tails.
7. Switch your Air Fryer to 'broil' mode and cook for 15 minutes at 350°F.
8. Serve warm.

612. CHEESECAKE DELUX

Prep & Cook Time: 30 minutes | Servings: 15

INGREDIENTS

1 lb. of cream cheese
½ tsp. of vanilla extract

1 cup of graham crackers, crumbled
2 tbsp. of butter

2 eggs
4 tbsp. of sugar

INSTRUCTIONS

1. Combine the crackers with the butter inside a mixing bowl.
2. Spread the cracker mix on the bottom of a lined cake pan.
3. Place the pan inside your Air Fryer & cook at 350°F for 5 minutes.
4. In another bowl, combine the sugar with cream cheese, eggs, vanilla. Whisk until fully combined.
5. Smoother the filling over the cracker crust.
6. Cook the cheesecake in your Air Fryer at 310°F for 13 minutes.
7. Leave the cake in the refrigerator for 3 hours.
8. Slice & serve!

613. MACAROONS

Prep & Cook Time: 20 minutes | Servings: 20

INGREDIENTS

2 tbsp. of sugar

2 cups of coconut, shredded
4 egg whites

1 tsp. of vanilla extract

INSTRUCTIONS

1. Combine the egg whites with the sugar in a mixing bowl.
2. Toss in the coconut & vanilla extract. Mix until fully combined.
3. Sculpt macaroon shapes using the mixture.
4. Place inside your Air Fryer & cook at 340°F for 7 minutes.
5. Let cool and serve cold.

614. ORANGE CAKE DELUX

Prep & Cook Time: 25 minutes | Servings: 12

INGREDIENTS

1 orange, peeled & cut quartered
1 tsp. of vanilla extract
6 eggs
3 tbsp. of orange zest

4 oz. of cream cheese
1 tsp. of baking powder
9 oz. of flour

1 oz. of sugar
3 oz. of yogurt

INSTRUCTIONS

1. Mix the oranges and break them down using a mixer.
2. Toss in 2 tablespoons of flour, sugar, eggs, baking powder & vanilla extract. Mix until fully combined.
3. Pour the mixture into two spring form pans.
4. Whack the pans inside your Air Fryer & cook at 330°F for 15 minutes
5. Combine the cheese with orange zest, yogurt & the rest of the sugar inside a mixing bowl. Stir well.
6. Put one cake layer on a plate and pour roughly half of the cream cheese mixture on top.
7. Add the remaining cake layer & top with the remaining cream cheese mixture. Smoother well.

8. Slice and serve into portions!

615. AMARETTO

Prep & Cook Time: 15 minutes | Servings: 12

INGREDIENTS

1 lb. of bread dough
1 cup of heavy cream
11 oz. of chocolate chips
1 cup of sugar
½ cup of butter, melted
1 tbsp. of amaretto liqueur

INSTRUCTIONS

1. Add a dusting of flour to the countertop and roll out the dough on top.
2. When rolled, cut the dough into around 20 slices. Cut each slice into two smaller slices.
3. Using a brush, coat each dough slice with butter & sprinkle with sugar.
4. Whack the slices inside your Air Fryer and fry at 350°F for 4 minutes.
5. When done, flip the slices and fry the other side for a further 2 minutes.
6. When fried, take the slices out of your Air Fryer and place them onto a plate to cool.
7. On the stove top, pour the heavy cream inside a skillet and cook on medium heat, adding the chocolate chips & stirring until the mixture is melted and fully combined. Add the liqueur and stir.
8. Pour the mixture into a bowl & serve the bread dippers with this sauce.

616. CARROT CAKE DELUX

Prep & Cook Time: 55 minutes | Servings: 6

INGREDIENTS

5 oz. of flour
¾ tsp. of baking powder
¼ tsp. of nutmeg, ground
½ tsp. of baking soda
½ tsp. of cinnamon powder
½ cup of sugar
⅓ cup of carrots, grated
⅓ cup of pecans, toasted & chopped.
¼ cup of pineapple juice
½ tsp. of allspice
1 egg
2 tbsp. of yogurt
4 tbsp. of sunflower oil
⅓ cup of coconut flakes, shredded
Cooking spray

INSTRUCTIONS

1. Combine the flour with the baking soda, salt, allspice, cinnamon & nutmeg. Mix until fully combined and place to the side.
2. Inside another bowl, mix the egg with the yogurt, sugar, pineapple juice, oil, carrots, pecans & coconut flakes. Combine well.
3. Pour the two mixtures together and mix until fully combined.
4. Pour this combined mixture into a greased spring form pan.
5. Place the pan inside your Air Fryer and cook at 320°F for 43 minutes.
6. When cooked, let the cake cool, cur and serve!

617. BANANA BREAD

Prep & Cook Time: 50 minutes | Servings: 6

INGREDIENTS

¾ cup of sugar
⅓ cup of butter
⅓ cup of milk
1 tsp. of vanilla extract 1 egg
3 bananas, mashed
2 tsp. of baking powder
1 ½ cups of flour
½ tsp. of baking soda
1 ½ tsp. of cream of tartar
Cooking spray

INSTRUCTIONS

1. Combine the cream of tartar, sugar, butter, egg, vanilla & bananas inside a mixing bowl until sully combined and place to the side.
2. Inside another bowl, combine the flour with the baking powder & the baking soda.
3. Then, pour the two mixtures together and combine them well.
4. Grease a cake pan with the cooking spray and place it inside your Air Fryer.
5. Pour the combined mixture into the pan and cook at 320°F for 45 minutes.
6. When cooked, take out the bread and let it cool down. Slice into portions and serve!

618. MOUNTAIN GRANOLA

Prep & Cook Time: 45 minutes | Servings: 4

INGREDIENTS

1 cup of coconut, desiccated
½ cup of almonds
½ cup of pecans, chopped.
1 tbsp. of sugar
½ cup of pumpkin seeds
½ cup of sunflower seeds
1 tbsp. of sunflower oil
2 tsp. of nutmeg, ground
1 tsp. of apple pie spice mix

INSTRUCTIONS

1. Combine the almonds, pecans, pumpkin seeds, sunflower seeds, coconut, nutmeg & apple pie mix inside a large mixing bowl.
2. On a medium heat, heat a pan with the oil inside on your stove top. Add the sugar and stir.

3. Pour this over the nuts inside the bowl and mix until fully combined.
4. Grease a baking sheet with butter and pour this nutty mixture on top.
5. Place inside your Air Fryer and cook at 300°F for 23 minutes.
6. When cooked, let the granola slab cool and cut into slices and serve!

619. PEARS & ESPRESSO CREAM

Prep & Cook Time: 40 minutes | Servings: 4

INGREDIENTS

4 pears, halved & cored
1 tbsp. of water
3 tbsp. of lemon juice
1 tbsp. of sugar

1 tbsp. of butter
For the cream:
1 cup of whipping cream

1 tbsp. of espresso, cold
1 cup of mascarpone
⅓ cup of sugar

INSTRUCTIONS

1. Combine the pears with the lemon juice, sugar, butter & water until fully combined.
2. Place the mixture inside your Air Fryer and cook at 360°F for 25 minutes.
3. In the meantime, combine the whipping cream with the mascarpone, sugar & espresso inside a mixing bowl.
4. Store this mixture inside your refrigerator to keep cool until the Air Fryer stops cooking.
5. When cooked, take the pears out of your Air Fryer and portion them onto plates. Top with the cool expresso mixture.
6. Serve!

620. PARMESAN MUFFINS

Prep & Cook Time: 20 minutes | Servings: 4

INGREDIENTS

3 oz. of almond milk
3 oz. of white flour
3 oz. of parmesan cheese, grated

2 eggs
2 tbsp. of olive oil
1 tbsp. of baking powder

A dash of Worcestershire sauce

INSTRUCTIONS

1. Inside a large mixing bowl, combine the eggs with the olive oil, milk, baking powder, flour, Worcestershire sauce & the parmesan. Stir well.
2. Grease a muffin pan and place it inside your Air Fryer.
3. Pour the mixture on top and spread it evenly. Cook at 320°F for 14 minutes.
4. When cooked, take out the muffins and let them cool.
5. Serve!

621. ANGEL FOOD CAKE

Prep & Cook Time: 40 minutes | Servings: 12

INGREDIENTS

¼ cup of butter, melted
1 cup of powdered erythritol

2 tsp. of strawberry extract
12 egg whites

1 tsp. of cream of tartar
A pinch of salt

INSTRUCTIONS

1. Preheat your Air Fryer at 380°F for 5 minutes.
2. In the meantime, combine the egg whites & cream of tartar. Whisk until fluffy peaks form.
3. Toss in the remaining ingredients except for the butter. Whisk until fully combined.
4. Pour the mixture inside a greased baking dish.
5. Place the dish inside your preheated Air Fryer and cook at 380°F for 30 minutes.
6. When cooked, take out, let cool and drizzle with some melted butter.

622. UPSIDE DOWN CAKE

Prep & Cook Time: 40 minutes | Servings: 9

INGREDIENTS

¼ cup of almond butter
¼ cup of sunflower oil
½ cup of walnuts, chopped
¾ cup & 2 tbsp. of coconut sugar

¾ cup of water
1 ½ tsp. of mixed spice
1 cup of plain flour
1 lemon, zest

2 tsp. of baking soda
1 tsp. of vinegar
3 baking apples, cored & sliced

INSTRUCTIONS

1. Preheat your Air Fryer at 380°F for 5 minutes.
2. Inside a mixing bowl, combine the almond butter & 3 tbsp. of sugar.
3. Grease a baking dish and pour the mixture inside.
4. Place the dish inside your Air Fryer.

5. Inside another bowl, mix the flour, remaining sugar and baking soda together. Toss in the mixed spice.
6. Inside another bowl, combine the oil, water, vinegar, & lemon zest. Toss in the chopped walnuts and stir well.
7. Mix both bowls together until fully combined. Arrange the apple slices on top.
8. Bake at 380°F for 30 minutes.

623. BLUEBERRY LEMON CAKE DELUX

Prep & Cook Time: 40 minutes | Servings: 4

INGREDIENTS

2 eggs
1 cup of blueberries
Zest from 1 lemon
Juice from 1 lemon

1 tsp. of vanilla
Brown sugar for coating
2 ½ cups of self-rising flour
½ cup of monk fruit

½ cup of cream
¼ cup of avocado oil

INSTRUCTIONS

1. Inside a mixing bowl, combine the wet ingredients together.
2. Add in the dry ingredients and stir until fully combined.
3. Grease a baking dish and place it inside your Air Fryer.
4. Pour in the mixture and cook at 330°F for 10 minutes.
5. When cooked, take out and let cool.
6. Cut inside portions and serve!

624. STRAWBERRY COBBLER

Prep & Cook Time: 30 minutes | Servings: 4

INGREDIENTS

2 tsp. of butter
1 ½ cup of strawberries
1 tsp. of sugar
1 tbsp. of butter

½ cup of flour
¼ cup of heavy whipping cream
1 tsp. of cornstarch
½ cup of water

½ tsp. of salt
¾ tsp. of baking powder

INSTRUCTIONS

1. Grease a baking dish with butter and place it inside your Air Fryer.
2. Into the dish add the water, cornstarch & sugar. Cook at 390°F for 8 minutes until a gooey mixture is formed.
3. Add the strawberries to the mixture. Stir well.
4. Inside a mixing bowl, combine the salt, baking powder, sugar & flour. Pour in the cream. Add a little butter.
5. Spoon the mixture on top of the strawberries.
6. Bake for 13 minutes at 390°F until golden brown.

625. CHOCOLATE SOUFFLE

Prep & Cook Time: 18 minutes | Servings: 2

INGREDIENTS

3 oz. of baking cooking chocolate
¼ cup of butter
2 eggs, yolks & whites separated

2 tbsp. of sugar
½ tsp. of vanilla extract
2 tbsp. of flour

1 tsp. of powdered sugar for dusting

INSTRUCTIONS

1. Inside a microwaveable proof bowl, combine the butter and chocolate. Place inside your microwave and cook for 1 ½ minutes until melted.
2. Remove the mixture from your microwave and stir until smooth.
3. Inside another bowl, add the egg yolks. Whisk well until fully combined.
4. Add in the sugar & vanilla extract. Again, whisk well.
5. Add in the chocolate mixture and mix until fully incorporated.
6. Toss in the flour and mix well.
7. This time, in a mixing bowl, add the egg whites and whisk until fluffy peaks are formed.
8. Fold the fluffy egg whites into the chocolate mixture and place to the side.
9. Grease two ramekins and sprinkle with sugar for taste.
10. Place the final mixture into the ramekins and smooth off the top to form a flat and even surface.
11. Place the ramekins inside your Air Fryer and bake at 330°F for 15 minutes.
12. When baked, take out carefully and let cool. Sprinkle with the powdered sugar and serve warm/

CATALOGUE OF NUTRITIONAL INFORMATION

In this table, you'll find a breakdown of the nutritional information for each recipe inside this book. This information includes standard nutritional macros for calories, proteins, fats & carbs. There are 625 entries representing a total of 625 recipes featured in this book. Values are given in whole numbers for 1 serving or portion, unless otherwise stated.

RECIPE#	CALORIES	PROTEIN	FAT	CARBS
1	443	11	12	20
2	171	17	19	6
3	388	12	5	14
4	135	18	4	23
5	379	9	15	7
6	474	11	20	17
7	93	9	20	23
8	488	7	14	10
9	436	10	18	18
10	197	18	5	13
11	202	3	12	23
12	120	13	25	8
13	265	11	15	22
14	260	17	6	15
15	145	10	21	8
16	381	4	13	22
17	132	11	9	16
18	372	8	21	24
19	209	7	23	12
20	121	19	20	24
21	495	17	14	6
22	368	18	10	7
23	319	5	4	15
24	357	10	3	24
25	492	6	5	3
26	348	4	19	9
27	355	16	10	10
28	367	20	21	6
29	206	15	17	13
30	131	15	13	19
31	194	16	22	9
32	90	20	24	6
33	147	6	25	13
34	86	10	23	8
35	161	19	15	7
36	438	12	3	22
37	334	9	4	22
38	348	10	20	19
39	278	11	18	20
40	481	5	14	21
41	500	8	9	15
42	448	7	24	5
43	159	11	18	10
44	323	9	13	14
45	222	2	5	24
46	389	7	17	23
47	184	12	3	19
48	419	10	8	18
49	497	18	3	11
50	193	17	15	11
51	258	17	23	20
52	367	6	24	7
53	444	11	17	3
54	456	13	3	14
55	211	3	15	11
56	456	7	4	16
57	278	5	7	13
58	309	19	18	17
59	429	3	15	20
60	483	3	9	18
61	283	17	19	10
62	363	5	24	4
63	182	14	21	21
64	500	10	20	16
65	472	10	22	14
66	94	2	7	19
67	135	16	15	19
68	172	10	10	7
69	184	18	23	17

RECIPE#	CALORIES	PROTEIN	FAT	CARBS
70	388	4	11	13
71	307	7	21	6
72	433	19	25	8
73	478	19	13	12
74	195	13	13	10
75	90	3	17	14
76	82	12	24	15
77	473	18	11	13
78	372	16	22	20
79	345	7	7	12
80	433	15	15	24
81	329	19	14	11
82	322	16	10	10
83	291	8	11	8
84	225	9	12	19
85	175	10	19	7
86	330	9	12	16
87	99	16	9	5
88	335	19	14	16
89	462	9	3	19
90	348	7	6	4
91	345	19	19	14
92	448	20	3	8
93	351	3	10	20
94	155	12	8	7
95	143	10	21	11
96	494	4	17	6
97	480	19	24	16
98	247	8	19	23
99	447	5	5	4
100	256	6	10	21
101	228	9	4	4
102	114	13	5	3
103	127	10	20	5
104	262	17	5	10
105	171	15	12	23
106	74	6	21	15
107	301	15	5	9
108	229	4	22	3
109	295	16	10	13
110	121	12	10	22
111	253	15	22	6
112	453	11	23	15
113	95	2	15	20
114	120	6	12	10
115	350	6	19	10
116	72	14	21	24
117	457	20	12	4
118	327	7	23	24
119	395	9	9	20
120	294	5	11	7
121	203	18	5	24
122	133	12	14	13
123	131	18	20	6
124	195	2	23	12
125	355	14	10	19
126	473	11	17	3
127	431	20	16	16
128	407	6	24	21
129	222	6	15	13
130	130	13	18	9
131	294	18	19	10
132	380	7	22	19
133	412	9	21	13
134	198	16	7	8
135	146	9	16	17
136	453	4	19	10
137	93	3	5	16
138	357	5	24	13

#					#				
139	165	17	23	21	222	215	8	24	4
140	462	9	12	19	223	154	2	22	10
141	103	16	16	12	224	144	3	12	22
142	391	7	12	15	225	109	10	12	12
143	363	8	19	12	226	315	11	15	23
144	154	4	12	10	227	397	18	8	22
145	396	17	14	13	228	303	19	8	11
146	131	20	18	6	229	284	11	23	7
147	211	5	16	9	230	76	8	16	9
148	394	8	18	9	231	400	15	3	13
149	199	15	22	20	232	432	7	3	12
150	306	7	14	20	233	500	18	18	6
151	412	19	17	3	234	238	20	10	24
152	306	13	13	20	235	171	7	25	12
153	118	6	10	21	236	355	13	11	4
154	453	20	11	9	237	186	19	13	11
155	193	17	10	23	238	291	13	9	6
156	157	2	11	23	239	411	7	7	17
157	469	5	14	7	240	462	17	18	4
158	308	7	10	3	241	225	10	25	17
159	282	16	10	13	242	392	19	8	17
160	323	13	5	17	243	130	3	4	7
161	99	10	6	13	244	396	13	3	9
162	339	4	10	16	245	346	2	19	18
163	478	15	25	23	246	316	3	18	15
164	447	2	19	9	247	456	3	15	20
165	255	14	10	15	248	399	8	23	5
166	486	15	11	18	249	417	14	7	21
167	81	16	10	12	250	450	7	9	23
168	367	11	7	22	251	162	8	10	5
169	267	17	16	9	252	457	15	19	13
170	464	7	9	7	253	273	18	18	14
171	281	2	10	12	254	341	2	8	13
172	417	5	4	16	255	344	9	8	19
173	339	3	21	19	256	222	3	11	15
174	358	16	20	19	257	242	17	10	11
175	322	5	25	9	258	287	4	18	14
176	390	5	4	18	259	313	10	8	22
177	434	17	25	5	260	454	6	5	22
178	385	12	17	16	261	336	20	11	16
179	163	15	11	24	262	208	3	17	24
180	83	19	18	4	263	270	12	25	7
181	272	15	13	18	264	117	10	19	13
182	102	9	4	14	265	79	14	17	11
183	100	18	14	16	266	284	13	24	10
184	115	18	18	23	267	148	5	10	7
185	382	8	12	17	268	189	6	14	16
186	147	3	21	16	269	294	19	22	14
187	140	10	21	15	270	82	18	10	14
188	189	2	21	21	271	381	11	13	10
189	462	4	15	6	272	279	14	7	16
190	353	2	10	6	273	141	12	7	10
191	245	11	15	5	274	101	14	3	20
192	169	6	15	24	275	299	10	5	20
193	271	17	9	3	276	253	20	17	13
194	488	15	6	7	277	481	11	14	21
195	232	10	18	24	278	445	11	18	14
196	398	19	23	24	279	485	19	15	7
197	104	15	20	18	280	465	4	21	5
198	430	10	3	5	281	443	13	23	9
199	460	3	19	19	282	315	15	20	7
200	500	20	21	21	283	183	19	4	8
201	321	6	15	19	284	310	7	6	3
202	178	3	13	14	285	84	7	5	3
203	483	4	8	12	286	496	6	6	24
204	469	7	14	8	287	396	12	4	7
205	394	4	17	5	288	129	11	7	17
206	235	19	16	16	289	448	4	15	21
207	368	4	13	21	290	222	9	13	3
208	244	13	17	20	291	471	13	10	9
209	309	8	16	15	292	491	15	5	14
210	142	20	21	20	293	89	11	17	16
211	184	16	25	13	294	137	13	7	24
212	145	11	14	14	295	476	17	18	20
213	94	14	19	16	296	218	3	10	13
214	92	7	6	15	297	111	20	6	8
215	279	5	25	14	298	387	8	20	14
216	235	8	16	21	299	374	17	16	23
217	308	4	21	5	300	280	8	25	11
218	254	14	20	11	301	73	2	5	12
219	457	20	7	24	302	258	18	17	16
220	236	10	5	11	303	193	6	17	10
221	242	11	15	19	304	423	4	12	17

305	192	7	24	5
306	434	15	18	7
307	465	6	25	12
308	429	13	8	9
309	211	6	6	24
310	392	2	7	10
311	318	16	8	8
312	235	2	22	19
313	283	3	7	16
314	500	18	9	14
315	117	11	18	7
316	211	13	11	7
317	204	8	10	11
318	479	16	19	22
319	123	16	24	5
320	308	9	10	13
321	271	8	3	6
322	80	2	4	14
323	471	13	15	9
324	245	2	21	17
325	299	19	19	13
326	475	5	16	22
327	437	5	15	18
328	251	18	12	3
329	240	6	11	18
330	392	5	19	11
331	497	9	14	24
332	490	20	21	17
333	431	9	11	23
334	291	12	25	14
335	445	17	19	23
336	484	12	18	6
337	419	19	3	7
338	257	17	22	15
339	477	19	24	6
340	361	3	25	7
341	310	9	6	16
342	495	12	21	5
343	319	15	23	7
344	236	10	9	15
345	401	15	14	7
346	481	16	11	7
347	255	6	14	12
348	131	10	20	24
349	327	16	11	21
350	174	10	25	8
351	161	19	20	21
352	194	17	25	7
353	144	12	14	19
354	484	10	15	11
355	261	11	7	5
356	108	8	24	21
357	178	8	10	16
358	174	13	19	12
359	345	17	23	24
360	119	5	20	20
361	442	10	18	19
362	135	8	6	4
363	493	20	19	24
364	107	6	12	17
365	480	7	19	15
366	421	11	21	13
367	446	2	8	4
368	407	5	6	21
369	379	12	15	15
370	455	13	6	17
371	484	5	9	15
372	111	13	9	15
373	229	15	5	19
374	390	2	21	24
375	319	3	5	24
376	151	7	25	10
377	186	16	11	19
378	478	16	7	12
379	218	8	22	10
380	137	15	15	4
381	398	8	7	15
382	167	14	11	8
383	460	20	18	11
384	85	2	21	14
385	363	4	9	11
386	227	2	17	17
387	340	17	24	4
388	413	14	17	11
389	462	8	5	12
390	349	20	11	10
391	401	12	24	19
392	189	11	8	8
393	215	18	21	18
394	201	10	3	24
395	398	5	16	3
396	131	9	5	15
397	391	3	13	15
398	437	13	9	8
399	136	20	22	20
400	351	12	25	13
401	187	5	13	16
402	244	15	12	17
403	183	2	11	19
404	165	3	17	6
405	311	4	21	21
406	492	2	23	22
407	90	17	18	16
408	424	8	22	7
409	250	10	20	15
410	437	13	19	13
411	464	5	25	8
412	435	15	15	18
413	463	2	4	16
414	123	18	22	10
415	411	10	12	23
416	136	20	16	13
417	481	19	21	9
418	296	8	19	14
419	77	14	20	19
420	468	5	18	16
421	72	14	17	15
422	362	16	22	10
423	76	4	12	6
424	359	14	6	11
425	178	3	11	18
426	415	7	20	9
427	325	18	10	5
428	433	10	15	16
429	160	6	13	3
430	225	8	6	21
431	196	3	20	13
432	399	4	11	19
433	314	18	5	17
434	225	18	5	22
435	334	19	11	12
436	343	17	22	19
437	93	17	7	11
438	138	5	10	16
439	340	13	14	5
440	406	8	9	15
441	368	20	18	17
442	427	13	9	7
443	462	8	14	13
444	394	16	15	22
445	366	16	21	16
446	168	3	10	22
447	277	16	6	23
448	268	19	22	17
449	155	15	19	8
450	466	17	23	11
451	140	12	22	10
452	294	14	17	4
453	76	6	11	15
454	491	6	23	11
455	103	8	15	8
456	344	17	17	20
457	79	12	23	13
458	281	19	20	7
459	338	16	13	19
460	144	7	3	9
461	308	5	15	23
462	483	9	16	17
463	462	3	11	15
464	146	17	22	21
465	276	8	6	7
466	122	15	21	9
467	203	11	3	23
468	313	13	13	11
469	282	6	8	17
470	439	7	21	5

471	394	3	13	20
472	401	10	15	23
473	196	12	21	18
474	255	7	5	5
475	445	18	21	3
476	260	14	22	20
477	260	20	17	16
478	353	9	21	3
479	328	12	19	7
480	74	9	20	6
481	106	8	12	22
482	296	16	11	19
483	133	10	11	7
484	312	19	15	13
485	252	2	24	17
486	431	17	10	5
487	346	9	12	3
488	317	18	23	14
489	167	9	23	8
490	457	19	8	6
491	74	5	12	8
492	263	3	19	21
493	302	19	7	20
494	419	3	3	7
495	140	13	16	4
496	397	9	17	14
497	286	8	22	22
498	500	10	9	22
499	329	17	4	14
500	329	10	22	4
501	454	4	10	24
502	74	13	17	14
503	399	9	13	5
504	496	17	3	22
505	104	19	5	24
506	175	20	5	21
507	362	19	10	13
508	489	5	11	16
509	377	19	23	22
510	260	5	20	14
511	293	14	18	11
512	248	16	3	24
513	110	11	17	13
514	402	8	9	19
515	351	15	12	17
516	136	17	17	5
517	481	3	16	16
518	327	19	13	21
519	483	2	6	3
520	325	15	25	14
521	204	10	9	9
522	217	7	20	22
523	373	16	4	13
524	225	13	25	22
525	325	7	8	3
526	316	14	6	18
527	223	13	22	19
528	403	14	18	12
529	210	3	17	21
530	127	4	9	15
531	118	20	6	7
532	260	14	13	5
533	490	15	20	16
534	193	8	21	7
535	128	7	8	21
536	239	4	9	10
537	154	18	17	21
538	319	18	20	7
539	141	15	17	23
540	356	2	3	17
541	336	6	14	8
542	368	2	10	6
543	104	17	13	16
544	455	4	17	5
545	241	8	18	21
546	108	6	11	6
547	225	20	12	10
548	79	10	21	19
549	408	8	13	8
550	232	7	22	21
551	251	3	18	9
552	315	18	24	4
553	93	3	11	18
554	85	17	20	7
555	272	13	20	4
556	185	19	4	13
557	357	15	11	5
558	385	3	19	18
559	225	2	19	21
560	449	11	25	11
561	128	7	7	18
562	327	6	12	21
563	157	5	11	17
564	111	7	15	24
565	169	16	4	15
566	395	13	8	17
567	387	7	13	8
568	398	18	7	18
569	424	17	14	7
570	122	3	10	22
571	105	18	8	17
572	342	3	9	4
573	83	6	23	11
574	94	13	16	6
575	220	9	18	23
576	335	10	23	9
577	421	10	5	23
578	142	6	9	9
579	158	3	24	13
580	331	3	24	10
581	373	7	16	16
582	438	8	18	22
583	131	6	18	17
584	439	10	17	6
585	181	19	4	24
586	277	15	12	17
587	293	9	21	3
588	87	14	19	21
589	403	6	18	15
590	437	8	3	7
591	342	4	7	23
592	290	7	12	3
593	244	3	18	16
594	365	2	9	6
595	126	2	9	3
596	100	15	23	3
597	342	15	13	16
598	411	14	19	9
599	130	14	10	3
600	387	2	21	8
601	331	8	21	18
602	397	5	11	16
603	342	7	12	4
604	490	10	15	6
605	135	16	18	10
606	233	2	11	14
607	365	8	14	19
608	192	10	15	12
609	78	18	20	16
610	119	7	15	11
611	309	8	22	3
612	256	17	7	24
613	261	16	7	5
614	73	7	3	24
615	106	17	25	18
616	151	10	7	4
617	234	9	12	13
618	273	16	15	19
619	194	3	13	13
620	176	7	18	12
621	382	17	17	10
622	233	5	23	5
623	206	3	23	8
624	279	7	20	9
625	410	5	14	6
END	0	0	0	0

CPSIA information can be obtained
at www.ICGtesting.com
Printed in the USA
BVHW010927301121
622858BV00027B/869